Inherited Land

Inherited Land

The Changing Grounds
of Religion and Ecology

edited by

Whitney A. Bauman

Richard R. Bohannon II

Kevin J. O'Brien

PICKWICK *Publications* · Eugene, Oregon

INHERITED LAND
The Changing Grounds of Religion and Ecology

Copyright © 2011 Wipf and Stock Publishers. All rights reserved. Except for
brief quotations in critical publications or reviews, no part of this book may be
reproduced in any manner without prior written permission from the publisher.
Write: Permissions, Wipf and Stock Publishers, 199 W. 8th Ave., Suite 3, Eugene,
OR 97401.

Pickwick Publications
An Imprint of Wipf and Stock Publishers
199 W. 8th Ave., Suite 3
Eugene, OR 97401

www.wipfandstock.com

ISBN 13: 978-1-60899-989-7

Cataloging-in-Publication data:

Inherited land : the changing grounds of religion and ecology / edited by Whitney A.
Bauman, Richard R. Bohannon II, and Kevin J. O'Brien.

xiv + 264 p.; 23 cm—Includes bibliographical references and index.

ISBN 13: 978-1-60899-989-7

1. Human Ecology—Religious Aspects—Christianity. 2. Environmentalism—Social
Aspects. I. Bauman, Whitney A. II. Bohannon, Richard (Richard R.). III. O'Brien, Kevin J.
IV. Title.

BT659 .I54 2011

Manufactured in the USA.

This book is dedicated to all of our mentors and teachers in Religion and Ecology, without whom our work would be impossible, including:

John Grim

Laurel Kearns

Catherine Keller

Jay McDaniel

Sallie McFague

Bobbi Patterson

Larry Rasmussen

Rosemary Radford Ruether

Bron Taylor

Mary Evelyn Tucker

Contents

Acknowledgments

No book emphasizing complexity and interdisciplinarity can hope to acknowledge all those who have influenced and shaped it, but there are nonetheless some individuals and groups that deserve special recognition.

First, we want to thank the American Academy of Religion for a grant that enabled many of the authors in this volume to come together for a colloquium in February of 2009 at Florida International University (FIU). Thanks also go to the Religious Studies Department and College of Arts and Sciences at FIU for hosting the colloquium. Thanks most of all to the scholars who gathered and took this work seriously enough to devote their time and considerable talents to it —Evan Berry, Brian Campbell, Forrest Clingerman, Eleanor Finnegan, Sarah Fredericks, Laura Hartman, Lucas Johnston, Gavin Van Horn, and Joe Witt—and to those who contributed papers for discussion—Willis Jenkins, Elizabeth McAnally, Sam Mickey, Tovis Page, Samuel Snyder, David Wright, and Greg Zuschlag.

We would also like to thank our reviewers and guides who helped us to move from colloquium to book, and our contacts at Pickwick for guidance and professionalism in the publication process. We were reassured by our publisher and the reviews we received that this project was worth the work so many people put into it and that a conversation about the changing grounds of Religion and Ecology deserves extended, book-length attention.

Third and finally, we would like to acknowledge the many different conferences, groups, and spaces that have brought the people in this volume together: without such habitat creation and preservation, our ideas would never have taken shape. So, special thanks go to the places, conferences, and support found in The Forum on Religion and Ecology, The International Society for the Study of Religion, Nature and Culture, the Religion and Ecology Group of the American Academy of Religion, and the Transdisciplinary Theological Colloquia at Drew University. These groups made the scholarly conversation leading up to this book possible, and we are particularly grateful for the teachers and mentors who organized and welcomed us into them.

Many of those organizers have also been teachers and mentors to the editors and authors of this volume, and it is to them that we have dedicated this work in gratitude for all they did to help us become scholars capable of writing it.

Contributors

Whitney Bauman is Assistant Professor of Religion and Science at Florida International University in Miami, Florida. He is the author of *Theology, Creation, and Environmental Ethics* (2009) and coeditor with Richard Bohannon and Kevin O'Brien of *Grounding Religion: A Field Guide to the Study of Religion and Ecology* (2010). He is currently the book-review editor for *Worldviews: Global Religions, Culture, and the Ecology* and serves as co-chair of the Religion and Ecology Group at the American Academy of Religion.

Evan Berry is Assistant Professor of Philosophy and Religion at American University and Co-Director of the Ethics, Peace, and Global Affairs master's program. His research interests focus on ideas of nature in modern Western culture, particularly on the religious roots of contemporary environmental discourse. Berry has trained in both social-scientific and theoretical methodologies. His current scholarship includes an ethnographic study of intentional communities in the Pacific Northwest, a critique of the philosophical assumptions of climate change ethics, and a book project on the role of religious ideas, language, and practice in the birth of the American environmental movement.

Richard R. Bohannon II teaches in the Environmental Studies department at the College of St. Benedict and St. John's University (Collegeville, Minnesota), and holds a PhD in Religion and Society from Drew University. He is the coeditor, along with Whitney Bauman and Kevin O'Brien, of *Grounding Religion: A Field Guide to Religion and Ecology* (2010). Richard received an MA in theological studies from Andover Newton Theological School, and worked with a small architecture firm in Boston for two years. He is a steering committee member for the Religion and Ecology Group at the American Academy of Religion.

Brian G. Campbell is a PhD candidate in American Religious Cultures at Emory University, where his research and teaching have focused on the history of race and environmental justice in Atlanta and Emory's place in this social and ecological context. His dissertation, "Alone in America: Solitude, Nature, and the Sacred from Walden to the World Wide Web," is a cultural and environmental history of American hermits and solitaries. Brian has a Masters of Divinity degree from Pacific School of Religion in Berkeley, California.

Elonda Clay is completing her PhD in Religion and Science at the Lutheran School of Theology at Chicago. A graduate of Kansas State University in Physical Science, she holds a master's degree in library and information science as well as a Master of Divinity degree. She is a former graduate of the Summer Leadership Institute at Harvard University. Elonda is a recipient of the GreenFaith Fellowship, the United Methodist Women of Color Scholarship, and the North American Doctoral Fellowship from the Fund for Theological Education. Her research areas include religion and ecology, African Diaspora religions, and DNA ancestry and race in the media.

Eleanor Finnegan is a lecturer at Coastal Carolina University and a PhD candidate in the Religion Department at the University of Florida. Ms. Finnegan received an undergraduate degree in religious studies with minors in economics and environmental studies from Colgate University and a Master of Theological Studies degree from Vanderbilt University, with a focus on Islamic studies. Her scholarly interests include American Islam and Muslims and the impact of the Islamic tradition on environmental ethics and practices. The recipient of several Foreign Language and Area Studies (FLAS) fellowships, Ms. Finnegan is a contributor to *Environmental Ethics* and the *Encyclopedia of Environment and Society*. She has presented research on American Muslims at international and national conferences. Her dissertation will be focused on farming among American Muslim communities.

Sarah E. Fredericks is an Assistant Professor in the Department of Philosophy and Religion Studies at the University of North Texas. Fredericks earned her PhD in Science, Philosophy, and Religion from Boston University. Her research explores the intersection of these three fields, particularly relating to worldview analysis, or the study of the ways that ethical values, metaphysical and epistemological commitments, and culture inform decision-making and action. Fredericks particularly focuses upon sustainable energy and indicators, methods of measuring progress toward goals such as energy sustainability that encompass technical and ethical dimensions.

Lucas Johnston is Assistant Professor of Religion and Environmental Studies at Wake Forest University. His research is interdisciplinary, investigating contemporary environmental and sustainability-oriented social movements and cross-cultural political dialog related to ideas about nature. Current projects include a history and analysis of the religious dimensions of sustainability, an examination of the relationship between sustainability, security and religious violence, and an exploration of case studies illustrating strategies for introducing sustainability into higher education curricula. Dr. Johnston is the Assistant Editor and Book Reviews Editor for the *Journal for the Study of Religion, Nature and Culture.*

Kevin J. O'Brien is Assistant Professor of Christian Ethics at Pacific Lutheran University, where he teaches in the religion and environmental studies departments. He is the author of *An Ethics of Biodiversity: Christianity, Ecology, and the Variety of Life* (2010), and coeditor with Whitney Bauman and Richard R. Bohannon II of *Grounding Religion: A Field Guide to the Study of Religion and Ecology* (2010). His current research focuses on the intersection of the Christian peace tradition and ecological ethics. In addition to pursuing his academic work, Kevin serves on the Board of Directors of the Christian environmental organization Earth Ministry.

Tovis Page received her PhD from the Committee on the Study of Religion at Harvard University in 2008 with a dissertation titled, "'The Problem of the Land is the Problem of the Woman': A Genealogy of Ecofeminism at Grailville." She is also the author of "Has Ecofeminism Cornered the Market? Gender Analysis in the Study of Religion, Nature, and Culture" in the *Journal for the Study of Religion, Nature and Culture.* Her academic work focuses on the intersection of religion, gender, and ecology.

Samuel Snyder is the Director of the Bristol Bay Fisheries and Watershed Protection Campaign for the Alaska Conservation Foundation, a non profit working to build strategic leadership and support for Alaskan efforts to take care of wild lands, waters, and wildlife, which sustain diverse cultures, healthy communities, and prosperous economies. In his position, he coordinates the work of roughly fifteen organizations—ranging from local non-profits representing Alaska Natives, commercial fishermen, and sportsmen to national non-profits such as Trout Unlimited—in their collective work to protect the world's largest salmon ecosystem in Bristol Bay, Alaska, from the threats of large-scale, open-pit, mining and mineral development, notably the Pebble Mine. He received his doctorate from the University of Florida's Graduate Program on Religion and Nature. His research engages the role of cultural values amid grassroots environmental decision-making, collaborative conservation, and the resolution of environmental conflict—particularly in the contexts of trout, salmon, and cold-water ecosystem conservation. He is interested in the relationship between pro-environmental values and pro-environmental behavior and takes seriously the effort to close the gap between the worlds of theory and practice. This latter question is most pressing as he has moved from studying conservation as an academic inquiry to working on the ground in the fight for the last great salmon ecosystem.

Gavin Van Horn is the Director of Midwest Cultures of Conservation at the Center for Humans and Nature (www.humansandnature .org), a nonprofit organization dedicated to exploring and promoting moral and civic responsibilities to human communities and to natural ecosystems and landscapes. As the Midwest Director, Gavin is responsible for developing and directing a series of interdisciplinary projects relevant to the sustainability, resilience, and restoration of human and natural communities in the Chicago and Midwest region. Before taking the post at the Center for Humans and Nature, Van Horn was the Brown Junior Visiting Professor in Environmental Studies at Southwestern University in Georgetown, Texas. Van Horn received a Bachelor of Arts from Pepperdine University, a Master of Divinity degree from Princeton Theological Seminary, and his doctorate from the University of Florida, with a specialization in Religion and Nature. His dissertation research examined the religious, cultural, and ethical values involved in the reintroduction of wolves to the southwestern United States. Van Horn continues to explore cultural perceptions of wildlife; place-based pedagogy; endangered species recovery, ethics, and policy; and the values involved in ecological restoration projects, community gardening, and wildlife management.

1

The Tensions and Promises of Religion and Ecology's Past, Present, and Future

WHITNEY A. BAUMAN, RICHARD R. BOHANNON II,
AND KEVIN J. O'BRIEN

Mountains and waters right now are the actualization of the ancient
Buddha way. Each, abiding in its phenomenal expression, realizes
completeness. Because mountains and waters have been active since
before the Empty Eon, they are alive at this moment. Because they have
been self since before form arose they are emancipation-realization.

—Dogen (1240)[1]

He showed me something small, about the size of a hazelnut, that
seemed to lie in the palm of my hand as round as a tiny ball. I tried to
understand the sight of it, wondering what it could possibly mean. The
answer came: "This is all that is made." I felt it was so small that it could
easily fade to nothing; but again I was told, "This lasts and it will go on
lasting forever because God loves it."

—Julian of Norwich (1373)[2]

1. Dogen, *Mountains and Waters*, 75.
2. Julian, *Revelation of Love*, 9–10.

1

But I'm in the woods woods woods, & they are in me-ee-ee. The
King tree & me have sworn eternal love—sworn it without swearing &
I've taken the sacrament with Douglas Squirrel drank Sequoia wine,
Sequoia blood, & with its rosy purple virtue of Sequoia juice . . . I wish
I was so drunk & Sequoical that I could preach the green brown woods
to all the juiceless world, descending from this divine wilderness like a
John Baptist eating Douglas Squirrels & wild honey or wild anything,
crying, Repent for the Kingdom of Sequoia is at hand.

—John Muir (1870)[3]

As buds give rise by growth to fresh buds, and these, if vigorous,
branch out and overtop on all sides many a feebler branch, so by
generation I believe it has been with the great Tree of Life, which fills
with its dead and broken branches the crust of the earth, and covers
the surface with its ever branching and beautiful ramifications.

—Charles Darwin, *On the Origins of Species* (1859)[4]

What people do about their ecology depends on what they think about
themselves in relation to things around them. Human ecology is deeply
conditioned by beliefs about our nature and destiny—that is, by religion.

—Lynn White (1967)[5]

In the course of organizing this volume and the conference that pre-
ceded it,[6] the unity and diversity of our field both became strikingly
clear. There is a coherent and growing group of scholars engaged in the
productive and vitally important study of what many of us refer to as
Religion and Ecology. However, there are remarkable differences not
only in the methodologies we use and the disciplines we locate ourselves
within, but also in the lineages of scholarship in which we place our-

3. Muir, "Letter to Jean Carre."

4. Darwin, *Origin of Species*, 105.

5. White, "Historic Roots," 1205.

6. Florida International University, in Miami, hosted a small colloquium of scholars
from February 27th to March 1st, 2009, generously supported by a research grant from
the American Academy of Religion.

selves. We work with a broad range of texts, sources, and inspirations, and we see ourselves and our work within a diverse range of traditions. This book is written to celebrate and explore those differences, which enable us to have sustained, academic, and fruitful conversations about the intersection of religious and environmental issues.

The quotes above represent some of the diverse sources and the breadth of inspirations that contribute to this work. The Japanese Zen master Dogen's *Mountains and Waters Sutra* builds on a tradition that was longstanding in Buddhism before he taught in the thirteenth century: teaching lessons about spiritual practice using examples from the natural world. This teaching emphasizes the importance of nature by identifying the mountains and waters as active, living selves who can share insight about the path to enlightenment. A century later, in another part of the world, the English mystic Julian of Norwich connected the religious to the natural in another way, envisioning the entirety of the cosmos in God's palm, simultaneously emphasizing the majesty of the divine and the importance and fragility of the creation. John Muir came from a vastly different context in the nineteenth century, and no longer appeals to the language of any explicit religious tradition in explaining his experiences of nature. Yet he depends upon religious language to capture the transformations he experienced in his studies of the nonhuman world. Writing about the natural world around the same time, Charles Darwin generally did not appeal to explicitly religious language, but he nevertheless wrestled with the theological implications of his ideas about the origin of species and the evolving tree of life.

Each of these accounts demonstrates the broad truth of historian Lynn White's assertion that there is a connection between the ways human beings relate to the nonhuman world and the faith traditions that inspire and structure thinking and beliefs. White's essay has been used ever since it was published in 1967 to demonstrate that religion is a vital conversation partner in the project of understanding and wrestling with how human beings relate to the rest of the world.[7] This assertion—that religion matters in environmental conversations—has been foundational to the field of Religion and Ecology, and it continues to be foundational for this book.

---

7. For a helpful discussion of White's influence and how it has changed over time, see Jenkins, "After Lynn White."

Along these lines, Mary Evelyn Tucker and John Grim assert that the environmental crisis:

> . . . is not only the result of certain economic, political, and social factors. It is also a moral and spiritual crisis which, in order to be addressed, will require broader philosophical and religious understandings of ourselves as creatures of nature, embedded in life cycles and dependent upon ecosystems. Religions, thus, need to be reexamined in light of the current environmental crisis.[8]

This contention set the context for a groundbreaking series of books in the field that traced environmentalist themes and suggested environmentalist changes to Buddhism, Christianity, Confucianism, Daoism, Hinduism, Indigenous Traditions, Islam, Jainism, Judaism, and Shinto. These books offered responses to the complex and enormous "environmental crisis" by examining and critiquing a selection of humanity's "philosophical and religious understandings" of its relationships to the nonhuman world.

Tucker and Grim, the scholars they gathered in their ten volume series, and many other thinkers in the field of Religion and Ecology have succeeded in establishing two vital, foundational claims within religious studies and theology: first, there is a complex and wide-ranging environmental crisis, and, second, this crisis is at least in part a moral and spiritual issue. While some religious people may dismiss environmental degradation as a myth or an irrelevant distraction from their faith, these believers are well outside the mainstream. While some environmentalists may believe that religion is a backwards and problematic way of living in the world, they are encouraged to keep quiet by their movement's leaders. Environmental degradation is widely recognized to involve moral and spiritual issues, and the leaders of moral and spiritual communities widely recognize that environmental degradation is real and requires a response.

Thus, over the last four decades, arguments from Religion and Ecology have convinced a wide range of religious leaders, with widely-heralded environmental statements emerging over the last twenty years from the Vatican, evangelical Christians, the Dalai Lama, Native American leaders, and many other religious authorities and communi-

---

8. This quote comes from the foreword to the series. See Tucker and Grim, *Religions of the World and Ecology.*

ties.[9] In response, many environmentalists who had previously identified themselves as secularists or pessimists about religion as a force for positive change have actively reached out to religious people and organizations, recruiting faith communities to join with and become part of their work.[10]

The occasion for this book is our awareness as emerging scholars in the field that these realities—that environmental degradation is widely accepted as real, and that the relationship between religion and environmental issues is generally understood—change the conversations scholars should have about these issues. These successes suggest that Religion and Ecology is developed, established, and matured enough to reflect on itself and to add new questions and concerns to the ones we inherit from the past. Such reflective questioning is the task of *Inherited Land*.

This is not a book written to replace the *Religions of the World and Ecology* series or to supersede those who created and work out of its impressive accomplishments. Rather, *Inherited Land* depends on that work and seeks to introduce it to readers who do not know this field even as we build upon it. Along those lines, we set this volume's contributors to three primary tasks. First, appreciatively and critically examine the academic field of Religion and Ecology—the land we have inherited. Second, discuss the changing grounds for this field: the debates over how religious traditions and environmental issues are related to one another, the increasing awareness of how diverse and complicated religion can be in these contexts, and the ever-expanding challenges of understanding the natural world and its degradation. Third and finally, discuss future directions, proposing a set of responses to these changing grounds and envisioning the field of Religion and Ecology that will take shape in light of its history and the challenges it now faces. We model those three tasks in the sections that follow, aiming to contextualize the essays to come with an understanding of the past, present, and possible futures of our field.

---

9. The Evangelical Declaration on the Care of Creation, for instance, was signed by a number of evangelical leaders in 1994, and was widely seen as an important sign of broad changes in religious attitudes toward this issue. See also John Paul II, "Ecological Crisis"; and Dalai Lama, "Buddhism and the Protection of Nature."

10. See for instance Sagan et. al., "Open Letter," in which scientists invited the religious community to collaborate on environmentalist work; Wilson, *Creation*, a book-length argument from a biologist to evangelical Christians to care for "the Creation": and Gardner, *Inspiring Progress*, an analysis from the Worldwatch Institute of the prospects for religious contributions to the movement for sustainable development.

Introducing Religion and Ecology: Constructive-Critical Engagements with Our Inheritance

Religion and Ecology has always been what Catherine Keller calls a "pluri-singular" phenomenon: it is established enough to have a coherent identity but broad enough that it has no single definition.[11] The established identity of the field is most clearly demonstrated by noting its increasing representation throughout the religious academy. "Religion and Ecology," or some variation thereof, has a substantial presence at major professional organizations in the study of religion, including the American Academy of Religion and the Society for Biblical Literature (see Figure 1). There are also specialized academic conferences and consortia: The Forum for Religion and Ecology (FORE), the Canadian Forum for Religion and Ecology, the European Forum for the Study of Religion and the Environment, and the International Society for the Study of Religion, Nature, and Culture (ISSRNC). These groups pursue Religion and Ecology broadly construed, and the growing membership and work of each are testaments to the current energy in the field. So is the frequent engagement with this field by other academics and scholarly organizations that do not specialize in religion, such as the International Association for Environmental Philosophy, the Society for Conservation Biology, the Society for Human Ecology, the Institute for Religion in an Age of Science (IRAS), and the Association for Environmental Studies and Sciences. The study of Religion and Ecology also maintains two refereed journals, *Worldviews: Global Religions, Culture, and Ecology*, first published in 1997, and the *Journal for the Study of Religion, Nature and Culture*, which began publication in 2007 and replaced the journal *Ecotheology*, in print from 1996 to 2006.

Graduate programs have begun offering degrees specializing in this field, the most prominent example being the program in Religion and Nature at the University of Florida.[12] It is also common to find specialists emerging from more general graduate programs in theology, ethics, sociology, and comparative religions.[13] There are an increasing number

11. See Keller, *Face of the Deep*. The central image of our title and this introduction—that the field of Religion and Ecology is a "ground" we have in common—also emerges from Catherine Keller's work ("Talking Dirty").

12. The University of Florida offers masters and doctoral degrees in Religion and Nature and holds the offices for the ISSRNC. Its first class of students enrolled in the Fall of 2003, several of whom have contributed to this volume.

13. Graduate programs in religion that have concentrations on Religion and Ecology within traditional religious disciplines include Drew University, the Graduate

Figure 1: Institutional Incorporation of Religion and Ecology
in Academic Associations

Association	Members[a]	Organized Component Uniting Environmental Issues and Religion[b]
American Academy of Religion	10,000	Religion and Ecology Consultation/Group (1991-current) Animals and Religion Consultation (2003-current)
Catholic Theological Society of America	Not published	Theology and Ecology (2002–2007)
International Association for Environmental Philosophy	Not Published	Society for Nature, Philosophy, and Religion (2005-current)
Society of Biblical Literature	8,500	Ecological Hermeneutics Section (2004-current)
Society of Christian Ethics	950	Interest Group on Environmental Ethics and Theology (1991-current)
Society for Conservation Biology	10,000	Religion and Conservation Biology Working Group (2007-current)

[a] Membership numbers are approximate, based on numbers published on each organization's website.

[b] As an indication that this is nonetheless still a new field, smaller organizations (e.g., the Society for the Scientific Study of Religion or the North American Academy of Liturgy) do not programmatically integrate Religion and Ecology in their annual meetings, though papers are often presented on the topic, nor is there an institutional presence within the Evangelical Theological Society.

of job openings in religion departments and environmental studies programs that explicitly request expertise in this subject matter, and faculty at other schools have demonstrated growing interest in developing such expertise. Furthermore, there is increasing awareness in the media, with particular attention paid to the growth of interfaith efforts at conservation, the growing evangelical Christian presence in these discussions, and the role of religious groups in responses to climate change.[14]

Theological Union and, most recently, Yale University, which currently houses the Forum for Religion and Ecology.

14. This includes groups such as the Evangelical Environmental Network (EEN) and Interfaith Power and Light (also known as the Regeneration Project). On religious responses to climate change, see Kearns (2007).

At least as important as external, institutional articulations of Religion and Ecology is the fact that the field has an *internal* coherence. There is a growing and increasingly established canon of literature that scholars in our field read and discuss. Inspired by these texts, we come to share an array of common questions, such as: What do major religious traditions contribute to solving the problems of environmental degradation?[15] What new or adapted religious traditions are emerging in response to our environmental realities?[16] What new connections and common grounds between religious traditions and practices are developing as communities of faith come together in light of these problems?[17] What practices and attitudes in the environmental movement can be understood and classified using the tools of religious studies or theology?[18]

While raising and discussing such questions, Religion and Ecology has also provided a set of answers, albeit intentionally only partial and tentative. Anthropocentrism, greed, consumerism, dominion, segregated thinking, and dualism are widely assumed to be unwelcome trends in human societies that contribute to environmental problems.[19] World religions and new religious movements are commonly thought to offer a wide range of resources and ideas that can contribute to a more sustainable future. Many scholars have come to see environmental degradation as not just a serious problem facing the human species, but also an opportunity for ecumenical and interfaith dialogue and common ground between these faiths. The most intensive effort along these lines is certainly the aforementioned *Religions of the World and Ecology* series. A second major publication has been the two-volume *Encyclopedia of Religion and Nature* edited by Bron Taylor, which self-consciously takes a broader view of both religion and nature than the Forum for Religion and Ecology.

---

15. See especially Tucker and Grim, *Religions of the World and Ecology* and Taylor, *Encyclopedia of Religion and Nature*.

16. See especially Albanese, *Nature Religion in America* and *Reconsidering Nature Religion*.

17. See especially Tucker and Grim, *Worldviews and Ecology* and Gottlieb *Greener Faith* and *Handbook of Religion and Ecology*.

18. See especially Taylor, *Ecological Resistance Movements* and *Encyclopedia of Religion and Nature*.

19. See Ruether, *Gaia and God*; Cobb and Daly, *For the Common Good*; Keller, *Apocalypse Now and Then*; and Plumwood, *Environmental Culture*.

The very fact that there is now an existing corpus of literature and wide infrastructure for academic discourse is a major and significant shift within Religion and Ecology. A scholar interested in these subjects in the 1960s or even the 1990s faced a substantially different task within the religious academy than those entering the field today. Religion and Ecology has an identity: we know who we are, where to meet together, and what broad subjects we will talk about when we do. These internal and external signs of establishment lead us to characterize Religion and Ecology as a "field" of study in the sense meant by sociologist Pierre Bourdieu: there are set parameters establishing who is in and who is out, there is a form of capital (knowledge about the "canonical" literature and figures), there is a basic set of assumptions and beliefs shared by those in the field, and Religion and Ecology vies for status and power within the larger fields of religious studies, environmental studies, the humanities, and public policy.[20] Finally, and perhaps most importantly for this volume, the limits of Religion and Ecology are constantly being both reinforced and questioned. Religion and Ecology is an established, pluri-singular field.

This book is clear evidence of that fact, reinforcing the boundaries of the field by citing the texts and questions we have inherited but also working to expand and clarify our shared tasks. Throughout the book, we test the boundaries of Religion and Ecology, above all by bringing together a variety of sometimes-conflicting perspectives among contributors. *Inherited Land* is intended to balance a genuine appreciation for Religion and Ecology as we have inherited it with a critical, careful, methodological attention to how our academic field is and should be changing.

Identifying "Religion and Ecology" — A Field without a Definition

A variety of factors that unite Religion and Ecology have already been mentioned: scholars in our field pay attention to contemporary environmental degradation and connect these challenges to the beliefs and practices of religious communities and traditions. We share a history, canon, and the institutional establishments noted above. Three other unifying characteristics can be further noted. First, ours is an inherently *interdisciplinary* field of study, drawing from a wide array of traditional

20. Bourdieu, *Homo Academicus*.

disciplines within religious and theological studies including the sociology of religion, history, ethics, theology, comparative religions, textual analysis, and philosophy. Furthermore, we bring religious and theological disciplines into dialogue with economics, social sciences, environmental sciences and natural sciences. Scholars who seek to think about faith traditions in light of contemporary environmental degradation are all agreed that no single academic discipline—and therefore no single academic—can do this work alone. Our work is necessarily dialogical and broad ranging.

Second, Religion and Ecology is an *activist* field: virtually all who work within it are motivated to some extent by a concern for how human communities impact Earth's ecosystems, with a commitment to not only conserve the natural world but also improve conditions for the human beings who depend upon it. One dimension of this activism is a widespread rejection of the idea that concern for the environment is discontinuous with concern for fellow humans. Influenced by environmental justice and civil rights traditions, the anti-globalization movement, eco-feminist insights, and post-colonial contributions, scholars in our field are not only convinced that we must respond to the realities of environmental degradation, but also that such issues have social, human impacts that must be carefully considered.

This activism does not detract from the third characteristic, the deliberately *academic* aspect of work in this field, which is characterized by critical analysis of assumptions and beliefs about environments and environmentalisms. Religion and Ecology has taken shape at scholarly meetings, in books with extensive footnotes, through long hours of research in libraries and over months rigorously studying religious and environmental communities. The relationship between this academic work and the activist bent of our field creates some tensions, but these tensions have largely been productive and energizing as careful research is done to contribute to a worthy cause.

Thus, our field is interdisciplinary, activist, and academic. However, this common ground must not disguise the considerable differences and disagreements that also characterize Religion and Ecology. Out of respect for this diversity, this book contains many different approaches, sometimes competing and sometimes mutually enhancing—another demonstration of our confidence that Religion and Ecology is an established enough field is our confidence that its boundaries can be questioned and debated.

Perhaps the most obvious disagreement within our field concerns what to call it: scholars engaged in these discussions variously study religion, theology, and/or spirituality in conversation with ecology, environment, and/or nature. As editors, we refer to our field as "Religion and Ecology" to signal its established identity, but some authors in this text will choose to use other language. One reason we have chosen to capitalize the name of our field is to distinguish it from the complex concepts that make it up, two sights of further tension within the field. "Religion," of course, conjures lists of "world traditions" and belief systems, but anyone who has studied or thoughtfully practiced any of these traditions knows that it is very difficult to conclusively characterize a religion, to identify what beliefs and practices within it are central and normative, and to establish clear understandings of who is included and who is not. Furthermore, the concept of "religion" is itself a western construction, and may mischaracterize cultural and philosophical traditions outside the west.[21] Nevertheless, we use the word as shorthand here in an effort to both signify an area of inquiry and disrupt it through new definitions and understandings of what "religion" might be.

As numerous chapters in this volume make clear, no responsible discussion of religion can focus singularly on the texts and ideas of religious leaders without also paying attention to the practices of other believers. Nor should scholars of religion ignore the prevalence of new and non-traditional systems of belief and action in the contemporary world, systems that act like religions despite not being traditionally recognized as such. Capitalist consumerism acts in some ways like a religion, as do fly-fishing, surfing, and kayaking.[22] Aware of this diversity, the contributors to this volume do not all share a common definition of religion, though they do all wrestle with the importance of religion in our world and struggle to understand the term as broadly as possible while also attending to the nuances of particular religious traditions.

Because we emphasize the definition and discussion of religion as a methodological issue, *Inherited Land* is in some sense a departure from the common approach to the study of Religion and Ecology, especially comparative works. This project is not organized by or focused on particular

21. Masuzawa, *Invention of World Religions.*

22. For an argument that consumerist capitalism is a religion, see David Loy (2002). For discussions of the religious character of water sports, see Bron Taylor (2007), A. Whitney Sanford (2007), and Samuel Snyder (2007).

religious traditions and religious practices; we do not offer a Christian, an Islamic, and a Taoist set of responses to common questions or concerns. Rather, the tradition and practices we analyze first and foremost are those of our own scholarly field. We are writing about Religion and Ecology rather than any particular religion, and what unites us is a commitment to understand where our field has come from and where it should be heading. To use chapter 6 as an example, Tovis Page does not provide a feminist theological argument, an analysis of gender norms within a particular religious tradition, or a critique of gendered approaches to the natural world by people of faith. Instead, she offers a discussion of how gender has been used in Religion and Ecology, developing a proposal for how our field can responsibly and fruitfully engage in contemporary discussions about sexuality and gender. *Inherited Land* builds on all that has come before, depending on the existing scholarship that has carefully analyzed particular traditions, but adding a layer of self-reflexive methodology. We hope that this book's contribution will be not to call for particular religious constructions, but rather to continue a scholarly engagement with the broad phenomena of Religion and Ecology.

Like religion, the word "ecology" raises a number of questions. Ecology means balance and equilibrium in the natural world to some, while it suggests imbalance and disequilibrium to others. To avoid the complexity of all these meanings, some scholars prefer to write about the interaction between religion and "nature," "the Earth," "ecosystems," or "environments" rather than "ecology." Of course, any one of these terms can similarly be understood to have a wide range of evolving meanings.[23]

We recognize this complexity and remain open to a variety of terms to signify these realities. As editors, we have chosen for sake of clarity to refer to the reality with which religious traditions engage in our field with a single term, ecology, primarily because of its historical import within the academy. We hope that this term is inclusive enough that all scholars in the field will recognize their work as part of this broad project. Again, however, the focus of this book is on methodology and self-reflection, and so the chapters that follow include discussions and debates about the strengths and weaknesses of these terms and how they identify the work we do together.

---

23. For a variety of perspectives on how the word "ecology" and its moral implications change, see Lodge and Hamlin, *Religion and the New Ecology*.

Changing Grounds: Religion and Ecology in New Contexts

The work of this book could not take place without the fertile ground prepared by scholars who have come before us, and our emphasis on this fact is more than an attempt to be polite. We owe a genuine debt to previous scholars who have established the reality of environmental degradation and the relevance of religion in responding to it. However, the points of agreement established by Religion and Ecology create new questions, which we believe will shape the future of our field.

Thanks to a wide array of activists and scholars, the reality of environmental degradation is beyond serious doubt in academic circles, as are the complexity and variety of the problems inherent in it. There is no longer any serious debate about whether human activity is changing the climate. However, those who understand this issue do recognize many uncertainties about how, how much, and how quickly the climate is changing and what should be done about it. No credible source denies that human beings are driving other species extinct at an alarming rate. However, the specific causes of this decline and the best remedies to it are both highly disputable. It is beyond question that the pollution and consumption accompanying industrialized human societies have disproportionately negative impacts on the poor and marginalized of our world. However, the best way to deal with the illnesses, drought, and food scarcities that result remain contentious. We know that the current global population cannot sustainably live on this planet with the levels of consumption to which people in the U.S. have grown accustomed. But whether this problem can be solved by a reduction in population, drastic changes in consumption patterns and habits, or technological innovation is the subject of ongoing, lively, and serious discussions. What is the role of religious people and scholars of religion in such discussions?

Environmental activism and religion are widely seen as belonging together, and this is an enormous accomplishment. However, given that "religion" *matters* to ecological discourse and given that "ecology" *matters* to religious scholars and practicing faith communities, what is the purpose and task of Religion and Ecology as an academic field today?

The essays in this volume discuss these questions at length. We assume that there is no single answer, no one approach to studying the intersection of religious traditions and environmental issues; instead we embrace a plurality of methodologies, goals, and objects of study. The authors of *Inherited Land* work from a variety of methods and assumptions, demonstrating the changed grounds of our discipline even as we reflect upon them. With our common inheritance serving as our meeting ground, we have the chance to be more reflexive about Religion and Ecology, questioning and critiquing the field in which we find ourselves. Along these lines, authors in this volume ask: What should we include in the categories of "religion" and "ecology"? What has been left out of this field, and what will be the cost of broadening our perspectives? How has the implicit advocacy in this field shaped its scholarship? How are sciences such as ecology, evolutionary biology, and cosmology used and abused by scholars in this field? How do the concerns of marginalized and minority communities influence Religion and Ecology, and how can we take these concerns more seriously? How should changes in the environmental community—increasing emphases on pragmatism, place, and cities—and in the scholarship of religion—increasing emphases on practices, lived religion, and nonhuman animals—shape our field? How should post-colonial and post-structural discourses influence the ways we think about Religion and Ecology?

These questions about our field coexist alongside long-established questions about religious traditions and environmental realities—questions of how humans relate to the nonhuman world and how religious people and scholars of religion can contribute to helping that relationship become more sustainable. We continue to ask these questions because, while the grounds of this field are changing, the land we have inherited requires continued work.

In the next eleven chapters, this volume seeks to contextualize, investigate, and extend Religion and Ecology. In chapter 2, Evan Berry addresses what Religion and Ecology means by "religion," offering lessons from the attempt to authenticate Nature Religion applicable to a wide range of scholars in our field. In chapter 3, Sarah Fredericks and Kevin O'Brien bring the same sort of perspective to "ecology," extending from that discussion to an argument about how natural science should be taken more seriously in our field, and then reflecting on the uncertainties that will come along with this move. In chapter 4, Eleanor Finnegan offers an argument about the breadth of attention in our field, first noting that the categories we generally use are heavily influenced by the Christian foundations of religious scholarship and then suggesting a different approach by drawing on a study of how particular Muslims in particular places relate to environmental issues.

After these reflections on the starting points of our field come a series of chapters discussing dialogue partners with which Religion and Ecology should critically and carefully engage. In chapter 5, Whitney Bauman argues that poststructuralist thought offers new perspectives for a nonfoundationalist Religion and Ecology. Tovis Page chronicles the influence of feminist and gender studies on the field and then proposes a different approach to gender and sexuality for future work in chapter 6. In chapter 7, Sam Snyder and Lucas Johnston draw lessons from philosophical pragmatism and apply them to a more grounded and useful scholarly approach to studies of religion and nature. Elonda Clay argues in chapter 8 that African American religion is an important category for Religion and Ecology, to be studied on its own complicated, rich, and informative terms rather than as a stand-in for environmental justice. Building on this suggestion in chapter 9, Richard Bohannon and Kevin O'Brien propose a more deliberate and cautious approach to environmental justice in our field, one that differentiates it from the broader and more holistic category of ecojustice. In chapter 10, Brian Campbell notes the growing importance of "practice" and "place" in the field and develops a perspective on how the two can correct one another in order to enhance Religion and Ecology. Richard Bohannon argues in chapter 11 that our field must study environmental crises and religious attitudes not merely in the abstract, but in the particular places in which most people experience both: cities. Finally, in chapter 12, Gavin van Horn discusses the field of Religion and Animals, which has roots in Religion and Ecology but now addresses the complexities of how religion relates to the nonhuman world with its own set of tools and approaches.

This volume obviously includes a wide range of ideas and academic discourses. Our common ground is a commitment to persistent questions about this academic field of Religion and Ecology, about where we situate ourselves within and around it, and about what we should do to help it to thrive and grow. The task of this book is ambitious: to map the field that we inherit and to stake out some possibilities of how it might continue to bear fruit as the climate and attitudes of the world around it shifts. In this sense, we hope that the contributions in this volume will point our intellectual and sensory attention toward some of these shifts in a way that is constructive for the future of the field. Ultimately, the aim of the volume is to build on what we have inherited, to use it to continue developing the questions, concepts, insights, and tools required for the perpetual human quest of discerning what types of worlds we want to help co-create and co-inhabit.

Bibliography

Albanese, Catherine L. *Nature Religion in America: From the Algonkian Indians to the New Age*. Chicago: University of Chicago Press, 1990.

————. *Reconsidering Nature Religion*. The Rockwell Lecture Series. Harrisburg, PA: Trinity, 2002.

Bourdieu, Pierre. *Homo Academicus*. Translated by Peter Collier. Stanford: Stanford University Press, 1988.

Dalai Lama XV. "Buddhism and the Protection of Nature: An Ethical Approach to Environmental Protection." In *Buddhist Peace Fellowship Newsletter*, Spring 1998.

Daly, Herman E., and John Cobb Jr. *For the Common Good: Redirecting the Economy Toward Community, the Environment, and a Sustainable Future*. 2nd ed. Boston: Beacon, 1994.

Darwin, Charles. *The Origin of Species by means of Natural Selection, or the Preservation of Favoured Races in the Struggle for Life*. 6th ed. London: John Murray, 1872.

Dogen. "Mountains and Waters Sutra." In *Dharma Rain: Sources of Buddhist Environmentalism*, edited by Stephanie Kaza and Kenneth Kraft, 65–76. Boston: Shambhala, 2000.

Gardner, Gary T. *Inspiring Progress: Religions' Contributions to Sustainable Development*. A Worldwatch Book. New York: Norton, 2006.

Gottlieb, Roger S. *A Greener Faith: Religious Environmentalism and Our Planet's Future*. Oxford: Oxford University Press, 2006.

————. *The Oxford Handbook of Religion and Ecology*. Oxford: Oxford University Press, 2006.

Jenkins, Willis. "After Lynn White: Religious Ethics and Environmental Problems." *Journal of Religious Ethics* 37 (2009) 283–309.

John Paul II, Pope. "Peace with God the Creator, Peace with All Creation." Message for the Celebration of the World Day of Peace, January 1, 1990. Online: http://www.vatican.va/holy_father/john_paul_ii/messages/peace/documents/hf_jp-ii_mes_19891208_xxiii-world-day-for-peace_en.html/.

Julian, of Norwich. *Revelation of Love*. Edited and translated by John Skinner. New York: Image, 1996.

Kearns, Laurel. "Cooking the Truth: Faith, Science, the Market, and Global Warming." In *Ecospirit: Religions and Philosophies for the Earth*, edited by Laurel Kearns and Catherine Keller, 97–124. Transdisciplinary Theological Colloquia. New York: Fordham University Press, 2007.

Keller, Catherine. *Apocalypse Now and Then: A Feminist Guide to the End of the World*. Boston: Beacon, 1996.

————. *The Face of the Deep: A Theology of Becoming*. London: Routledge, 2003.

———. "Talking Dirty: Ground Is Not Foundation." In *Ecospirit: Religions and Philosophies for the Earth*, edited by Laurel Kearns and Catherine Keller, 63–76. Transdisciplinary Theological Colloquia. New York: Fordham University Press, 2007

Lodge, David M., and Christopher Hamlin, editors. *Religion And the New Ecology: Environmental Responsibility in a World in Flux*. Notre Dame: University of Notre Dame Press, 2006.

Loy, David R. *A Buddhist History of the West: Studies in Lack*. Albany: State University of New York Press, 2002.

Masuzawa, Tomoko. *The Invention of World Religions, Or, How European Universalism Was Preserved in the Language of Pluralism*. Chicago: University of Chicago Press, 2005.

Muir, John. "Letter to Jeanne Carr." (Fall, 1870) John Muir Correspondence Collection at the University of the Pacific. Online: http://digitalcollections.pacific.edu/cdm4/document.php?CISOROOT=/muirletters&CISOPTR=12500&REC=4/.

Plumwood, Val. *Environmental Culture: The Ecological Crisis of Reason*. Environmental Philosophies Series. London: Routledge, 2002

Ruether, Rosemary Radford. *Gaia & God: An Ecofeminist Theology of Earth Healing*. San Francisco: HarperSanFrancisco, 1992.

Sagan, Carl et. al. "An Open Letter to the Religious Community." In *Ecology and Religion: Scientists Speak*, edited by John E. Carroll and Keith Warner, ii–vi. Quincy, IL: Franciscan, 1998.

Sanford, A. Whitney. "Pinned on Karma Rock: Whitewater Kayaking as Religious Experience." *Journal of the American Academy of Religion* 75 (2007) 875–95.

Snyder, Samuel. "New Streams of Religion: Fly Fishing as a Lived, Religion of Nature." *Journal of the American Academy of Religion* 75 (2007) 896–922.

Taylor, Bron Raymond. *Ecological Resistance Movements: The Global Emergence of Radical and Popular Environmentalism*. SUNY Series in International Environmental Policy and Theory. Albany: State University of New York Press, 1995.

———. "Surfing into Spirituality and a New, Aquatic Nature Religion." *Journal of the American Academy of Religion* 75 (2007) 923–51.

——— et al., editors. *The Encyclopedia of Religion and Nature*. 2 vols. London: Thoemmes Continuum, 2005.

Tucker, Mary Evelyn, and John A. Grim, editors. *Worldviews and Ecology: Religion, Philosophy, and the Environment*. Ecology and Justice Series. Maryknoll, NY: Orbis, 1994.

———, editors. *Religions of the World and Ecology*. 10 vols. Cambridge: Harvard University Press, 1997–2004.

White, Lynn, Jr. "The Historic Roots of Our Ecologic Crisis." *Science* 155 (1967) 1203–7.

Wilson, Edward O. *The Creation: An Appeal to Save Life on Earth*. New York: Norton, 2006.

2

Nature Religion and
the Problem of Authenticity

EVAN BERRY

Introduction

In a 1975 essay, Charles Lemert attempted to define "non-church religion," a category he believed captured the object of an emerging scholarly interest in the "religiosity" of presidential speeches, small town high school football games, town meetings, etcetera.[1] Lemert opened by forgiving readers who approached his article with "skepticism," evidencing his anxiety about the degree to which this inquiry remained at the margins of religious studies. His apologetics are a reminder that the concept "religion" has almost always been expressed in institutionalized, theistic traditions. Despite the fact that the kinds of phenomena Lemert intended (civil religion, implicit religion, nature religion, etc.) are almost certainly more familiar to contemporary scholars of religion—though few would use the term "non-church religion"—researchers in these areas continue to anticipate skeptical receptions of their work. For example, Bron Taylor has argued that explorations of "aquatic nature religions," like surfing and fly-fishing, are important because they illuminate "beliefs and practices that might not be considered religious by

1. Lemert, "Defining Non-Church Religion."

18

those presuming more conventional understandings of the term."[2] Why is it that such "conventional understandings" of religion have proven so enduring and how does this present a theoretical challenge for scholarship on "non-traditional" religious topics?

This volume's appraisal of a maturing field of research affords an opportunity to situate Religion and Ecology vis-à-vis the disciplinary status of scholarship on "non-church religions." Specifically, this chapter investigates the engagement of the conceptual category "nature religion" with the ever-present debates about the meaning and limits of religion itself. These debates have created a challenge for contemporary scholars of Religion and Ecology because, especially where human relationships with the natural environment are concerned, it is not always clear if and whether there should be any restrictions on what can meaningfully be called "religion." The contention of this essay is that there is a viable middle ground for scholarship on "non-church religions" that mediates between overly restrictive definitions of religion and overly inclusive ones. Less a definition of religion than a demand for particular kinds of scholarly evidence and argument, the theoretical approach explored here is a genealogical conception of "nature religion."

The Study of Nature Religion

The term *nature religion* came into widespread scholarly use following the publication of Catherine Albanese's *Nature Religion in America*.[3] Albanese imagined nature religion as a "useful construct" that captures the "intrinsic" relationship among the diverse social expressions that draw on nature as a symbolic resource.[4] Although Albanese's treatment is in many ways the definitive analytical approach to "nature religion," other scholars have used the term to designate similar, though not entirely congruent, objects. There are at least five different, though variously overlapping, ways that contemporary scholars define "nature

2. Taylor, "Focus Introduction: Aquatic Nature Religion."

3. This essay is confined to a discussion of nature religion as a key category of analysis for scholars interested in the interface of religion and ecology. The term also has deep conceptual connections with the "natural religion(s)," a notion that has permeated western analyses of religion since the early modern era. For a more thorough exploration of these connections and of their significance for the study of Religion and Ecology see Taylor, "Ecology and Nature Religion."

4. Albanese, *Nature Religion in America*, 6-8.

religion." First, the term might be used to refer to a diverse assemblage of cultural phenomena that have in common the use of "religious" terminology to describe, conceptualize, and shape experiences of and engagements with the natural world.[5] Second, "nature religion" also can designate social phenomena structured around certain kinds of acts said to be characteristic of "religion" and related closely to the natural world, for example rituals, the division of sacred and profane, or metaphysical beliefs.[6] Third, nature religions are said to be those cultural phenomena that fulfill their environmental function "religiously".[7] Fourth, although research on "religious environmentalism" is sometimes developed separately from work on "nature religion," terms like "religions of nature" are intended to be as broadly inclusive of "conventional" religious phenomena as possible.[8] Finally, the category identifies a strain of discourse within the larger history of (typically American) religions that draws on nature as symbolic resource.[9]

"Nature religion," however, has an authenticity problem, which concerns whether the diverse cultural phenomena designated by the term are *authentically* religious. When scholars use the phrase "nature religion," in what sense do they intend that such phenomena be taken as *religious*? Is the use of the term intended as a mere heuristic or in a more provocative sense? More to the point, is nature religion anything more than a theoretical construct? Does it point to something fundamental about the meaning of religion as it shapes the social landscape of the modern world? Scholars in this quickly expanding conversation about the interface of religion and ecology—especially social scientists—need to be vigilant about this fundamental methodological question. How do they, and how should they, position themselves with regard to the more fundamental question as to what counts as religion?

Given the diversity of sub-fields within religious studies, it is not surprising that there is ample room for disagreement as to the meaning of religion; it is even less surprising that emerging research areas would not conform with the theoretical explanations and expectations

5. Dunlap, *Faith in Nature*; Gottlieb, *Oxford Handbook on Religion and Ecology*.

6. Taylor, "Surfing into Spirituality"; Snyder, "New Streams of Religion"; Sanford, "Pinned on Karma Rock."

7. Rappaport, *Ecology, Meaning, and Religion*; Brinkerhoff and Jacob, "Mindfulness and Quasi-Religious Meaning Systems."

8. Bron Taylor, "Ecology and Nature Religion."

9. Albanese, *Nature Religion in America*; Gould, *At Home in Nature*.

of more established fields. However, the fact that many scholars of religion "might not consider" nature religion to belong to the discipline's constitutive category seems somewhat more a cause for concern than mere wrangling over theoretical details. Three principal concerns are apparent: *intra*disciplinary conviviality, the long-term viability of Religion and Ecology as a field of research, and its reception and impact outside the academy.

The first concern is that the changing landscape of theoretical possibilities within the study of religion may ultimately widen the gap between the social scientific and confessional poles that have long anchored the discipline. Not all discourse about what counts as religion needs pander to "conventional understandings of the term," but such discourse ought consider what it means to expand the theoretical horizons of "religion" working independently of such conventionalism. Although they are theoretically iconoclastic, categories like nature religion and "implicit religion" were not developed to occlude traditional perspectives; rather, they were designed to bring those perspectives into sharp relief—to challenge them, to provide alternative perspectives, and to address their shortcomings.[10] This chapter hopes for an *intra*disciplinary conviviality and begins to articulate some of the ways that the growing body of literature on nature religion can be put in dialogue with such "conventional understandings" in productive ways.

The second concern is more manifestly theoretical. Scholars of Religion and Ecology share an intellectual space with "conventional understandings of religion," beyond which lie potential objections and counterarguments to the category "nature religion." However, much of the scholarly work to date on nature religion has focused on the "positive case"—building an argument for the validity of the category—and there has been less direct engagement with detractors. Perhaps because of the ever-widening space between subfields in the contemporary academy, scholars of the "conventional" view have not developed a robust theoretical critique of "nature religion." Nonetheless, the explicit acknowledgement of the discipline's internal disagreements about basic theoretical questions begs for a rebuttal of potential critiques. Although it is beyond the scope of this essay to definitively defend the category "nature religion," the basic features of such an argument would plausibly be structured around several specific objections. Anticipating these

10. Bailey, *Implicit Religion in Contemporary Society.*

objections and developing meaningful responses to them will hedge against theoretical insularity and academic esotericism.

The third concern, to paraphrase one of former President George W. Bush's more charming claims about the nature of democracy, is that "theories have consequences." What are the consequences of the theoretical category "nature religion"? Certainly, the interpretive approaches deployed by scholars of Religion and Ecology have important ramifications for the academic study of religion, for the college classroom, and for the popular reception of scholarship on religion and the environment. This latter import—the influence of academic discourse on public conversations about religion and nature—calls to mind what the editors of this volume have dubbed the "double apologetic" of Religion and Ecology: the need to convince both "religious actors" and "environmental activists" of the validity of this particular field of study. The existence of such a dual audience presupposes, however, who is "religious" and who is "secular" among our readers, students, and research subjects. Considering the abundance of recent scholarship that interrogates the boundary between religiosity and irreligiosity,[11] this "double apologetic" takes on a heightened significance. The theoretical maneuvers employed by scholars of Religion and Ecology have greater significance than simply choosing among potential objects of analysis: they also profoundly shape the audience, reception and impact of such analysis.

Debating the "Religion" in Religion and Ecology

At the heart of the question surrounding the term religion is a long-standing disagreement between scholars who employ substantive definitions of religion and those whose work utilizes functionalist perspectives (Berger 1974). Put crudely, substantive theories of religion demand that phenomena manifest some kind of "belief in spiritual beings" in order to properly called "religious." Prominent substantivist theorists include E. B. Tylor, James Frazer, and Rodney Stark. Such an approach is deemed "substantive" because it asserts that religion should be classified with respect to its referent (variously understood as the sacred, the divine, or, more generically, the supernatural). Functionalist theories of religion argue that religions should be understood in terms of what they *do*

---

11. Saler, *Conceptualizing Religion*; Chidester, *Authentic Fakes*.

rather than what they *believe*.[12] Variously, theorists have argued that the function of religion is the legitimation of social hierarchy (Marx), the establishment of "moral community" and social solidarity (Durkheim), the acceptance of death (Malinowski), the orientation of individuals amidst the complexity of the symbolic order (Geertz), or the negotiation of what it means to be human (Chidester).

Perhaps the most basic point of disagreement between substantivists and functionalists concerns how restrictive definitions of religion should be. From the substantivist perspective, functional definitions are too broad: any phenomenon generative of certain social arrangements is not necessarily "religion." For example, fellow passengers on a cruise ship likely experience an enhanced sense of solidarity, but this seems unconvincing evidence that Norwegian Cruise Lines is a religious organization. From the functionalist perspective, substantive definitions are too narrow: the religious character of modern era, with its attendant proliferation of cultural forms, cannot be accurately captured by looking only to those forms centered on supernatural phenomena. For example, what better lens than religion have scholars to interpret something like the devotion to Star Trek, with its coherent vision of humankind, ritualized conventions, and mythic characters?[13]

The tension between substantive and functional theories of religion has tangibly shaped the development of Religion and Ecology as a field of study. The application of restrictive definitions of religion has limited scholars of Religion and Ecology to an analysis of the ecological dimensions of "world religions." Although Mary Evelyn Tucker and John Grim's influential *Religions of the World and Ecology Series* never explicitly defines "religion," and although it espouses a somewhat functionalist approach (that religions "generate worldviews and ethics"), the series cleaves to the parameters of religious studies charted by the

12. The divergence between functional and substantive definitions of religion, then, is reflective of a deeper, cross-disciplinary divergence between etic and emic modes of social scientific analysis. Should religions be studied and interpreted according to their 'internal' logic or are they better left to the analytical scrutiny of 'outsiders'? It should be clear here that the definitional and theoretical problems about which scholars of nature religion are concerned are quite closely related to the fundamental questions of religious studies. Is "religion" an inherently theological category that necessarily implies normative assumptions about the social order or is it more useful as a flexible analytical category for the social sciences?

13. Jindra, "Star Trek Fandom as a Religious Phenomenon."

substantivist perspective. Roger Gottlieb's important work shares much of this trajectory, asking about "how religious institutions have committed themselves to environmental causes."[14] It is worth noting that these groundbreaking scholars of Religion and Ecology are not focused on "nature religion": rather, their work seeks to articulate the emergence of "religious environmentalism" as a distinct moment in the contemporary history of religions. To evaluate the environmental efforts of the "world's religions," however, does not address the deeper theoretical and definitional questions prompted by inquiry about the relationship between religion and nature in the first place.[15]

These questions are particularly important in Religion and Ecology, where the proliferation of books about "eco-spirituality,"[16] the canonical place of Henry David Thoreau and John Muir as "prophets" of the environmental movement,[17] and the widespread location of "faith in science"[18] suggest that the "religion" in Religion and Ecology demands considerable conceptual flexibility. Restrictive definitions of religion, with their emphasis on "faith-based institutions," present an authenticity problem in that they impose unnecessarily stringent limits on what counts as religion. "Inauthenticity," in this sense, echoes Heidegger's use of the term: what is to be counted as religion is dictated by disciplinary inertia, the "they-self" of scholarly convention.

At the other extreme, broad definitions of religion risk relegating Religion and Ecology to the realm of scholarly abstraction. One emphasis within Religion and Ecology has been to identify the implicit religious

---

14. Despite his privileging of "world religions" in texts like *Deep Ecology and the World's Religions* (2001) and the *Oxford Handbook on Religion and Ecology* (2006), Gottlieb's 2006 monograph, *A Greener Faith*, does include a chapter appraising "environmentalism as spirituality."

15. Itself a category currently under intense criticism (see Masuzawa, *The Invention of World Religions*), the association of "world religions" with canonical, institutionalized communities understood primarily in comparison to hegemonic European traditions, seems an inadequate lens through which to survey the rapidly changing religious landscape of the modern world. Similar critiques of "organized religion" and "religious traditions" cast doubt on the validity of those categories as well; see McCutcheon, *Manufacturing Religion*; Herview-Leger, *Religion as a Chain of Memory*.

16. Carroll, *Sustainability and Spirituality*; Kearns and Keller, eds., *Ecospirit*; Bergmann, et. al., *Nature, Space and the Sacred*.

17. Cohen, *The Pathless Way*; Thomas Dunlap, *Faith in Nature*.

18. Midgley, *Science as Salvation*.

character of various features of "green culture,"[19] but to classify all aspects of contemporary culture that share significant "commonalities" with phenomena generally agreed upon as "religious" threatens to detach religion from its historical contexts. In its most radical expression, this approach counts as religion anything reminiscent of religion; for social scientists and humanists trained to see religion everywhere, this sets a low threshold. This theoretical perspective is a sloppy application of Jonathan Z. Smith's dictum that because religion "is a term created by scholars for their intellectual purposes [it] therefore is theirs to define."[20] Smith insists that those "intellectual purposes" must be self-reflexively and self-critically justified; he is not offering a theoretical equivalent of "anything goes." Privileging the subjective position of scholars of religion destabilizes the already slippery category "religion," making it difficult, if not impossible, to construct persuasive arguments about what is *authentically* religious. The ability to make and dispute such arguments is critical to religious studies as a field, and to Religion and Ecology in particular.

Take for example the suggestion that gardening might be counted as a form of nature religion. For some, the idea that gardening has a spiritual dimension would be unsurprising; it can certainly serve an important, even religious, role in the lives of dedicated gardeners. It can be personally enriching, socially fulfilling, and is widely associated with religious concepts, metaphysical propositions, and a host of stories and myths.[21] Gardening, however, is not synonymous with "religion" and to categorize it as such fails to accurately and fully capture a great deal of what it is. For many, gardening is no more than a hobby. For others, it is a simple necessity of food production or perhaps even a business enterprise. Of course, the attempt to theorize gardening as religious practice does not require all gardeners agree with such a classificatory maneuver, but it seems reasonable to mount a more restrained argument, interpreting gardening as a practice that, for some, has religious qualities. This is much more in line with Smith's assertion: it requires that in order to classify phenomena as religious, scholars must carefully delineate their intellectual purposes and the limits of their arguments. The alternative,

19. See Taylor, *Ecological Resistance Movements*; Bloch, "Alternative Spirituality and Environmentalism"; Brinkerhoff and Jacob, "Mindfulness and Quasi-Religious Meaning Systems"; Thomas Dunlap, *Faith in Nature*.

20. Smith, "Religion, Religions, Religious," 281.

21. Sobosan, "Cultivating Autonomy," 53-59; Michael Jamison, "The Joys of Gardening."

to identify gardening as something exhibiting the general properties of religion, reduces the category "religion" to a mere heuristic. To do so is the theoretical equivalent of the "Midas touch": if everything one touches turns to religion, then the term looses its currency. Overly broad definitions of religion have thus created an authenticity problem for Religion and Ecology as well, in the sense that they foreclose the possibility of "actual" religion: religion that exists as such beyond the purposeful touch of theorists.[22]

If a cultural phenomenon like gardening (or surfing or fly-fishing) can be said to have "religious dimensions," yet is not "religion" in the same sense as is Islam or Shinto, then what is its appropriate classificatory status? If gardening can be classified as "leisure" or "entrepreneurialism" in the same measure as it can be "religion," how do we account for the junctures, layers and overlaps that allow gardening to exist as a "composite" phenomenon?[23] From this perspective, the basic theoretical question of nature and religion changes: for whom is gardening "religious," and why? How can the boundaries between the religious and secular aspects of gardening be thoughtfully treated? A generation of intellectual trailblazers in Religion and Ecology have made phenomena like gardening accessible to scholars of religion, but the theoretical challenge now facing the subfield concerns the limits of the category "religion." Gardening *can* be interpreted as "religious," but *should* it be? The wellspring of intellectual energy currently devoted to the interface of Religion and Ecology situates contemporary scholars at an appropriate moment in which to think candidly about the limits of "religion."

Given that scholarship on nature religion is closely tied to the conceptual basis of "religion," satisfactory theoretical work in this area needs to do more than rely on analogical arguments for religion. Arguments that a phenomenon "resembles" religion, is "implicitly religious," or

22. It is not my intention to imply that there is such a thing as "religion" that exists entirely independent from the scholarly enterprise. The aim of this argument is to suggest that there are ways of delimiting the term "religion" between the two extremes identified above. Perhaps a simpler way to point beyond the "touch of theorists" is to ask when and how something would *not* be religion, even if it were to be identified by scholars as such.

23. Here the word composite is used to indicate the simultaneous applicability of different theoretical categories. The term "hybrid" might be equally useful, especially considering the abundant literature on hybrid religiosity in the late modern era. See Latour, *We Have Never Been Modern*; Canclini, *Hybrid Cultures*; Appadurai, *Modernity at Large*.

is "quasi-religious" do not seem sufficiently rigorous to justify the use of the category religion. In fact, although it substantially expands the theoretical reach of religious studies, the notion of "implicit religiosity" heightens the authenticity problem under discussion. Theories of "implicit" and "quasi-religion" are resultant of the idea that the scholar of religion—and *not* the adherent of religion—figure most prominently in determining the religious character of social phenomena. In these approaches religion is something that is seen by and recognized as such by expert social scientists, yet there is a lack of clarity about how such vision is acquired or exercised.

Among scholars whose work engages "implicitly religious" phenomena, there are two primary apologies for the taxonomic procedure. One is the concept of "family resemblances," which draws on the work of linguistic philosophers like Ludwig Wittgenstein and George Lakoff in support of a flexible, inclusive definition of religion. The class of phenomena called "religion" is, according to this perspective, not necessarily populated by things that share common characteristics; rather, "religion" designates a loose assortment of practices, ideas and symbols that may only be akin to one another by mutual relation to distant "cousins" (for example, solitaire and football both belong to the category "game," although they share few if any common properties).[24] The other line of defense of "implicit religiosity" is articulated most clearly by David Chidester, who obfuscates the line between "authentic" and "inauthentic" religious phenomena by arguing that even fake religions "do real religious work."[25] Chidester's claim is that because the conditions of the modern era make it difficult, perhaps impossible, to delineate between the actual and the artificial, membership in the group "religion" ought be determined solely with regard to function. Neither of these accounts of how scholars can utilize their ability to designate a thing as religious offers much in the way of checks and balances to this power; neither offers a coherent vision about what the limits of the category of religion might be.

---

24. The most thoroughgoing development of "family resemblance" theory in the study of religion can be found in Saler's *Conceptualizing Religion*. Though this approach is associated primarily with Saler's work, other prominent theorists of religion have also taken similar approaches (e.g. Smith, "Religion, Religions, Religious"; Spiro, "Religion: Problems of Definition and Explanation").

25. Chidester, *Authentic Fakes: Religion and American Popular Culture*.

Nature Religion in Theoretical Relief

The term nature religion offers an appropriate point of entry into debates about the meaning and limits of religion because it typically designates a point of conjunction between "religious" and "secular" affairs. At its core, nature religion refers to a marriage of phenomena conventionally understood as religion (metaphysical beliefs, ritual practices, sacred institutions, etc.) to phenomena not conventionally understood as such (biochemical feedback loops, recreational activities, etc.). The field of Religion and Ecology can be mapped as a variety of conversations about the inseparability of conventional and unconventional forms of religiosity, or, more bluntly, the inseparability of religious tradition and environmental practice. Around the category "nature religion" scholars have developed three distinct ways of discussing the conjunction of religion with environmental beliefs and behaviors. To survey how these perspectives shape the field of Religion and Ecology is helpful for seeing—and thinking—the way forward.

First, theologians and ethicists have deployed numerous conceptual and symbolic resources with the purpose of overcoming the ecological limitations of traditional religious ethics. In the Abrahamic traditions this "greening of religion" is commonly known as "ecotheology," but equivalent conversations and communities of activism can be found in every globalized religious system. Ecotheological discourse has a secular corollary: for many environmentalists, ecological sustainability necessarily requires the cooperation of religious communities.[26] Although the last several decades have produced a rich variety of "religious environmentalisms," ranging from the practical to the revolutionary, these various threads of theological and ethical conversation rarely address the authenticity question at hand. Moreover, the scholarly literature analyzing religious environmentalism has engaged only peripherally in theoretical reflection about meaning of "religion" itself.[27] This genre of

26. It is worth noting that there has been substantial resistance to the alignment of institutional religion and environmental causes. Reactionary forces within religious traditions have responded negatively to some or all of the claims advanced by ecotheologians (e.g. Nash, "The Bible vs. Biodiversity") and skeptics, both within and without religious communities, have worried that the environmental movement has, at times, exploited the moral and political force of religious authority, see Callicott, *Earth's Insights*; Larson, "Conceptual Resources in South Asia."

27. See Kearns, "Saving the Creation"; Kearns and Keller, eds, *Ecospirit*; Wolkomir, et al., "Denominational Subcultures of Environmentalism."

Religion and Ecology scholarship simply underscores the authenticity problematic: are these religious merely because the textual sources and ritual traditions upon which ecotheologians draw are included in "conventional understandings" of religion?

The second kind of approach to Religion and Ecology comes from sociologists of the structural functionalist school. Reasoning from the Durkheimian perspective that religion is that which serves to bind societies together in "moral community," many social scientists labor to identify the religious dimensions of nominally secular environmental practices. This functionalist perspective saturates much of the literature on religion and nature, essentially arguing that environmentalism is "like" a religion.[28] Taken literally, this line of analysis seems to suggest that that the resemblance between "actual religions" and "quasi-religions" is coincidental, rather than causal. Though it offers a powerful descriptive tool for ethnographers and social scientists, unreflective functionalism asks more than it answers the question concerning the authenticity of "nature religion."

The third type of scholarship on Religion and Ecology is largely the domain of historians and human geographers. Figures like Roderick Nash, Catherine Albanese, Mark Stoll, and Rebecca Kneale Gould trace the continuities between modern environmentalism and historical religious forms, such as Romanticism, Metaphysicalism, the Protestant Ethic, and the Social Gospel movement. Clearly, though, the range of phenomena grouped together as nature religion cannot be reduced to mere recapitulations of religious history. In taking historical religious communities or traditions as the starting point for their analyses, these— and other like-minded—scholars take historicity as the fundamental grounds upon which nature religion can be interpreted as "religion."

That a field as eclectic and interdisciplinary as Religion and Ecology should serve as a home to discordant voices and conceptual divergences is not surprising. Yet these divergences frequently affect shared conceptual territory. A specific example will help point the way to the kinds of theoretical concision demanded by competing notions of what counts as religion. Although the term nature religion serves a central conceptual category shaping scholarly work on Religion and Ecology, its application remains uneven and ambiguous. This uneven application leaves important and fundamental research questions unaddressed. For

28. Dunlap, *Faith in Nature: Environmentalism as Religious Quest.*

example, what are the relations between "religious environmentalisms" (i.e. the environmental dimensions of religion as it is "conventionally understood") and environmentalism as implicit religion? What are the broader social, historical and cultural patterns that have shaped these two divergent—but nonetheless clearly related—phenomena?

One example of where this definitional confusion arises can be found in the way nature religion is simultaneously equated with and juxtaposed to "civil religion." Such ambiguity about the relation between nature religion and other forms of "non-church religion" is evident in Amanda Porterfield's review of *Nature Religion in America*. She writes,

> [Albanese's] study of nature religion challenges Robert Bellah's well-known argument that 'civil religion' is the great tradition of American culture. From Albanese's perspective, nature religion is the morally superior tradition in American cultural history, while civil religion has often been the agent of Anglo-Protestant imperialism and the antagonist of democratic pluralism. Albanese suggests that nature religion is more often harmonious than patriarchal and that, unlike the repressively homogenizing effect of civil religion, the purest examples of nature religion have been as open, accommodating, and pluralistic as nature herself.[29]

This is suggestive of a dualism between nature religion and civil religion, an antagonism between the "Anglo-Protestant" hegemony of civil religion and the "accommodating, pluralistic" structure of nature religion. The former is a phenomenon derivative of religious orthodoxy, conditioned by the maintenance of tradition and a project of social orthodoxy. The latter is a fluid stream running through American life and letters; nature religion acts, as Porterfield would have it, as a counterbalance to religious "imperialism." Nor is Porterfield's approach uncommon. In his forward to *Nature Religion in America*, Martin Marty refers to this same tension, framing nature religion as the "countercovenant" to the American "covenant" of civil religion. Against the theoretical backdrop of this chapter—the question of what counts as religion—it appears that civil religion is associated with "church religion," but that the radical pluralism of nature religion keeps it outside this category.[30]

---

29. Porterfield, "Nature Religion in America," 156.

30. The reification of nature religion as anti-institutional provides much of the impetus for scholarship that grapples with the "quasi-religious" character of many environmental practices. It is, perhaps, the idea that nature religion is a "countercovenant"

However, the relationship between nature religion and civil religion is sometimes described in much less polar terms. The entry on nature religion in the *Encyclopedia of Religion and Nature* invokes civil religion because of its shared "extra-institutional" expression:

> Like Robert Bellah's notion of civil religion, Albanese's idea of nature religion can help make visible practices in popular culture and political activity of all religions as religious expressions, and thus broaden the understanding of religion beyond its most identifiable institutional expressions, and help religionists more easily to understand religious activities that do not easily correspond to categories of study derived from religious institutions like churches and scriptures.[31]

The comparison here utilizes the legacy of scholarship on civil religion as justification for contemporary attentions to extra-ecclesial phenomena like ecospirituality or wilderness experiences. In the same way that civil religion designates a variety of practices, ideas, beliefs, literary moments, speech acts, and dispositions that suggest themselves to scholars of religion as deserving of the classification "religion," so too does nature religion. Perhaps Porterfield's and Davy's comparisons of the categories nature religion and "civil religion" differ because they diverge in their interpretation of Bellah's argument. Whether or not that is the case, both Porterfield and Davy highlight a tension in Albanese's seminal text between nature religion and the "republicanism" of civil religion.

In contrast with her interpreters, Albanese never describes nature religion as opposed to organized religion or religious traditionalism, nor does she pursue an analogical explanation as to why nature religion is "religious." Where Bellah's original explanation of civil religion argues that the symbolic elements he identifies "have played a crucial role in the development of American institutions and still provide a religious dimension for the whole fabric of American life, including the political sphere,"[32] Albanese does not privilege the functionalist approach. Her direct comparison of nature religion and civil religion states,

> Like the term civil religion, which has become part of our academic language in religious studies since 1967, nature religion is a

---

that has established the theoretical tensions between implicit religiosity and conventional religiosity in Religion and Ecology studies.

31. Davy, "Nature Religion," 1174.

32. Bellah, "Civil Religion in America," 3.

contemporary social construction of past and present American religion . . . when I speak of nature religion I do not mean a religious genre that is divorced from human history or society. It is, of course, tempting to subsume [these kinds of phenomena] into familiar comparative categories, to view the practice of nature religion as an example, on American terrain, of the 'cosmic' opposite to the Judeo-Christian religions of history. But that is hardly what I have in mind.[33]

Here Albanese anticipates and directly rebuts the polarization of nature religion with "church religion." Nature religion is like civil religion because it deploys the symbolic resources of religious tradition(s) as a means to grapple with emergent social and historical questions. For Albanese neither nature religion nor civil religion is synonymous with "church religion": both are deeply and variously spread throughout American culture. From her view, nature religion and civil religion, however, are each intimately linked with religious tradition and bear the traces of institutionalized religious forms and theological patterns. Though nature religion is, as Albanese puts it, "unorganized, non-institutional, and largely intuitive," it flourishes in particular "denominations" that are traceable through time and space, derivative of enduring conceptual and behavioral patterns, and genealogically descended from existing religious systems.[34] In other words, even though nature religion is often a diffuse cultural phenomenon, its religiosity is attributable less to its function that to its form. For Albanese, whose voice carries significant weight regarding this category, nature religion is a historical, genealogical category, not a functional, analogical one.

Academic investigations about the relationship of Religion and Ecology must develop a more robust theoretical framework if it is to meaningfully capture the continuities and discontinuities between the environmental movement and "traditional" religion. The modern realization that human activity can, and has, profoundly affected natural systems at global, local, and regional scales provoke questions that establish a new context for religious thought and behavior. It is around this context that scholars of Religion and Ecology need to construct a theoretical perspective that accounts for developments across the various areas of research to which the field attends. The "authenticity problem"

33. Albanese, *Nature Religion in America*, 8.
34. Ibid., 199.

described above presents a challenge to scholars of Religion and Ecology to seek out theoretical models that accurately describe the social change and cultural plasticity that animates nature religion but advance within coherent limits about what can and should be counted as religion.

When deployed abstractly, structural functionalism and other social scientific theories of "quasi-religion" actually obscure the religiosity of nature religion. In making the case for the religiosity of nature religion, the analogical argument is less convincing to the "conventionalists" mentioned at the outset of this chapter than would be a genealogical one. The insufficiency of functional approaches, however, cannot adequately be corrected by a wholesale reversion to theologically essentialist arguments that favor strictly delimiting religion as practices and beliefs pertaining to supernatural beings. In between the two theoretical extremes that bifurcate contemporary scholarship in Religion and Ecology, there are a wide variety of possible alternatives. Rather than choose among all these potential ways of theorizing the field, it is more reasonable to establish some basic limits of what can be authentically called nature "religion." The remainder of this essay sketches the parameters of an approach flexible enough to steer a middle course between the Scylla of quasi-religiosity and the Charybdis of theological narrow-mindedness.

Conceptualizing Nature Religion Genealogically

In 1905, the well-known naturalist John Burroughs wrote that

> the forms and creeds of religion change, but the sentiment of religion—the wonder and reverence and love we feel in the presence of the inscrutable universe—persists. Indeed, these seem to be renewing their life today in this growing love for all natural objects and in this increasing tenderness towards all forms of life. If we do not go to church as much as did our fathers, we go to the woods much more, and are much more inclined to make a temple of them than they were.[35]

Burroughs's take on American religiosity at the outset of the twentieth century embodies the same conceptual problems that face contemporary scholars of nature religion. Are the woods a kind of temple? What is the relationship between "worship" at this temple and so-called "church religion"? Or, as Burroughs goes on to argue in *The Gospel of*

35. Burroughs, *The Gospel of Nature*, 4.

Nature, does this "growing love for all natural objects" signify a return to religious life in its most "authentic," "primordial" formulation? Is the "sentiment of religion" visible in the "increasing tenderness towards all forms of life" the result of a radical break with traditional religion or a transformation of religious tradition itself? Against the backdrop of Burroughs's words, the salience of debates about the meaning of religion for scholars of nature religion is distinctly evident.

The power of Burroughs's analysis lies in the fact that he frames the emergence of what might now be called "nature religion" in historical relation to "church religion." Do the new and emerging modalities of religion that take nature as their fundamental ground assume the "form" of extant religious traditions or do they grow directly from the "content" of such traditions? If religion is defined functionally, then "form" serves as the primary vehicle for its historical transmission, and contemporary nature religion can be said to be functionally *analogous* to "church religion." If religion is defined substantively, then nature religion is only religious to the degree to which it shares content with "church religion": it is religious only so far as it is *genealogically* descended of historical traditions. Simply put, the theoretical approach required for this field of study needs to be rigorously historical and at the same time committed to identifying the patterns and moments that account for why, as Burroughs put it, "the forms and creeds of religion change."

This essay proposes that a solution to the "authenticity problem" can be found by grounding the "religiosity" of nature religion genealogically, rather than analogically. Simply stated, this means that scholars working on nature religion should be burdened with the task of historically situating any given example of nature religion, accounting for its religious roots and its relationships to sacred histories. Does this mean that only "church religion" and its offspring can be counted as religious? Absolutely not; in fact, it means something much more radical. A genealogical approach conceptualizes religion as gene sequence, which, though unique and enduring, can be found throughout a population, can be recessive or dominant, can be concentrated or diffuse. Like a gene sequence, religion is infinitely repeatable, but not infinitely repeated; each instantiation requires verification that is traceable through earlier generations. Unlike a gene sequence, however, "religion" can be transmitted in a variety of ways: religious histories can tell stories of mutation, hybridization, recapitulation, decay, influence, substitution, resuscitation or ossification.

By situating nature religion in historical context, the engagement of scholars of Religion and Ecology with definitional debates favors narration over classification. This is theoretically advantageous in that it offers conceptual clarity about what properly belongs to the study of religion. It adjudicates between the different classificatory approaches of functionalists and substantivists. For example, functionalist scholarship (i.e., analogical theories of religion) has interpreted Greenpeace as a religious movement because it organizes a community around a moral center and is replete with ritual behavior.[36] This maneuver remains intractably unconvincing for substantivists,[37] but a genealogical approach might provide a more convincing basis for classifying the organization as "religious." The fact that Greenpeace's founders, Irving and Dorothy Stowe, were committed Quakers offers a much stronger point of leverage into conversations about the organization's religious character. Why Greenpeace's official history downplays the way that its roots in the Religious Society of Friends shaped the group's trajectory becomes an important research question.[38] If religion as it is "conventionally understood" is central in Greenpeace's genesis, what does it mean that this is not an important part of the organization's contemporary identity? Any genealogical approach to this question would, in repudiation of an a priori concept of religion, be compelled to reconstruct a narrative that traced Greenpeace's history from "conventionally religious" to "implicitly religious." This kind of historical work should bring to the fore the theological and ethical concepts that played a role in the group's foundation, the ways and reasons that Greenpeace members have understood their participation as religious, and, perhaps more importantly, the ways and reasons that group members have not understood their participation as religious. A genealogical perspective should replace the question as to whether or not Greenpeace qualifies as "religion" with the question as to how the organization embodies and is embedded in broader patterns of religious history. The status of Greenpeace as an implicitly religious organization ought not rest on a definitional abstraction; that

36. Glass, "Producing Patriotic Inspiration at Mount Rushmore"; Greil and Robbins, eds. *Between the Sacred and the Secular.*

37. Stark, "Reconceptualizing Religion."

38. The group's description by some contemporary commentators as "originated by Quakers, now independent" belies the need for more critical historical analysis, see King, "Transformative Nonviolence."

members might not see the group as religious is something that needs to be built into the explanatory framework.

The strength of analogical theories is that they manifestly reject the idea that religion is a static category and work to defend against the normative (and subtly theological) claim that only certain kinds of belief and behavior can be considered "authentically" religious. Despite this strength, the preceding pages have attempted to outline some of the problems faced by theories of religion that rely on analogy for the heavy-lifting of their classificatory enterprise. A converse weakness of substantive theories is that they offer little insight about how religions grow and change over time; as long as a phenomenon has "the sacred" at its core it is and always will be "religion." But what of secularization? Do the vestiges of religious tradition, stripped of their once sacred character, remain appropriate objects for the scholar of religion? Do social movements with religious origins remain "religion" beyond the point they continue to meet substantive definitions of the category?

The degree to which theories of religion are able to grapple with this issue is a useful measure of their suitability for scholars of Religion and Ecology. In aiming to interpret popular forms of religiosity, analogical theories of religion have been particularly attentive to practices "outside the formal structures provided by most societies for [religious] activity' because [those] structures have become inadequate."[39] Built into the theoretical perspective of implicit religiosity, quasi-religions, and, by extension, nature religions, is an unspoken affirmation of secularization theory. Confusingly, these theories assert that "religiosity" is something scholars must look for outside the confines of "Religion" because "Religion" no longer houses all examples of the category "religion." Where functionalist and analogical theories posit that popular culture does "religious work," they also raise questions concerning the displacement of conventional forms of religion. The genealogical approach asserts that scholarship on nature religion ought to reflexively engage with its implications for secularization theory. Because the conceptual framework for scholarship on "non-church religions" is premised on the idea that such religious forms displace, replace or can substitute for "church religions," scholars working on such forms need to account for the historical position of their data. Whether or not the religious practices and ideas studied under the heading of nature religion "do actual religious

39. Albanese, "Religion and American Popular Culture."

work" suggests an empirically verifiable research question. Although it will not always be demonstrable that "non-church religions" displace (or supplement) "church religions," serious theoretical reflection about the meaning of nature religion must account for such relations.[40]

To assert that particular modern phenomena should be counted as members of the class of objects called "religion" is to say that those phenomena have joined that class; their belonging to that class can thus most appropriately be determined by narrating that process of joining. Despite the shortcomings of analogical approaches, the genealogical perspective also looks beyond the limits imposed by "conventional understandings" of the term religion. The standard of evidence required to establish a genealogical explanation for religious phenomena is not so burdensome as to exclude everything but "traditional religion." The genealogical method encourages scholars—in the field of Religion and Ecology and elsewhere—to look to the ways that cultural phenomena inherit their religious context, to understand how religion serves as a critical source for contemporary social forms, ecological and otherwise.[41]

As should be clear in the above, genealogically oriented scholarship is suited to look for "nature religion" both inside and outside the confines of "church religion." Inside "church religion," through its demand that all cases of "nature religion" need be accounted for historically, the genealogical approach reframes the way that "religious environmentalism" is to be understood. Such phenomena emerge out of religious communities, but do so in ways that shift the center of gravity for those same communities. The category "nature religion" should ask challenging questions about how religious institutions maintain tradition and how they adapt to evolving cultural and ecological landscapes. Outside "church religion," the genealogical approach is easily lent to a variety of "extra-ecclesial" phenomena, as long as those phenomena are not abstractly rendered as religion. Religion can be found scattered throughout the fabric of modern life, though never disconnected from the threads of history and tradition. A thing is not religious because it looks religious;

40. The demand that analogical theories of religion must account for the historical relationships between tradition and emergent practices also holds true for work on related cultural forms like civil religion, popular religion, and industrial religion, see Callahan, et. al., "Allegories of Progress."

41. Excellent scholarship in this direction includes Danielle Hervieu-Leger's *Religion as a Chain of Memory* (as well as her more focused treatment of nature religion) and Kelly Besecke's work on religious discourse.

rather, it looks religious because it embedded in a particular religious history. It is this embeddedness that qualifies a thing as religion, and to which scholars of religion working outside the confines of "conventional understanding" must be attentive.

Whatever its bearing on Religion and Ecology scholarship, a genealogical approach fails to solve the definitional problems that have confronted religious studies for generations. This perspective does not provide an adequate tool for deciding what counts as religious history in the first place, and, in essence, kicks the definitional question down the road. However, the burden to engage in explicit, historical justifications of the use of the term religion establishes clearer parameters for how scholars ought approach, interpret, and explain phenomena marginalized by "conventional understandings" of religion. This holds particularly true for scholarship on nature religion, where a disparate collection of cultural phenomena have been assembled into a whole that may or may not be "religious" in the same way. Through its insistence on narrative, context, and relationship, the genealogical approach outlined here offers an effective way to account for the religiosity of nature religion. Only insofar as nature religion can be placed in the context of broader patterns of religious history can it be said to be authentically religious.

Bibliography

Albanese, C. L. *Nature Religion in America: From the Algonkian Indians to the New Age.* Chicago: University of Chicago Press, 1990.

———. "Religion and American Popular Culture: An Introductory Essay," *Journal of the American Academy of Religion* 44 (1996) 733–42.

Appadurai, Arjun. *Modernity at Large: The Cultural Dimensions of Globalization.* Public Worlds 1. Minneapolis: University of Minnesota Press, 1996.

Bailey, E. I. *Implicit Religion in Contemporary Society.* Leuven: Peeters, 1997.

Bartkowski, John P., and W. Scott Swearingen. "God Meets Gaia in Austin, Texas: A Case Study of Environmentalism as Implicit Religion." *Review of Religious Research* 38 (1997) 308–24.

Bellah, Robert. "Civil Religion in America." *Daedelus* 96 (1967) 1–21.

Berger, Peter L. "Some Second Thoughts on Substantive versus Functional Definitions of Religion." *Journal for the Scientific Study of Religion* 13 (1974) 125–33.

Bergmann, Sigurd et al. *Nature, Space and the Sacred: Transdisciplinary Perspectives.* Farnham, UK: Ashgate, 2009.

Besecke, Kelly. "Speaking of Meaning in Modernity: Reflexive Spirituality as a Cultural Resource." *Sociology of Religion* 62 (2001) 365–81.

———. "Seeing Invisible Religion: Religion as a Societal Conversation about Transcendent Meaning." *Sociological Theory* 23 (2005) 179–96.

Bloch, J. P. "Alternative Spirituality and Environmentalism." *Review of Religious Research* 40 (1998) 55–73.

Brinkerhoff, Merlin B., and Jeffery C. Jacob. "Mindfulness and Quasi-Religious Meaning Systems: An Empirical Exploration within the Context of Ecological Sustainability and Deep Ecology." *Journal for the Scientific Study of Religion* 38 (1999) 524–42.

Burroughs, John. *The Gospel of Nature.* Chester: Applewood Books, 1905.

Callahan, Richard J. et al. "Allegories of Progress: Industrial Religion in the United States." *Journal of the American Academy of Religion* 78 (2010) 1–39.

Callicott, J. Baird. *Earth's Insights: A Survey of Ecological Ethics from the Mediterranean Basin to the Australian Outback.* Berkeley: University of California Press, 1994.

Canclini, Néstor García. *Hybrid Cultures: Strategies for Entering and Leaving Modernity.* Minneapolis: University of Minnesota Press, 1995.

Carroll, John E. *Sustainability and Spirituality.* Albany, State University of New York Press, 2004.

Chidester, David. *Authentic Fakes: Religion and American Popular Culture.* Berkeley: University of California Press, 2005.

Cohen, Michael P. *The Pathless Way: John Muir and American Wilderness.* Madison: University of Wisconsin Press, 1984.

Davy, Barbara Jane. "Nature Religion." In *The Encyclopedia of Religion and Nature*, edited by Bron Raymond Taylor et al, 2:1173–75. 2 vols. London: Thoemmes Continuum, 2005.

Dunlap, Thomas. *Faith in Nature: Environmentalism as Religious Quest.* Weyerhaeuser Environmental Books. Seattle: University of Washington Press, 2004.

Glass, Matthew. "Producing Patriotic Inspiration at Mount Rushmore." *Journal of the American Academy of Religion* 62 (1994) 265–83.

Gottlieb, Roger S. *A Greener Faith: Religious Environmentalism and Our Planet's Future.* New York: Oxford University Press, 2006.

———. *The Oxford Handbook on Religion and Ecology.* Oxford: Oxford University Press, 2006.

Gould, Rebecca Kneale. *At Home in Nature: Modern Homesteading and Spiritual Practice in America.* Berkeley: University of California Press, 2005.

Greil, Arthur L., and Thomas Robbins, editors. *Between Sacred and Secular: Research and Theory on Quasi-Religion.* Religion and the Social Order 4. Greenwich, CT: JAI Press, 1994.

Hervieu-Leger, Danièle, editor. *Religion et Ecologie.* Sciences humaines et religious. Paris: Cerf, 1993.

———. *Religion as a Chain of Memory.* Translated by Simon Lee. New Brunswick, NJ: Rutgers University Press, 2000.

Jamison, Michael. "The Joys of Gardening: Collectivist and Bureaucratic Cultures in Conflict." *Sociological Quarterly* 26 (1985) 473–90.

Jindra, Michael. "Star Trek Fandom as a Religious Phenomenon," *Sociology of Religion* 55 (1994) 27–51.

Kanagy, Conrad L., and Hart M. Nelson. "Religion and Environmental Concern: Challenging the Dominant Assumptions." *Review of Religious Research* 37 (1995) 33–45.

Kearns, L. "Saving the Creation: Christian Environmentalism in the United States." *Sociology of Religion* 57 (1996) 55–70.

Kearns, Laurel and Catherine Keller. *Ecospirit: Religions and Philosophies for the Earth.* Transdisciplinary Theological Colloquia. New York: Fordham University Press, 2007.

King, Sallie B. "Transformative Nonviolence: The Social Ethics of George Fox and Thich Nhat Hanh." *Buddhist-Christian Studies* 18 (1998) 3–36.

Larson, Gerald J. "Conceptual Resources in South Asia for 'Environmental Ethics.'" In *Nature in Asian Traditions of Thought: Essays in Environmental Philosophy*, edited by J. Baird Callicott and Roger T. Ames, 267–77. SUNY Series in Philosophy and Biology. Albany: State University of New York Press, 1989.

Latour, Bruno. *We Have Never Been Modern*. Translated by Catherine Porter. Cambridge: Harvard University Press, 1993.

Lemert, Charles C. "Defining Non-Church Religion." *Review of Religious Research* 16 (1975) 186–97.

Masuzawa, Tomoko. *The Invention of World Religions*. Chicago: University of Chicago Press, 2005.

McCutcheon, Russell T. *Manufacturing Religion: The Discourse of Sui Generis Religion and the Politics of Nostalgia*. New York: Oxford University Press, 1997.

Midgley, Mary. *Science as Salvation: A Modern Myth and Its Meaning*. London: Routledge, 1992.

Nash, James A. "The Bible vs. Biodiversity: The Case against Moral Argument from Scripture." *Journal for the Study of Religion, Nature and Culture* 3 (2009) 213–37.

Porterfield, Amanda. Review of *Nature Religion in America from the Algonkian Indians to the New Age*, by Catherine L. Albanese. *Journal of the American Academy of Religion* 59 (1991) 155–57.

Rappaport, Roy A. *Ecology, Meaning, and Religion*. Richmond, CA: North Atlantic, 1979.

Saler, Benson. *Conceptualizing Religion: Immanent Anthropologists, Transcendent Natives, and Unbounded Categories*. Studies in the History of Religions 56. Leiden: Brill, 1993.

Sanford, A.W. "Pinned on Karma Rock: Whitewater Kayaking as Religious Experience." *Journal of the American Academy of Religion* 75 (2007) 875–95.

Smith, Jonathan Z. "Religion, Religions, Religious" in *Critical Terms for Religious Studies*, edited by Mark C. Taylor. Chicago: University of Chicago Press, 1998.

Snyder, Samuel. "New Streams of Religion: Fly Fishing as a Lived, Religion of Nature," *Journal of the American Academy of Religion* 75 (2007) 896–922.

Sobosan, Jeffrey G. "Cultivating Autonomy." *Journal of Religion and Health* 18 (1979) 53–59.

Spiro, Melford E. "Religion: Problems of Definition and Explanation." In *Anthropological Approaches to the Study of Religion*, edited by Michael Banton, 85–126. A. S. A. Monographs 3. London: Tavistock, 1966.

Stark, Rodney. "Reconceptualizing Religion, Magic, and Science." *Review of Religious Research* 43 (2001) 101–20.

Stoll, Mark. *Protestantism, Capitalism, and Nature in America*. Albuquerque: University of New Mexico Press, 1997.

Taylor, Bron Raymond. *Ecological Resistance Movements: The Global Emergence of Radical and Popular Environmentalism*. SUNY Series in International Environmental Policy and Theory. Albany: State University of New York Press, 1995.

———. "Ecology and Nature Religion." In *The Encyclopedia of Religion*, edited by Lindsay Jones et al., 4:2664–68.15 vols. 2nd ed. Detroit: Macmillan Reference USA, 2005.

———. "Exploring Religion, Nature, and Culture." *Journal for the Study of Religion, Nature, and Culture* 1 (2007) 5–18.

———. "Focus Introduction: Aquatic Nature Religion." *Journal of the American Academy of Religion* 75 (2007) 863–74.

———. "Surfing into Spirituality and a New, Aquatic Nature Religion." *Journal of the American Academy of Religion* 75 (2007) 923–51.

Tucker, Mary Evelyn, and John Grim, editors. *Religions of the World and Ecology*. 10 vols. Cambridge: Harvard University Press, 1997–2004.

Wolkomir, Michelle et al. "Denominational Subcultures of Environmentalism." *Review of Religious Research* 38 (1997) 325–43.

3

The Importance and Limits of Taking Science Seriously

Data and Uncertainty in Religion and Ecology

Sarah E. Fredericks and Kevin J. O'Brien

Introduction

Environmental degradation raises a complex and daunting set of questions about how contemporary people, especially in industrial societies, live. The natural first response to such questions is to look for clear and straightforward answers. Most people seek these answers from natural scientists, researchers who can cite quantifiable data to support their claims about how the world works, how human activity has changed it, and what can be done to alleviate environmental degradation. This puts those of us in the field of Religion and Ecology in an odd position: When we seek to address the challenges of environmental degradation and to challenge the search for easy answers, how will we gain attention from a public that may assume insight will come only from scientists?

One option is to demonstrate that scientific experts seek our input. Along these lines, scholars in our field frequently cite texts like the "Open Letter to Religious Communities" spearheaded by Carl Sagan in 1990, which appeals to religious people "to commit, in word and deed, and as boldly as is required, to preserve the environment of the Earth," noting that a problem as enormous as the degradation of the global environment "must be recognized from the outset as having a religious as well as a scientific dimension."[1] Scientific acknowledgement that religious communities are deeply influential helps to authorize the work of our field, giving religious work and studies of religion the imprimatur of the widely accepted experts on environmental issues.

However, taking our charge from scientists implicitly affirms their authority over environmental issues, assuming that the conversation about environmental degradation begins with science. An alternative authorization for our field rejects the authority of natural scientists in favor of humanistic, social scientific, and/or traditionally religious ways of knowing. Proponents of this position challenge the public trust in "data" and those who cite it by noting that science and its technological products have contributed to—perhaps even caused—contemporary environmental degradation. An important source for this argument is Carolyn Merchant's classic text in environmental history, *The Death of Nature*, which argues that contemporary Western science is based on a reductionist belief that nature is mechanistic and can be mastered by scientists with "objective, value-free, and context free knowledge of the external world."[2] Merchant points out that these assumptions represent not just the outcome of careful and rational experimentation, but also the expression of a particular cultural ideology, inscribing the desire to control the natural world into the structures of its sciences. For many in Religion and Ecology, this viewpoint leads to a critique of scientific expertise and an affirmation of the humanistic and social scientific study of culture as checks on and corrections of the excesses of natural science.[3]

Unfortunately, both these broad approaches take a reductive view of science. The first treats scientists as experts who authorize and provide raw material for a separate project by religionists. The second sees science as merely the product of its least constructive foundations. We

1. Sagan, "Open Letter."
2. Merchant, *The Death of Nature*, 290.
3. It is worth noting that Merchant herself does not dismiss science completely, and in fact understands ecology as a "restorative" and "subversive" science capable of criticizing not only the mechanism of other forms of scientific rationality but also the technology such thinking has produced, the capitalism that such technology has spread, and the attitudes toward women and the natural world that all three have perpetuated (ibid., xx).

propose that Religion and Ecology should adopt a nuanced, balanced, and dialogical approach to science. This chapter develops such a perspective, hoping to both learn from and raise questions about science; we call for attention to science in the field of Religion and Ecology by accepting that science has vitally important perspectives and unavoidable limitations, both of which must be faced realistically.

Our central argument is that Religion and Ecology should engage science dialogically; our field should work to raise questions and challenges about environmental degradation alongside scientists. We should not treat science as a simplistic source of answers. The scientific method itself emphasizes the importance of continual correction and insight rather than an unquestioning acceptance of expertise. Nor are scientific perspectives competition against the perspectives developed by Religion and Ecology; on the contrary, science is a conversation partner that helps us to ask and engage the right sorts of questions.

As scholars of Religion and Ecology learn to engage in dialogue with the details and processes of natural science, our field will not only gain a better understanding of environmental degradation, but will also be better prepared to accept our own limitations and engage in a more open dialogue about environmental issues, a dialogue that includes scientists as well as communities and cultures that are too-often left out of academic discourse. Taking science seriously, we argue, is a path to recognizing the limitations of *all* knowledge, the uncertainties inherent in environmental issues, and the tools necessary to respond to these limitations and uncertainties.

Uses of *Ecology* in Religion and Ecology

Unsurprisingly, ecology is the science most often cited by scholars in our field as influential and vital to our work. However, a close reading of some key texts reveals that in Religion and Ecology the word *ecology* is most frequently used not to reference a scientific discipline, but rather to emphasize a general idea of interconnectedness and its moral value.

As the term is usually used in our field, all systems and communities have an ecology, and to note this is to identify and investigate the dynamic relationships between their influences, contexts, and participants. Human belief systems, for example, have an ecology because they are shaped by the environmental, cultural, and ideological factors that together shape what and how people think. One example comes from Sarah McFarland Taylor's study of environmental activism among Catholic women religious, *Green Sisters: A Spiritual Ecology.* Taylor defines this "spiritual ecology" as a meeting point of "Roman Catholicism, environmental activism, nature mysticism, social justice, feminism, and in some cases, even aspects of the metaphysical tradition [in] relationship with one another." The integration of these diverse influences is an ecology, a system of interrelatedness in which "We see a reshaping of religious culture, born of a system that draws simultaneously on a plurality of resources."[4] The word emphasizes the integrative nature of these women's lives and work; it calls attention to the intricate syntheses they make of the many influences and institutions of which they are a product. Ecology, here, is a characteristic of a system.

For many in our field, this ecological character of systems has a normative value. For example, offering a Confucian approach to environmental issues, Young-chan Ro appeals to a moral order of interconnectivity: "Ecology, thus, must be based on a reciprocal receptivity with nature and the universe, by 'seeing' and 'listening' to the wonder, mystery, and pain of the universe . . . [H]uman beings must be understood in light of the universe."[5] In this usage, ecology is a normative term, a statement about how people *should* or *must* live in, with, and as part of interconnected systems, conforming to the harmonies and relationships of the world.

Along similar lines, ecofeminist theologian Rosemary Radford Ruether argues that the central lesson of ecology is that "all the diverse animal and plant populations in an ecosystem are kept in healthy and life-giving balance by interdependency."[6] For Ruether, human beings act rightly as creatures of this world only when we live ecologically, participating in this planetary balance and interdependence. This understanding frequently leads to an understanding of ecology as an activist cause and movement that is broader than "environmentalism" because it not only advocates sustainability and responsibility toward nonhuman nature, but also emphasizes the inseparability of humanity from the rest of the world.

4. Taylor, *Green Sisters,* 205.

5. Ro, "Ecological Implications," 184.

6. Ruether, *Gaia & God,* 55.

Perhaps the quintessential usage of ecology as a morally-charged interconnected system that has been influential on our field is that of Brian Swimme and Thomas Berry's *Universe Story*, which ends its celebration of cosmic and evolutionary history by calling for a move into the "ecozoic era," which they hope will be characterized by a central commitment to the fact that "the universe is a communion of subjects rather than a collection of objects . . . Existence itself is derived from and sustained by this intimacy of each being with every other being of the universe."[7] This perspective is of course heavily informed by scientific perspectives—Swimme himself is a mathematical cosmologist and Berry frequently cites cosmology and ecology in his writings. However, *The Universe Story* does not represent a sustained dialogue with scientific ecologists; instead, Swimme and Berry draw upon a key ecological idea to make a moral and theological argument.

Such uses of ecology have important roles in Religion and Ecology, suggesting contributions that scholars in our field can make to the study of environmental problems and religious responses to these problems. However, we worry that if ecology is defined only or mainly as a moral affirmation of interrelatedness, if the central lessons of ecology are understood as ethical or philosophical, then the insights of the ecological sciences will be ignored or oversimplified. Thus, it is important for scholars of Religion and Ecology to recognize that ecology is not only a characteristic and value of systems, it is also a natural science that studies organisms in relationship to one another and to their nonliving contexts.

Understood as a science, ecology does not simplistically demonstrate that "everything is interconnected." Rather, it assumes relationships and then seeks to identify which are the most important and which will contribute to the most effective models of reality. Along these lines, ecological theorists Timothy Allen and Thomas Hoekstra write:

> The folk wisdom of ecology that says everything is connected to everything else is only true in an uninteresting way, for the whole reason for doing ecological research is to find which connections are stronger and more significant than others. We do not wish to show that everything is connected, but rather to show which minimal number of connections that we can measure may be used as a surrogate for the whole system in a predictive model. That is the strategy of the basic scientist in ecology.[8]

7. Swimme and Berry, *Universe Story*, 243.
8. Allen and Hoekstra, *Toward a Unified Ecology*, 284.

Ecology in this sense is a science dedicated to modeling the natural world in order to understand how it functions and predict how it will function in changing conditions. Scholars who emphasize the interconnectedness of all systems share a basic assumption with ecological scientists, but the science develops an analytical research program rather than a moral argument from this starting point.

Understanding ecology in scientific terms is important not only to get the science right, but also because it will complicate and ultimately enrich the morality and cosmology derived from it. Affirmations of ecological systems as morally interconnected must be brought into conversation with more scientific analyses because the latter reveal far more about ecosystems than the "healthy and life-giving balance" identified by Ruether and other proponents of ecology. As Lisa Sideris—an ethicist who has engaged in detailed dialogue with science—observes, a description of the natural world as harmoniously ecological "shuts out all the potentially unpleasant and (as a norm for humans) ethically problematic aspects of natural systems," ignoring the fact that life and ecosystems depend upon predation and destruction at least as much as harmony and relationship.[9] When ecologists study organisms in relationship, they observe competition and death alongside cooperation and harmony, and no attempt to derive morality from ecology should ignore this fact.

Religion and ecology has important lessons to teach about the interconnectedness of all systems and the implications of such interconnection for human morality. But these lessons will be far more relevant to the world and to contemporary environmental degradation if they are further developed in conversation with ecological science, the experimental investigation of organisms in their contexts.

Wrestling with the Data: Taking Science and Its Limits Seriously

Religion and ecology as a field is deeply concerned with environmental challenges, and this is a key reason to engage in dialogue with the scientists who have carefully studied issues like biodiversity loss, climate change, and environmental injustice.

---

9. Sideris, *Environmental Ethics*, 49.

The Importance of Scientific Data in the Study of Environmental Issues

The science of ecology is of particular and urgent importance to scholars of Religion and ecology interested in the degradation of biodiversity. Ecologists have spent years debating the extent to which diversity enhances the health and function of ecosystems, and continue to disagree about *how much* diversity is necessary and whether there can be such a thing as too much diversity within an ecosystem.[10] This is a much more nuanced perspective on the variety of life than that of ethicists who tend to assume that biodiversity preservation is unqualifiedly and always good, and may even define biodiversity itself as a core value or virtue.[11] Furthermore, a subtle scientific discussion of biodiversity notes that the variety of life can in some ways *increase* as landscapes are changed from "wilderness" to urban land.[12] For this reason, scientific research is increasingly focusing on the biodiversity of human neighborhoods, backyards, and bodies as well as on that of rainforests and coral reefs.[13] These expansions of ecological research have significant implications for all who take biodiversity seriously.

Of course, biodiversity is only one of many environmental issues attended to by scholars in our field, and for this reason the science of ecology is not the only relevant conversation partner for scholars of Religion and Ecology. For example, the growing centrality of climate change as an environmental, political, and moral issue calls for careful attention to geology, physics, and climatology, which have much to

10. See for instance Loreau et al., *Biodiversity and Ecosystem Functioning*.

11. For instance, Ivone Gebara extends an unqualified argument about "respect for biodiversity" into a plea for the value of interreligious collaboration, which she calls "religious biodiversity" (*Longing for Running Water*, 205). James Nash makes a similar move when he includes biodiversity in his list of virtues in *Loving Nature*. He later developed a much more nuanced discussion and, we think, a more appropriate term, when he focuses on "bioresponsibility" ("Theological Foundations for Ecological Responsibilities," 6). For an extended attempt to take biodiversity science seriously in the context of Religion and Ecology, see O'Brien, *Ethics of Biodiversity*.

12. Gorke, *Death of Our Planet's Species*, 79–80.

13. This is most clearly demonstrated in the field of conservation biology, which applies scientific research to the activist project of preserving biodiversity. Three conservation biologists note that this task calls ecology "to unembarrassedly examine human populated areas in the same way that it might approach any ecological system—as an arena to generate new patterns, to examine the structure and function of ecological systems, and to test general theories" (Pickett et al., "New Paradigm," 73).

contribute to any analysis of our impact on the planet's basic weather and climate systems. Scholars of Religion and Ecology frequently cite the reports of the Intergovernmental Panel on Climate Change (IPCC), which offers invaluable consensus views on the science of the subject from an international group of experts.[14] Because so many public debates centered for decades on whether climate change is real and whether it is anthropogenic, uses of these reports tend to emphasize the clarity and unanimity of scientists on these questions about climate change. It is therefore vital that Religion and Ecology take this science seriously by affirming the scientific consensus that anthropogenic climate change is a real and urgent problem.

However, while there is widespread agreement that anthropogenic climate change is occurring, there are also numerous areas of continuing research, particularly about the details of climate change: How exactly do the current climactic changes compare to prehistoric periods of change? Will droughts or floods be a more serious problem globally as the climate changes, and which regions of the world are the most at risk? At what point will or did the emissions of industrialized human societies cross a threshold at which fundamental and irreversible climactic change is inevitable? Is it possible to devise technologies whereby we can continue to produce energy from fossil fuels while sequestering the emissions of CO_2 and other climate changing by-products? Are there realistic technological strategies by which the climate can be intentionally altered in order to mitigate or reverse the processes we have already caused? To take climate data seriously means not only citing statistics about global average temperature and rates of change, but also wrestling with uncertainties that characterize the work of climate scientists.[15]

Taking science seriously should not only move us beyond ecology, but also beyond the natural sciences as a whole. This is particularly clear when attention turns to environmental injustice, the reality of inequality and exclusion that leaves oppressed peoples bearing more burdens of degraded environments while exercising less influence over the systems causing that degradation. The work of toxicologists and chemists is vital in studying this phenomenon, but the bulk of relevant research has been

14. The most recent report at the time of this writing is Pachauri and Reisinger, *Climate Change 2007.*

15. For one attempt to take climate science seriously in the context of Religion and Ecology, see Northcott, *Moral Climate.*

conducted by social scientists—particularly sociologists, political scientists, and geographers—who have carefully described and quantified the realities of inequality and the organized responses to it in communities around the world.[16] These scholars demonstrate clear evidence of injustice, vital data that should shape and inspire the field of Religion and Ecology.[17] However, taking such data seriously leads to a new set of questions: To what extent can common themes link very different examples of environmental injustice from across the world and to what extent does the uniqueness of each example need to be respected? Will environmental injustice be most effectively fought with appeals to existing national and international laws, or are new legal initiatives required? These and other questions emerge from a genuine dialogue with the sciences and they are a necessary part of taking scientific data seriously.

The Limits of Scientific Data in the Study of Environmental Issues

Whether helping us to study biodiversity, climate change, or environmental injustice, science is not simply a starting point or a source of information, but also a dialogue partner raising questions and challenges. The reverse is equally true: scholars of Religion and Ecology in dialogue with science should raise questions and challenges about the conclusions and methods of scientists. Taking science seriously means not only learning from it, but also understanding and grappling with its limitations.

The central limitation of science is the simple fact that scientists never have complete knowledge or infallible descriptions of any situation. The scientific method through which theories and data are found, developed, and revised over time is a core expression of this uncertainty; a characteristic of good science is the assumption that its models and ideas will be revised over time as systems and understandings change. Yet many nonscientists and scientists alike make the unscientific assumption that with time, research will lead to certainty, that with a bit more funding or patience experts will completely understand and thus be able to resolve all environmental problems. Those of us in dialogue

16. Two volumes representative of the work in this field are Bullard, *Quest for Environmental Justice* and Westra and Lawson, *Faces of Environmental Racism*. See also the journal *Environmental Justice*.

17. Perhaps the most work has been done on this subject in our field by Larry Rasmussen. See especially *Earth Community, Earth Ethics*; and "Environmental Racism and Environmental Justice."

with scientists must remind them (and ourselves) that their knowledge will always be limited by a lack of research as well as by the unpredictability and complexity of natural systems.

The three environmental issues already discussed demonstrate the inevitability of uncertainty. Even a preliminary study of environmental injustice reveals vast uncertainties, partly because the factors that make marginalized communities vulnerable to injustice also make careful studies of these communities less common. There are wide gaps in available scientific knowledge about how much lead paint there is in housing projects, the quantity and contents of toxic waste dumped in the neighborhoods of poor people and racial minorities, the implications of extractive mining in Native American reservations and third world countries, and the political processes contributing to environmental injustice. Further research could—and should—offer many answers to these questions, and further engagement with the local knowledge of people outside of traditional academe could likely expand our awareness of what can be known. However, such research would almost certainly reveal many more questions as well as answers, and so we must continually acknowledge important limits to what we know about the reality of environmental injustice.

The scientific study of climate change is much better funded and more prominent than the study of environmental injustice, but there nevertheless remain profound uncertainties here, as well. This is demonstrated most alarmingly by reports that the rate of global CO_2 emissions is rising even faster than predicted by most projections—including early IPCC reports.[18] Furthermore, there are some climactic processes that will have inevitably unpredictable effects: the rapid melting of arctic ice will change sea levels and ocean currents, but no one can say exactly how. The thawing of permafrost in northern regions will release long-sequestered carbon and methane, which will likely increase the rate of climate change, but it is not known exactly when this will happen or what its full implications will be. Studying climate change involves making estimates and predictions about the future of multiple dynamic systems, including future human behavior, and so there will always be uncertainties and limits to what can be known about it.

---

18. For example, Michael Raupach and colleagues found that "the emissions growth rate" in the early 2000s exceeded the *highest* estimate the IPCC had made in its report from 2000 ("Global and Regional Drivers of Accelerating CO_2 Emissions," 10289).

Uncertainty is also an inevitable aspect of any attention to biodiversity loss. Scientific studies can conclusively tell us that extinctions and degradation are occurring at alarming rates, but exactly how much will be lost if the expansion of industrial human cultures continues cannot be fully known. In large part, this is because no one knows how much biodiversity exists today. While taxonomists have named about 1.75 million different species, few doubt that at least twice that many exist, and highly respected estimates suggest that there may be 10 million or more distinct species in the world.[19] Furthermore, biodiversity is far greater than just a count of species, including the genetic diversity within each species and the wide array of ecosystemic systems through which species interrelate. Ecologists currently have no widely-agreed upon ways to define and measure genetic and ecosystemic diversity, a sign of even further uncertainty. The variety of life on earth is simply too vast and too complicated for human beings ever to hope to fully understand it, which means that our understanding of life's variety and its loss will always be limited.

Further limitations to science arise from the fact that scientists, as human beings, are susceptible to blinding biases or misdirecting corruption that can change their work and findings. Famous examples of studies sponsored by oil companies that downplay the risks of climate change represent only the most current expression of this reality. Scientists working for the nuclear industry frequently emphasize the safety of that technology and deemphasize the uncertainties surrounding disposal and treatment of nuclear waste; those working for the chemical industry tend to trust the safeguards of their companies without extensive analysis of the uncertainties and limits of what they know about these chemicals. These experts may be presenting sound information, but it is also possible that they have been manipulated or are simply wrong.[20] Some scientists may be dishonest, others may be misguided by the ideas of risk inherent in their disciplinary training.[21]

Sociological and scientific biases may also be combined as when technical, political, and financial limits to data collection enable significant factors to be overlooked in favor of those that are easily measurable

19. Eldredge, *Life in the Balance*, vii.

20. For a broad discussion of the ways scientific findings can be influenced, interpreted, and interfered with by industrial interests, see Michaels, *Doubt Is Their Product*.

21. For a discussion of disciplinary perspectives on risk, see Satterfeld et al., *Risk Analysis*.

or those for which data already exist. For example, most environmental data focuses on individual environmental pollutants, on their prevalence in industrialized nations, and on their economic effects. This means that the cumulative environmental damage resulting from the interaction of pollutants as well as damage in developing countries are under-studied topics. Additionally, harms to community well being that cannot be measured in standard economic terms are often ignored. So, few researchers studying the impacts of environmental damage focus on the fact that indigenous communities often can no longer safely bathe in sacred rivers, eat their traditional foods, or develop other sorts of relationships with their non-human relatives because of pollution and other environmental destruction.[22] Similarly, more data is available to examine national and economic impacts of environmental damage than local or social effects. This means that very severe, local damage may be overlooked (the contention of much environmental justice literature) and that social effects such as the loss of relationships with biota, the land, and bodies of water may be overlooked as short-term economic indicators are studied. Exacerbating these trends is the fact that new studies often focus on previously existing data so that expensive, potentially politically sensitive new data does not need to be collected. Thus, the cycle continues.

These limitations demonstrate both the imperfections and importance of science. After all, the limits of knowledge do not offer any excuse to dismiss the scientific enterprise over that of any other endeavor. All humans and therefore all scholars are influenced by personal agendas, institutional assumptions, and cultural norms; and every academic field deals with the complexities of funding pressures, disciplinary traditions, and the phenomena we study.[23] Thus, natural science and religious studies, like all other human endeavors, should be balanced by a dialogue with other forms of expertise and other ways of knowing.

The limitations of science are therefore a reason to engage not only with the facts of environmental degradation, but also with the work and

---

22. Cumulative risk studies are beginning to look at some of these questions but are still vastly outnumbered by traditional studies. See for example Harper et al., "Traditional Tribal Subsistence Exposure Scenario."

23. These broad claims are well established by the philosophy of science, science and technology studies, and science and religion. See Lakatos, "Falsification and the Methodology of Scientific Research Programmes"; Broad and Wade, *Betrayers of the Truth*; Vaughan, *Challenger Launch Decision*; Kuhn, *Structure of Scientific Revolutions*; Murphy, *Theology in an Age of Scientific Reasoning*; Barbour, *Religion and Science*.

insights of environmental scientists themselves.[24] This will not be easy. Scientific knowledge raises challenges for religion and ecology scholars because the existing or easily measurable data may not be the most important, and because most in our field are not trained to judge, critique, and work with the methods of the natural sciences. To meet these challenges, scholars of Religion and Ecology must become as familiar as possible with the methods and assumptions of the sciences most relevant to our areas of expertise. When we understand these modes of discourse, we will be better prepared to make our own contributions to broad dialogues about environmental degradation. Through deep study of and collaboration with scientists, Religion and Ecology could considerably expand its knowledge base and move forward despite the limitations inherent in every way of knowing and understanding the world.

Tools for Dealing with Uncertainty

When studying environmental degradation and taking science seriously as a source of questions and insight, we face uncertainty about information that has not been found, events that have not yet happened, and phenomena that are too complicated to be accurately modeled and understood. Religion and Ecology needs a set of tools with which to respond to these inevitable uncertainties. A few such tools can be found in the methods of the natural scientists and in the religious and philosophical traditions we study. More will emerge through a genuine dialogue between these perspectives and those of local and traditional communities.[25]

Openness to Change

The natural sciences are well suited to such a dialogue. In self-reflective and careful science that works from the methodological assumption of falliblism, scientists do not claim to have complete understanding or absolute truth. When science is done well, its practitioners are inherently aware of its own limitations, which means that science is fundamentally open to change as knowledge develops.

---

24. Zabinski, "Scientific Ecology and Ecological Feminism," 314–15.

25. For examples of such responses to scientific uncertainty, along with many others, see Vitek and Jackson, *The Virtues of Ignorance.*

To understand and support such openness, philosophers of science have long studied the ways that scientific theories and communities change over time.[26] For example, Imre Lakatos argues that scientific research programs consist of a "hard core" of propositions that researchers tend to see as unchanging as well as a "protective belt" of hypotheses, data, and methods that may be revised or jettisoned as new research challenges the existing theories.[27] Larry Laudan adds a helpful dimension to Lakatos's theory, recognizing the interconnection of theories, methods, and goals such that a change in one may spark a change in another. Laudan offers the revised claim that while some theories, methods, and interpretations of data are significantly protected in a scientific community, even these may be submitted to critique in extreme circumstances when new information is discovered or diverse fields of knowledge encounter one another.[28]

It is useful for scholars of Religion and ecology to understand religious beliefs and communities in a similar way: some ideas in a faith tradition are open to repeated revision (the protective belt) while others are much more rooted in and necessary, if not absolutely unchanging (the hard core). This model for understanding religion can help us to accept that all forms of knowledge, including religious beliefs and practices, can and will change at least to some extent. Religion, like science, is open to correction.[29]

This has, in fact, been a core assumption of many scholars in our field, who have sought to adapt religious traditions in light of environmental degradation. We have, however, disagreed about how much needs to change: some clearly believe that peripheral changes to the protective belt will reveal the green heart of traditional religions, while

26. Kuhn, *Structure of Scientific Revolutions*; Lakatos, "Falsification and the Methodology of Scientific Research Programmes"; and Laudan, "Dissecting the Holistic Picture of Scientific Change."

27. Lakatos, "Falsification and the Methodology of Scientific Research Programmes," 132–37.

28. Laudan, "Dissecting the Holistic Picture of Scientific Change," 146–47. A full discussion of such a combined theory would, of course, need to overcome the fact that all elements are up for correction in Laudan's theory while some are protected in Lakatos's. It seems that some elements would still be more protected though ultimately open to revision.

29. This understanding of religion is compatible with the argument Whitney Bauman makes about a nonfoundationalist religion in chapter 5 of this volume.

others argue that fundamental shifts in the hard core of religion are necessary in response to unprecedented crisis.

For instance, most Christian theologians have argued that the belief in God as Creator should be preserved, albeit possibly reinterpreted (a hard core, which may or may not be unchanging). Other ideas, such as a narrowly anthropocentric vision of God's love or salvation, have been revised or jettisoned (the protective belt). Most Buddhists engaged in environmental activism emphasize that their tradition's longstanding lessons about the link between suffering and desire have something to teach overconsumptive industrial cultures (a hard core), but they bring new ideas like carbon footprint analysis to bear in order to teach this lesson (the protective belt).

Environmental degradation is not the first or only occasion for religious change: faith systems changed during the civil rights movements, industrialization, colonialism and postcolonialism, the Enlightenment, and countless other periods of historical upheaval. In response to a changing world, religious people learn what can be known and adjust their ideas according to their best understanding of reality. Beliefs and practices shift over time.

To be religious in a world of limited knowledge requires a recognition that some beliefs and ideas must change. To study religion during an environmental crisis that we do not fully understand must similarly entail a willingness to recognize, chronicle, and even suggest changes to some aspects of religious belief. To accept the inevitability of religious change is to accept that no claim of or about religion will ever be absolutely final or beyond question. This may be controversial among some believers and scholars, but it is vital if we hope to engage in a mutual and mutually correcting dialogue with the natural sciences about environmental issue. If religions are to respond to environmental degradation, they must be open to adaptation and correction in conversation with the natural sciences and other ways of understanding what is happening to the earth's ecosystems.

Adapting to Uncertainty

Such openness, along with its foundation in uncertainty, raises a challenging question: Where is the line between utter ignorance and an informed uncertainty? In other words, given that we will never know everything, when do we know enough to make a change in tradition, or to take an action on behalf of environmental issue? Along these lines, the precautionary principle in environmental ethics sets one guideline: actions which may have destructive consequences should not be taken, even if full evidence for such effects is not established. [30] This principle hinges on the assumptions 1) that the implications of what we do to our environments frequently cannot or will not be fully understood, and so 2) our default position should be one of caution, of *not* taking actions that might cause harm.

An alternative principle might take a more positive approach, emphasizing that it is important to take action to protect the environment or mitigate harm even when our knowledge is not complete. Along these lines, Paul Ehrlich urges fellow scientists to support the conservation of biodiversity despite the many uncertainties that exist about it. He acknowledges that "more research is badly needed" to better understand the reality of and threats to biodiversity as well as its role in the systems of life on earth, but quickly adds, "we already know enough about the manifold values of biodiversity (of which involvement in biogeochemical cycles is just one) *to take action now*."[31] This assertion that uncertainty is not an excuse for inaction among environmentalists might be generalized into an "activist principle," a complementary counterbalance to the precautionary principle, stating that actions to repair or mitigate environmental degradation should be taken, even if the problems and potential solutions cannot be fully understood.

In balancing these two principles, scholars of Religion and Ecology might find helpful guidance in the concept of adaptive management developed by ecologists and ecosystem managers.[32] This approach to the interaction with and manipulation of environmental systems emphasizes the importance of reversibility and the opportunity to learn from experience, stressing that human interactions with ecosystems should be as adaptive as ecosystems themselves.[33] This approach involves making

30. Freestone and Hey, "Origins and Development of the Precautionary Principle."

31. Ehrlich, "Biodiversity and Ecosystem Function," vii.

32. While adaptive management theory may help people think through an interactive, tentative approach to interacting with environmental systems, we recognize that the language of management is problematically linked to assumptions of human domination and control. We hope that its lessons can be used without unquestionably adopting such a position.

33. Bryan G. Norton has developed and extended this approach with respect to ethics and participatory or democratic decision making. His *Searching for Sustainability* is a good entrance point to adaptive management for scholars of religion and

small, potentially reversible environmental decisions so that actions can be revised or repaired as we learn more about their consequences and the various ways ecosystem components interact.

For example, dam construction in the Grand Canyon has seriously degraded sand bars on the river and has had a significant impact on river biota. Though scientists seek to restore river ecosystems, most do not advocate completely destroying the dams. Rather, they are simulating pre-dam spring floods by letting more water flow through dam spillways for a short period of time to see if the sandbars and the life dependent on them can be restored.[34] As people learn more about their influences on the river system, this program can be stopped, slowed, or accelerated. As such, it is good example of adaptive management, a thoughtful response to the inevitabilities of uncertainty.

Scholars of Religion and Ecology aiming to identify or advocate ethical courses of action, even as scientific knowledge is limited and ecosystems and communities constantly change, could benefit from the tentative, revisionary style of adaptive management. This approach takes something from the precautionary principle, avoiding actions that irreversibly and permanently change a system whenever possible; but it also applies an activist principle, encouraging the use of small changes to improve a situation and/or learn more about how it might be improved. Learning from adaptive management, our field could be better equipped to articulate tentative ethical, theological, and cultural proposals about how religions can and should change, and how human attitudes and practices toward the nonhuman world should take shape.

Expanding the Dialogue

A final tool for responding to inevitable uncertainties is a more expansive dialogue that goes beyond natural science and Religion and Ecology. While this chapter has focused on what scholars in our field should learn from science, it is vital to note that a conversation between religionists and scientists is not expansive enough to respond to the uncertainties and complexities of environmental degradation. We must find ways to

---

philosophy. Other significant texts on adaptive management include Holling, *Adaptive Environmental Assessment*; Lee, *Compass and Gyroscope*; Walters, *Adaptive Management of Renewable Resources*; and Gunderson and Holling, *Panarchy*.

34. Gunderson, "Resilience, Recovery, Renewal."

invite other perspectives into the conversation, to fill gaps in our understanding and point out uncertainties we have not yet noticed.

Ecofeminists and environmental justice scholars have long recognized that most scholarly approaches to environmental problems have been limited by an emphasis on the ideas and traditions of developed countries, mainstream religious traditions, men, whites, and the rich while those of developing countries, traditional cultures, women, people of color, and the poor are ignored.[35] This can lead scientists and scholars of Religion and Ecology to overlook valuable community knowledge about flood patterns, medicinal plants, and agricultural methods of local ecosystems, as well as community values about the type of lives people want to live. Ignoring this wisdom and these values has helped contribute to the disruption of ecosystems and the denigration of community life around the world and continues to distort ethical analyses. Incorporating previously excluded persons and their forms of knowing into our dialogue is a vital step toward recognizing and responding to the uncertainties and complexities of these problems.

One possible objection to the serious engagement with natural science we advocate is that it closes the door to genuine conversation with the local communities who have other approaches in relating to and making sense of the natural world. There is certainly some reason for this suspicion: many scientists have casually and unjustly dismissed traditional ecological knowledge and local communities, and many emphasize quantitative data and expertise to an extent that makes an open conversation difficult. However, we have demonstrated that this is not the only way to understand science, and that in its core method and most creative expressions, natural science should be about one kind of limited knowledge that is open to learning from others. A genuine dialogue between science on the one hand and Religion and Ecology on the other emphasizes the necessity for openness in both, and thus makes it more possible to have a genuine dialogue with local communities and non-academic experts.

Such dialogue is of course a challenging aspiration. Community knowledge and values can be difficult to incorporate into an academic dialogue because they are multifaceted and may be difficult for an outsider to understand or accurately represent. Community members may also be rightfully wary of academics—religionists as well as scientists—for our

---

35. See for instance Rasmussen, "Environmental Racism and Environmental Justice"; and Warren, "Taking Empirical Data Seriously."

historical association with oppressive governments, business practices, or monolithic views of religious faith and practice. Community-based knowledge may also pose challenges to researchers insofar as it resists quantification, which has become the primary focus of so much contemporary academic work. Scholars and scientists who have been trained with certain standards for what to take seriously need to question and rethink these standards in light of what traditional peoples and communities can contribute to our discussions. As academics accept the limitations of our own fields and the inevitability of uncertainty, we must be open to different ways of knowing and responding to such uncertainty. Indeed, the more open scholars can be to diverse forms of knowledge, the more prepared scholarship will be for the inevitable uncertainties of environmental challenges.

Conclusion

We assert that Religion and Ecology should engage in ongoing, open dialogue with the natural sciences, and that such dialogue will help both scholarly enterprises to be more open to other approaches and to the inevitable limitations of all knowledge. Such dialogue is necessary because Religion and Ecology on its own does not and cannot know enough to respond to environmental degradation. Our field has developed creative and vital arguments about the interconnected character of reality, the historical and ideological roots of environmental degradation, and the responses of religious communities to these factors. These insights will be enhanced in a dialogue with scientists who bring data and experimentally tested claims about environmental degradation and mitigation strategies to the table. Our humanistic and social scientific approaches lead to conclusions and claims that natural scientists could not make, and vice versa. Environmental challenges like biodiversity loss, climate change, and environmental injustice can only be understood and addressed through a wide-ranging dialogue that takes all these elements seriously.

Furthermore, openness to such a dialogue could extend outward beyond Religion and Ecology and science, taking traditional and community-based forms of knowing seriously. This expansive conversation will be vitally important in responding to environmental challenges: the voices of local peoples without academic credentials must be heard, and such peoples must be empowered to advocate for themselves if a more just and sustainable social structure is ever to take shape.

No discussion of the past, present, or future relationship between human beings and the rest of the world is complete without the observation and analysis of natural scientists, just as no proposals about how human cultures should respond to environmental degradation is complete without a careful analysis of the religious elements of a culture and an attention to that culture's traditional relationship to the natural world. In order to take all these elements seriously, Religion and Ecology needs to attend to both religious belief systems and scientific ways of knowing, and to use a dialogue between these two to expand its attention outward even further. This is an impossibly broad and complex process, and so it will require constant openness to change. Such openness is, luckily, familiar to both religions and ecologies.

Bibliography

Allen, Timothy F. H., and Thomas W. Hoekstra. *Toward a Unified Ecology.* Complexity in Ecological Systems Series. New York: Columbia University Press, 1992.

Broad, William, and Nicholas Wade. *Betrayers of the Truth.* New York: Simon & Schuster, 1983.

Bullard, Robert D., editor. *The Quest for Environmental Justice: Human Rights and the Politics of Pollution.* San Francisco: Sierra Club Books, 2005.

Ehrlich, Paul R. "Biodiversity and Ecosystem Function: Need We Know More?" In *Biodiversity and Ecosystem Function*, edited by E. D. Schulze and Harold A. Mooney, vii–xiii. Ecological Studies 99. Berlin: Springer, 1994.

Eldredge, Niles. *Life in the Balance: Humanity and the Biodiversity Crisis.* Princeton: Princeton University Press, 1998.

Freestone, David, and Ellen Hey. "Origins and Development of the Precautionary Principle." In *The Precautionary Principle and International Law: The Challenge of Implementation*, 3–17. The Hague: Kluwer Law International, 1996.

Gebara, Ivone. *Longing for Running Water: Ecofeminism and Liberation.* Translated by David Molineaux. Minneapolis: Fortress, 1999.

Gorke, Martin. *The Death of Our Planet's Species: From Ecological Theory to a Concept of the Intrinsic Value of Nature.* Washington, DC: Island Press, 2003.

Gunderson, Lance H. "Resilience, Recovery, Renewal: Ingredients for Sustainability." Lecture to the School of Public Policy, Georgia Institute of Technology, Atlanta, GA January 16, 2008.

Gunderson, Lance H., and C. S. Holling. *Panarchy: Understanding Transformations in Human and Natural Systems.* Washington DC: Island, 2002.

Harper, Barbara L. et al. "Traditional Tribal Subsistence Exposure Scenario and Risk Assessment Guidance Manual." Corvallis: Oregon State University Printing and Mailing, 2007. Online: http://www.hhs.oregonstate.edu/ph/sites/default/files/xposure_Scenario_and_Risk_Guidance_Manual_v2.pdf/.

Holling, C. S., editor. *Adaptive Environmental Assessment and Management.* Caldwell, NJ: Blackburn, 2003.

Kuhn, Thomas S. *The Structure of Scientific Revolutions*. 3rd ed. Chicago: University of Chicago Press, 1996.

Lakatos, Imre. "Falsification and the Methodology of Scientific Research Programmes." In *Criticism and the Growth of Knowledge: Proceeds of the International Colloquium in the Philosophy of Science, London 1965*, edited by Imre Lakatos and Alan Musgrave, 91–196. Studies in Logic and the Foundations of Mathematics. Proceedings 4. Cambridge: Cambridge University Press, 1970.

Laudan, Larry. "Dissecting the Holistic Picture of Scientific Change." In *Philosophy of Science: The Central Issues*, edited by Martin Curd and J. A. Cover, 139–69. New York: Norton, 1998.

Lee, Kai N. *Compass and Gyroscope: Integrating Science and Politics for the Environment*. Washington DC: Island, 1993.

Loreau, Michel et al., editors. *Biodiversity and Ecosystem Functioning: Synthesis and Perspectives*. Oxford: Oxford University Press, 2002.

Merchant, Carolyn. *The Death of Nature: Women, Ecology, and the Scientific Revolution*. 2nd ed. San Francisco: Harper & Row, 1990.

Michaels, David. *Doubt Is Their Product: How Industry's Assault on Science Threatens Your Health*. Oxford: Oxford University Press, 2008.

Nash, James A. *Loving Nature: Ecological Integrity and Christian Responsibility*. Churches' Center for Theology and Public Policy. Nashville: Abingdon, 1991.

———. "Theological Foundations for Ecological Responsibilities: In the Coherent Core of Christianity We Will Not Find a Divine Mandate to Pollute, Plunder, or Prey on the Rest of Nature." *Christian Social Action* 10 (1997) 4–7.

Northcott, Michael S. *A Moral Climate: The Ethics of Global Warming*. Maryknoll, NY: Orbis, 2007.

Norton, Bryan G. *Searching for Sustainability: Interdisciplinary Essays in the Philosophy of Conservation Biology*. Cambridge Studies in Philosophy and Biology. Cambridge: Cambridge University Press, 2003.

O'Brien, Kevin J. *An Ethics of Biodiversity: Christianity, Ecology, and the Variety of Life*. Washington DC: Georgetown University Press, 2010.

Pachauri, R. K., and A. Reisinger, editors. *Climate Change 2007: Synthesis Report. Contribution of Working Groups I, II, and III to the Fourth Assessment Report of the Intergovernmental Panel on Climate Change*. Geneva, Switzerland: IPCC Secretariat, 2007.

Pickett, Steward, et al. "The New Paradigm in Ecology: Implications for Conservation Biology above the Species Level." In *Conservation Biology: The Theory and Practice of Nature Conservation, Preservation, and Management*, edited by Peggy Fiedler and Subodh Jain, 261–78. New York: Chapman and Hall, 1992.

Rasmussen, Larry L. *Earth Community, Earth Ethics*. Ecology and Justice Series. Maryknoll, NY: Orbis, 1996.

———. "Environmental Racism and Environmental Justice: Moral Theory in the Making?" *Journal of the Society of Christian Ethics* 24 (2004) 3–28.

Raupach, Michael R., et al. "Global and Regional Drivers of Accelerating CO_2 Emissions." *Proceedings of the National Academy of Sciences of the USA* 104 (2007) 10288–93.

Ro, Young-Chan. "Ecological Implications of Yi Yulogok's Cosmology." In *Confucianism and Ecology: The Interrelation of Heaven, Earth, and Humans*, edited by Mary Evelyn Tucker and John H. Berthrong, 169–86. Religions of the World and Ecology. Cambridge: Harvard University Press.

Ruether, Rosemary Radford. *Gaia & God: An Ecofeminist Theology of Earth Healing.* San Francisco: HarperSanFrancisco, 1992.

Sagan, Carl, et al. "An Open Letter to the Religious Community." Online: http://earth-renewal.org/Open_letter_to_the_religious_.htm/.

Satterfield, Terre A. et al. "Discrimination, Vulnerability, and Justice in the Face of Risk." *Risk Analysis: An International Journal* 24 (2004) 115–29.

Sideris, Lisa H. *Environmental Ethics, Ecological Theology, and Natural Selection.* Columbia Series in Science and Religion. New York: Columbia University Press, 2003.

Swimme, Brian, and Thomas Berry. *The Universe Story: From the Primordial Flaring Forth to the Ecozoic Era—A Celebration of the Unfolding of the Cosmos.* San Francisco: HarperSanFrancisco, 1992.

Taylor, Sarah McFarland. *Green Sisters: A Spiritual Ecology.* Cambridge: Harvard University Press, 2007.

Vaughan, Diane. *The Challenger Launch Decision: Risky Technology, Culture, and Deviance at NASA.* Chicago: University of Chicago Press, 1996.

Vitek, Bill, and Wes Jackson, editors. *The Virtues of Ignorance: Complexity, Sustainability, and the Limits of Knowledge.* Culture of the Land. Lexington: University Press of Kentucky, 2008.

Walters, Carl J. *Adaptive Management of Renewable Resources.* Caldwell, NJ: Blackburn, 2001.

Warren, Karen J. "Taking Empirical Data Seriously: An Ecofeminist Philosophical Perspective." In *Ecofeminism: Women, Culture, Nature,* edited by Karen J. Warren, 3–20. Bloomington: Indiana University Press, 1997.

Westra, Laura, and Bill E. Lawson, editors. *Faces of Environmental Racism: Confronting Issues of Global Justice.* 2nd ed. Studies in Social, Political, and Legal Philosophy. Lanham, MD: Rowman & Littlefield, 2001.

Zabinski, Catherine. "Scientific Ecology and Ecological Feminism." In *Ecofeminism: Women, Culture, Nature,* edited by Karen J. Warren, 314–26. Bloomington: Indiana University Press, 1997.

4

What Traditions Are Represented in Religion and Ecology?

A Perspective from an American Scholar of Islam

ELEANOR FINNEGAN

In establishing the field of Religion and Ecology, academics and activists have tried to create an area of study that is inclusive of many religious traditions. However, there has been a focus on traditions or aspects of traditions that would influence the largest number of people or carry the greatest authority, because of a desire to confront the environmental crisis and assumptions about the nature and role of religious traditions. These aims and assumptions, along with a tendency to organize scholarship within a schema of world religions, have limited the religions and aspects of religions studied within the field. Communities, institutions, beliefs and practices considered outside of mainstream conceptions of traditions have often been overlooked.

Looking at three American Muslim farm communities in the United States provides specific examples of what is lost when certain groups and types of religious production and experience are overlooked. Comparing the history of the academic study of religion to the aims and assumptions of Religion and Ecology point to the ways in which these omissions are unintentionally crafting a field that perpetuates historical biases from the larger discipline. The work within the field of Religion and Ecology will always be linked to activism, therefore it is important to recognize past oversights and biases in the field and to work to include scholarship that helps overcome these shortcomings, in order to avoid problems historically present in the study of religion.

Tradition and Traditions throughout the History of Religion and Ecology

The field of Religion and Ecology has mostly focused on the question of how humans can act in an ethically responsible way toward nature, and it has sought answers primarily in major world traditions. As discussed in the first chapter of this volume, "Religion and Ecology" was first used to refer to a consultation, which later became a group, at the American Academy of Religion in the early 1990s. Using interdisciplinary, inter-religious and intercultural approaches, this group of scholars sought to respond to emerging ecological realities by developing new ethics from within religious studies and theology.[1]

Another important event in the history of the development of the field of Religion and Ecology were the international conferences on "Religions of the World and Ecology," held at Harvard Divinity School's Center for the Study of World Religions between 1996 and 1998. These interdisciplinary conferences included historians, theologians, ethicists, scientists, grassroots workers, scholars, and graduate students and were organized around ten world religions: Judaism, Christianity, Islam, Hinduism, Jainism, Buddhism, Daoism, Confucianism, Shinto, and Indigenous religions. Using methods of "retrieval, reevaluation, and re-construction," the goal was to point to actual or potential sources of environmental awareness and action from within each tradition, because these religions were understood as "key shapers of people's worldviews and the formulators of their most cherished values."[2] These assumptions about the nature of religions and the format of these conferences have been an important template for the field ever since.

After these conferences, Harvard University's Center for the Study of World Religions published ten edited volumes between 1997 and 2003. These volumes were arranged by the ten world religions and included

1. Chapple and Blissman, "Religion and Ecology Group Five Year Report for Group Renewal."

2. Tucker, "Religion and Ecology: Survey of the Field," 407.

edited papers from the conferences, as well as other important papers not presented. These books aimed to provide a foundation for future research and to stimulate interest among scholars, religious leaders, and laypeople.

This work was developed further with the creation of the Forum on Religion and Ecology (FORE) in 1998, which, like the conferences, was organized by Mary Evelyn Tucker and John Grim. Its goals have been to continue research, activism, and education in the area of Religion and Ecology by encouraging outreach within and outside of academia, interdisciplinary environmental-studies programs, and to religious and policy groups. The Forum has pursued these goals by helping to develop the Earth Charter, becoming involved in the organization of many national and international conferences, and hosting a website (http://fore. research.yale.edu/) that provides resources for teachers, while fostering research and outreach.

The FORE website has been trying to provide a systematic record of work from and on traditions throughout the field of Religion and Ecology. The site features sections for each of the ten world traditions. Every one of these sections has a Bibliography page. These bibliographies provide a partial overview of the published work produced and claimed by the field of Religion and Ecology. Together the bibliographies chronicle books, chapters in edited volumes, articles in journals, statements from religious leaders, literature for believers, newspaper articles, and even some conference presentations. These bibliographies are not exhaustive, but they do provide some insight as to the resources in the field and how they have been categorized.

The FORE work is based on the assumption that religion is the foundation or font of many people's deepest moral values. It has also organized materials around the idea of distinct religious traditions that are presented as influential on the global stage. Several other compilations have been published since the Harvard books, and some of them point to other sources for study and ways of organizing the field. However most are still based on the assumptions that there is an environmental crisis, which is caused by human actions, that needs to be addressed and ended.

Roger Gottlieb's *This Sacred Earth* and Bron Taylor's *Encyclopedia of Religion and Nature* are notable because they address the issues of Religion and Ecology topically and engage unconventional sources of religious inspiration. *This Sacred Earth*, for instance, includes a selection of primary source texts from "nondenominational spiritual thinkers," such as nature writers who linked spirituality to environmental concerns and particular religious traditions.[3]

Another compilation of essays edited by Roger Gottlieb, *The Oxford Handbook of Religion and Ecology*, was published in 2006. Similar to projects associated with Harvard and the Forum, this work was concerned with reevaluating and transforming traditions. In the introduction, Gottlieb states that the two driving questions of Religion and Ecology are: "What have the world's faiths believed about the human relation to *nature*? And how must beliefs (and actions) change as we face the *environment*?"[4] Like his earlier volume, this compilation is not exclusively arranged by religions of the world. The first section addresses religious traditions, the second looks at conceptual issues, and the third section looks at the participation of religion in environmental politics.

Some of these newer compilations question the presumption that religion is the source of many people's deepest moral values. In 2005, Bron Taylor and several other scholars began a new scholarly society, the International Society for the Study of Religion, Nature, and Culture, which aimed to expand the range of critical analysis. Intended for scholars from diverse disciplines, this society has particularly encouraged naturalistic studies of religion, work that critiques religion as environmentally destructive, and "studies that examine nature-human-society relationships that have nothing to do with what today might be called ecological integrity or ecosystem health."[5] This group began holding meetings in 2006 and now publishes the *Journal for the Study of Religion, Nature, and Culture*.

Even this group, which has attempted to expand the areas of study in the field of Religion and Ecology, is still shaped by some overarching presuppositions about human-nature relations and religion. The field has been based on the idea that human actions have caused an environmen-

3. The term "nondenominational spiritual thinkers" comes from Gottlieb's preface to *This Sacred Earth*. It primarily seems to include works by writers who were concerned with illuminating the religious dimension of human-nature relations, although Gottlieb does include chapters by scholars who study the religious dimensions of seemingly secular environmental groups, such as deep ecologists and radical environmentalists. Gottlieb, *This Sacred Earth*, xi.

4. Gottlieb, "Introduction: Religion and Ecology," 6.

5. The International Society for the Study of Religion, Nature, and Culture, "Frequently Asked Questions."

tal crisis that needs to be addressed and ended. Therefore, the work of this field often has a normative aim or scholars themselves are activists. Even the *Journal for the Study of Religion, Nature, and Culture* encourages submissions that grapple with "what constitutes ethically appropriate relationships between our own species and the places, including the entire biosphere, which we inhabit."[6] Furthermore, some scholarship that is not intended as normative is used by practitioners to shape ideas and practices in relation to nature, giving it an unintended influence on believers.[7]

Problems with the "World Religions" Approach

The aims and types of classification systems predominantly found in the field of Religion and Ecology run the risk of perpetuating biases that have existed in religious studies. The idea of "world religions," tolerance, and comparative studies emerged from post-Reformation Christian experiences and missionary goals.

The idea of religion in the singular as opposed to religions in the plural arose from the split between Catholics and Protestants. With the creation of new forms of Christianity, there was a need to tolerate different forms of Christianity. Such tolerance, however, was initially extended only within Christianity, and in European colonies that had a "large numbers of non-Christian subjects, Christian missionaries were given free reign and encouragement to seek new converts . . . religious toleration in Europe was only extended to different varieties of Christianity; non-Christian religions did not receive this concession."[8] It was not until 1627 that non-Christian forms of religion were labeled as religions. However, this was done in a book that asserted Christianity's superiority to all other religions.

Within this history of the idea of religions, Carl Ernst argues, "one can see . . . in the overall trend from 'religion' to 'religions' a concept of competing beliefs and political communities in a context of imperialism and missions."[9] Christians labeled specific traditions as "world religions" because these traditions were seen as competitive with Christianity

6. The Journal for the Study of Religion, Nature, and Culture.

7. Bron Taylor has written about this in his article "Religious Studies and Environmental Concern."

8. Ernst, *Following Muhammad*, 43.

9. Ibid., 41.

on a global scale. Religions with higher numbers of practitioners were deemed more significant.

Many scholars in the field of Religion and Ecology have perpetuated this focus on significant world religions due to their aim of addressing the environmental crisis. In hopes of influencing as many people as possible, scholars and activists have focused on religions that are important on a global scale. They have also emphasized what they perceive to be the mainstream within those traditions.

Bron Taylor has highlighted some of the shortcomings of this approach. In critiquing the work of the Harvard conference and books, he has argued that a desire to appeal to members of mainstream or world religions has three repercussions for how traditions are represented within the field of Religion and Ecology. First, it has contributed to the exclusion of nature-based spiritualities, such as those found among environmentalists, Pagans, Wiccans, and New Agers. Second, the field has often focused on figures and scholars connected, if not committed, to the traditions being studied. Finally, he notes that "embedded in the series was not only a clear bias toward mainstream traditions but also ones favoring the mainstreams of these traditions," focusing on seemingly widely known and respected texts and leaders.[10] Taylor argues that these factors have made it difficult to find areas where religion could be changing or adapting to face environmental problems.

A desire to influence as many people as possible has also effected the materials studied within the field, causing many scholars to focus on the Christian or Jewish tradition. In *This Sacred Earth*, for instance, Roger Gottlieb decided to focus primarily on the Jewish and Christian traditions because he believed that the majority of his book's audience would be grounded in these two traditions. His work was then shaped by his goal of providing relevant information to readers: information that might help to inform their ideas and worldviews. Many authors in the field have used the same reasoning to justify exclusive focus on the Christian tradition: Christianity has the most adherents worldwide. It is also relevant, however, that many scholars of Religion and Ecology work in North America and Europe, which are both predominantly Christian.

The categorizes of world religions are in themselves an inflexible system of categorization that makes it difficult to include or chronicle traditions, ideas, or works that do not fit within the rubric of world

10. Taylor, "Critical Perspectives on 'Religions of the World and Ecology,'" 1375.

religions. The FORE website, for example, places some works which concern philosophy or scientific cosmologies in the section concerning Christianity. Presumably, they are included there because they are part of the Western tradition rather than Christianity, specifically.

Through the inclusion or exclusion of sources identified as within or outside of a tradition, scholars enable groups "to differentiate themselves both within the limit of their own group (i.e. to rank the many degrees of group membership) and in distinction from others. In the process, they are thereby enabled to allot or withhold resources and status accordingly."[11] Christianity has been dominant within the field of Religion and Ecology and an underlying focus on Christianity has affected the field. Often, studies of other religions are undertaken in part to inform Christians or Westerners—who are sometimes equated —about how other traditions can help shape their relations with nature. This is close to the early comparative system among missionaries and early scholars, where Christianity was the baseline against which other traditions were compared and contrasted.

The Forum bibliographies on Buddhism and Hinduism have the most resources outside of Christianity and Judaism. This does not, however, reflect trends in numbers of believers throughout the world. In fact, it has been argued that scholars have often focused on these traditions either to appropriate aspects of Asian religions that are understood as more environmentally sound or to figure out how to best export western environmentalism to the Asian world. George James, a scholar of Indian traditions, argues that much of the writing on Indian environmental ethics in particular has been informed by two contradictory Western views on Indian religion and culture – either Indian traditions are beneficial or they are harmful when confronting the environmental problems in the west. He argues that both these views are informed by an orientalist mindset that India or Asia is completely other from Western society and thought.[12] The inclusion of studies of Judaism within studies primarily

11. McCutcheon, *Religion and the Domestication of Dissent*, 1.

12. James, *Ethical Perspectives on Environmental Issues in India*. Gerald Larson, a scholar of Indian philosophy, has also critiqued Western scholars who mine Asian traditions for ideas that can be used by Westerners to create environmental ethics. He argues that this practice is exploitative in the same way that resource extraction is exploitive: in both cases, something is appropriated and removed from its context. However, Larson leaves open the possibility of comparative studies, and believes that studying Asian religions can offer a useful mirror for western society or provide new metaphors

aimed toward Christian audiences also poses some problems as to how the Jewish tradition is engaged.

The "World Religions" Approach versus the Example of Three American Muslim Farms

The world-religions approach has led to very narrow definitions of religious traditions and aspects of traditions worthy of study. The example of three American Muslim farms further demonstrates what can be overlooked when scholars only focus on the mainstream of a tradition. Although scholars within the field of Religion and Ecology have attempted to create a field that is inclusive of all religions and all types of believers, there are few studies on communities like these three farms, where members are a minority within their culture, country, and religious tradition. The majority of scholarship on Islam and ecology focuses on texts or the practices of Muslims in Muslim majority countries.[13] By focusing on the textual tradition and perceived mainstream, scholars miss the lived experience of many Muslims, the diversity of interpretations of Muslim texts, the other resources that influence Muslims' interactions with and ideas about the environment, the role of practice in the lives of many Muslims, and the negotiation that happens among religious believers as they attempt to live their religious and environmental ideas. Without studies of different communities, including small communities, scholars in the field of Religion and Ecology risk essentializing the

---

for environmental problems in the West. See Larson, "'Conceptual Resources' in South Asia for 'Environmental Ethics'," 267–77 and 325.

13. Several books and articles focus on the doctrines of Islam, such as Ahmad, *A Cosmopolitan Orientation of International Environmental Law*; Ammar, "Islam and Deep Ecology"; Ammar, "Islam and the Environment"; Callicott, "Historical Roots of Western European Environmental Attitudes and Values"; Haq, "Islam"; and Izzi al-Din, *Environmental Dimensions of Islam*. Several articles and books look at Muslims in Muslim countries, such as Afrasiabi, "Environmental Movement in Iran"; Aghajanian and Merhyar, "Fertility, Contraceptive Use and Family Planning Program Activity in the Islamic Republic of Iran," Foltz, *Environmentalism in the Muslim World*; Foltz, "Environmental Initiatives in Contemporary Iran"; Foltz, "Iran's Water Crisis"; Westcoat, "'Right of Thirst' for Animals in Islamic Law"; and Westcoat, "From the Gardens of the Qurʾan to 'Gardens' of Lahore." Foltz et al., *Islam and Ecology*; and Khalid and O'Brien, *Islam and Ecology* are compilations that include both types of analysis. Foltz's *Animals in Islamic Traditions and Muslim Cultures* does look at textual sources as well as practices among Western Muslims.

Islamic tradition, further losing sight of the diversity, flexibility, and change found within the tradition.

Since the forced migration of Muslim slaves to the Americas, groups of Muslims in North America have been involved with agriculture. Farming has allowed them to create and maintain religious identities and communities, and in some instances agriculture has been a part of their religious community. Within the past 30 years, three groups of Muslims in Pennsylvania and Illinois have established religious agricultural communities.

The Bawa Muhaiyaddeen Fellowship Farm is part of the Bawa Muhaiyaddeen Fellowship, a group of Sufi Muslims who follow the teachings of Muhammad Raheem Muhaiyaddeen. The fellowship began in 1971 when Bawa, a renowned spiritual teacher and healer in Sri Lanka, came to Philadelphia and established the fellowships headquarters there. In the United States, Bawa cultivated plants for healing and had his followers grow plants as well. In 1976 and 1977, he had community members come to work on his farm in Sri Lanka. In 1980 the community first bought farmland for a cemetery. Bawa also had his followers farm the land in order to learn religious lessons about cooperation and unity as well as lessons on how to provide materially for one's own self and community.

Currently, the community owns a 108-acre farm in Coatesville, Pennsylvania, and many members of the fellowship moved there and started their own branch of the fellowship in the early 1990s. Bawa's shrine is on the farm and some members still cultivate Bawa's garden. Eighty acres are in the federal government's Conservation Resource Environment Program. Members of the community plan to become certified organic in 2010, and they are crafting a plan to better embody their religious and environmental values at the farm.

The Dayempur Farm is one of the community institutions of another Sufi group, the Dayemi Tariqat. The Dayemi Tariqat is part of a larger Sufi community, the Dayera Sharif, which began 1,400 years ago in Bangladesh. Members of the Dayemi Tariqat follow the teachings of an American spiritual teacher, Sheik Din, who was trained by and remains connected to the lineage in Bangladesh. Sheikh Din began the Dayempur Farm when he moved seven people to Southern Illinois and bought farmland in 1995.

Although community members live in the town of Carbondale, Illinois (and there are also community groups in South Carolina, Texas,

Germany, and Bangladesh), they own 60 acres of farmland in nearby Anna, Illinois, 2.5 acres of which are cultivated. Four people are employed full time at the farm and every member of the community has to work on the farm at least one day a month. The farm grows medicinal herbs, cooking herbs, vegetables, fruit, and nuts, which are used within the community for things like communal meals and medicines and are also sold in some of the community's businesses, such as the restaurant, general store, and health clinic. The Dayemi Tariqat is not only involved with their farm but also with similar farm communities in Bangladesh.

The Farm of Peace is also a Sufi community, part of the Shadhiliyya Sufi Center East, which itself is a branch of a larger community of Shadhiliyya Sufis who follow the teachings of Sidi Muhammad Sa'id al-Jamal ar-Rifa'i ash-Shadhuli (Sidi), a spiritual teacher who lives in Jerusalem. This lineage has communities all over the United States and headquarters in California. The group began in California in the early 1990s after a follower of Sidi returned to the United States and began teaching.[14] Sidi himself began teaching in the United States in 1993.[15]

Covering 150 acres in Warfordsburg, Pennsylvania, the Farm of Peace began in 2000 as a gathering place for members of the Sufi Center East. Some of the land has been left wild, most of it is used for pastures, and there is also a garden. They support the garden by selling CSA (Community Supported Agriculture) shares primarily to members outside of the religious community. Members use the pastures to raise *halal* sheep that have been slaughtered according to the Islamic tradition. The land also houses a center for spiritual retreat and healing. There are several people living on the farm, but most community members reside in surrounding areas.

Together, these three communities represent a broad diversity of membership, experience, thought, and practice within American Islam and among religious farmers. They are inspired by different teachers, and all express different concerns and ideas about the place of religion and nature in a good, meaningful life. They also demonstrate unique attempts at intentional living and agriculture. Some of these communities, for instance, are only gardening and others have functional farms.

Amid the differences between these groups, there are also similarities. Most members of each community are American converts to Islam.

14. Meadow, "Shadhiliyya Order."
15. Shadhiliyya Sufi Center, "Biography of Sidi Muhammad Sa'id al-Jamal."

The groups also share Sufism, practicing a mystical form of Islam that usually is concerned with knowing and experiencing God. Sufis typically join a group associated with a lineage of teachers that is called a *tariqa*, which translates to mean "way," and follow a spiritual teacher called a sheik, who promotes specific religious practices.

Among studies of Islam and ecology, there has been some but not much scholarship on Sufi thinkers, practices, institutions, or beliefs.[16] Indeed, Sufis have often been considered on the margins, if not outside of the realm of the Islamic tradition. The development of the study of Islam has contributed to this perceived split. During the colonial period, Western scholars defined Sufism as fundamentally different from Islam. In fact, following orientalist themes, "the essential feature of the definition of Sufism that appeared at the time was that it had no intrinsic relation with the faith of Islam."[17] Although premodern Muslim societies usually saw no split, different groups of Muslims adopted this distinction between Sufism and Islam and have used it for various aims. Fundamentalists have seen Sufism as an internal threat to Islam, and Modernists have understood Sufism as an obstacle to modernity.

Within the American context, "there has been a tendency among academics, anticult groups, and traditional Muslims alike to lump the American-bred Sufi groups into categories such as 'cults,' 'New Age,' 'popular,' or 'unorthodox' . . . , [and] there are many Americans involved in Sufi movements who emphasize classical Sufism's goal of the transcendental unity beyond all distinctions (including religious differences) to the point of denying any essential connection of Sufism with the religion of Islam."[18]

Far from denying Islam, however, the communities and most of the members of the Bawa Muhaiyaddeen Fellowship Farm, the Dayempur Farm, and the Farm of Peace identify and practice as Sunni Muslims. It is vital to study such minority groups on their own terms and to turn our scholarly attention away from broad and generalizing categories and toward indigenous and local processes of identity formation and appropriations of tradition. Including these groups will help insure our understanding and definition of Islam reflect the reality of believers and practitioners.

16. Nasr, "Ecological Problem in Light of Sufism"; Clarke, "Universe Alive"; and Wescoat, "From the Gardens of the Qur'an to the 'Gardens' of Lahore."

17. Ernst, *Shambhala Guide to Sufism*, 9.

18. Webb, "Sufism in America," 249.

Often, scholars or activists within Religion and Ecology have focused on the textual traditions of each religion, which has continued and reinforced Protestant Christian assumptions about the primacy of texts. Such focus on texts has in part been an attempt to claim authority; and within studies of Islam and ecology, scholars and activists have focused on texts in an attempt to identify universal Islamic ideas about the environment. Some scholars, such as Nawal Ammar and Richard Foltz, have argued that the Muslim world is diverse and that it is impossible to talk about a monolithic Islamic view on anything unless focusing on common sources of meaning. However, they then debate which texts can be included. Ammar argues, "it is only justifiable to discuss the Islamic world as a homogenous community insofar as Muslims adhere to a defined textual literature." Although she does not spell out which texts these are, she focuses on the Qur'an, *hadith* (the recorded sayings and actions of the Prophet Muhammad), and *sharia* (Islamic law).[19] Foltz states that "for any idea to achieve anything approaching universal acceptance by Muslims as 'Islamic,' it must be convincingly demonstrated that it derives from the Qur'an or, failing that, from the example of the prophet Muhammad."[20]

The idea that only texts can be universally Islamic is part of a debate over how to define the Islamic tradition. In defining ideas, institutions, or practices as "Islamic," scholars and Muslims are creating a tension between texts and practices. Some who are concerned with definitions of Islam and the contours of the Islamic tradition, maintain that even the textual parts of the tradition, including the Qur'an and example of the Prophet, can only be understood through the filter of believers and their experiences.[21]

In explaining their work on the farms or the relationship between humans and the environment, members of the three Sufi farms introduced above do refer to the Qur'an, the example of the Prophet, and historical legal practices from the Middle East. So they do in some way fit the definitional limits proposed by Ammar and Foltz. However, these ideas are often, but not always, filtered through the teachings of each community's sheik, making their interpretations specific to their experience as American Sufis who are studying as part of a particular lineage.

19. Ammar, "Islam and the Environment."

20. Foltz, *Islam and Ecology*, 253.

21. Safi, *Progressive Muslims*; Curtis, *Black Muslim Religion*; and Ernst, *Following Muhammad*.

This does not make their interpretation unusual as compared to all other interpretation. Instead, it points out some of the variety in interpretation within the Islamic tradition.

Community members also refer to examples or resources specific to their Sufi orientation, as well as their experience as Americans and their ideas about the environment, food production, and alternative forms of society. If scholars of Religion and Ecology look only to texts and the mainstream of traditions, they may overlook some of the diverse sources that religious communities and believers use to shape their interaction with the environment.

It is important to study all of these sources of meaning and the complicated ways in which they are used by Muslims, so that scholars do not miss the process of negotiation and interpretation that takes place within a community of believers as it attempts to enact or explain its ethics. Studying diverse expressions of the Islamic tradition also help scholars avoid essentializing the Islamic tradition as a fixed thing that originated in Arabia and can be separated from the innovations and variations of diverse Muslim groups over the course of history.

The field of Religion and Ecology has also assumed that beliefs influence actions, which is a historic idea that has been traced to Protestant assumptions about the dominant role of belief in religious identity. However, members of these Muslim farm communities are not just drawn to farming or being involved with agricultural communities because of their beliefs. Some also explain the importance of farms in helping them to enact religious practices. Several note that the farm allows them to concretely live out ideas about surrendering to God and breaking attachments. One member explained that "working with the CSA elements or the orchard, when I can get outside and start making the land productive, I feel like I'm following the will of God." Farming has also influenced some members' ideas about religious practices and figures. Another member noted that "the more I study the life of the Prophet Muhammad, peace be upon him, and the more I'm able to see the wisdom of what he was able to create, the more he inspires this work for me. And, by doing that, what ends up happening is that [I] begin to see the work of the farm . . . as something that is not separate from your daily life. Like, this is a spiritual practice."

Therefore, it is important to remember, as scholars such as Bill Jordan, Jim Cheney, and Anthony Weston have noted, that when dealing with environmental ethics, practice may come before belief or practices may lead to new or changed beliefs.[22]

As the diverse forms of Sufi environmentalism discussed above reveal, there are many more diverse expressions of religion—even within the United States—deserving inclusion and careful study. These kinds of study are necessary for more fully understanding the lived experience of Muslims. These kinds of studies can also help scholars avoid further essentializing or narrowing the definitions of religions.

Conclusion

The work from the field of Religion and Ecology will likely always have some kind of impact on the traditions it studies. There will also likely continue to be scholars who intentionally are activists. However, as members of a field concerned with embracing and engaging religious diversity, scholars of Religion and Ecology must be aware of which traditions and aspects of traditions that have been included and emphasized by the field in service to this normative aim. They must also be conscious of the systems of organization that lead to the preference of particular kinds of scholarship and aspects of traditions. Finally, scholars need to make sure that there are more studies of everyday manifestations of religious practice and beliefs emerging from groups or aspects of religions outside of the mainstream of traditions.

Without these studies, ideas about religion and various religious traditions become too rigid, confined, and fixed. Studies of religious communities and groups on the margins demonstrate the more complicated connections between religious and environmental beliefs and practices. These studies can help our analysis of other aspects of religions, including texts. They can also identify other aspects of religion that should be studied, expanding the traditions that are included in the field.

Bibliography

Afrasiabi, Kaveh L. "The Environmental Movement in Iran: Perspectives from Below and Above." *The Middle East Journal* 57 (2003) 432–48.

22. Weston and Cheney, "Environmental Ethics as Environmental Etiquette," 115–34; and Jordan, *The Sunflower Forest*.

Aghajanian, Akbar, and Amir H. Merhyar. "Fertility, Contraceptive Use and Family Planning Program Activity in the Islamic Republic of Iran." *International Family Planning Perspectives* 25 (1999) 98–102.

Ahmad, Ali. *A Cosmopolitan Orientation of the Proces of International Environmental Lawmaking: An Islamic Law Genre*. Lanham, MD: University Press of America, 2001.

Ammar, Nawal H. "Islam and Deep Ecology." In *Liberating Faith: Religious Voices for Justice, Peace, and Ecological Wisdom*, edited by Roger S. Gottlieb, 551–64. Lanham, MD: Rowman & Littlefield, 2003.

——."Islam and the Environment: A Legalistic and Textual View." In *Population, Consumption, and the Environment: Religious and Secular Responses*, edited by Harold Coward. Albany: State University of New York Press, 1995.

——. "Islam and the Environment: A Legalistic and Textual View." In *Population, Consumption, and the Environment: Religious and Secular Responses*, edited by Harold Coward, 131–46. Albany: State University of New York Press, 2000.

Callicott, J. Baird. "The Historical Roots of Western European Environmental Attitudes and Values: Islam." In *Earth's Insights: A Multicultural Survey of Ecological Ethics from the Mediterranean Basin to the Australian Outback*, edited by J. Baird Callicott, 30–36. Berkeley: University of California Press, 1994.

Chapple, Christopher, and Beth Blissman. "Religion and Ecology Group Five Year Report for Group Renewal." Online: http://www.religionandnature.com/aar/R+E-Report2004.pdf.

Clarke, L. "The Universe Alive: Nature in the *Masnavi* of Jalal al-Din Rumi." In *Islam and Ecology: A Bestowed Trust*, edited by Richard Foltz et al., 39–65. Religions of the World and Ecology. Cambridge: Harvard Divinity School, Center for the Study of World Religions, distributed by Harvard University Press, 2003.

Curtis, Edward E., IV. *Black Muslim Religion in the Nation of Islam, 1960–1975*. Chapel Hill: University of North Carolina Press, 2006.

Ernst, Carl W. *Following Muhammad: Rethinking Islam in the Contemporary World*. Islamic Civilization & Muslim Networks. Chapel Hill: University of North Carolina Press, 2003.

——. *The Shambhala Guide to Sufism*. Boston: Shambhala, 1997.

Foltz, Richard. *Animals in Islamic Tradition and Muslim Cultures*. Oxford: Oneworld, 2006.

——. "Environmental Initiatives in Contemporary Iran." *Central Asian Survey*. 20:2 (August 2001) 155–65.

——. "Iran's Water Crisis: Cultural, Political, and Ethical Dimensions." *Journal of Agricultural and Environmental Ethics* 15 (2002) 357–80.

——, editor. *Environmentalism in the Muslim World*. New York: Nova Science, 2005.

Foltz, Richard et al., editors. *Islam and Ecology: A Bestowed Trust*. Religions of the World and Ecology. Cambridge: Harvard Divinity School, Center for the Study of World Religions, distributed by Harvard University Press, 2003.

Forum on Religion and Ecology. Online: http://fore.research.yale.edu/religion/.

Gottlieb, Roger S. "Introduction: Religion and Ecology—What Is the Connection and Why Does It Matter?" In *The Oxford Handbook of Religion and Ecology*, edited by Roger S. Gottlieb, 3–21. Oxford: Oxford University Press, 2006.

——, editor. *This Sacred Earth: Religion, Nature, Environment*. New York: Routledge, 1996.

Haq, S. Nomanul. "Islam." In *A Companion to Environmental Philosophy*, edited by Dale Jamieson, 111–29. Blackwell Companions to Philosophy 19. Malden, MA: Blackwell, 2001.

The International Society for the Study of Religion, Nature & Culture. "Frequently Asked Questions." Online: http://www.religionandnature.com/society/faq.htm/.

Izzi al-Din. *The Environmental Dimensions of Islam*. Cambridge: Lutterworth, 2000.

Khalid, Fazlun M., with Joanne O'Brien. *Islam and Ecology*. World Religions and Ecology. New York: Cassell, 1992.

James, George A., editor. *Ethical Perspectives on Environmental Issues in India*. New Delhi: APH, 1999.

The Journal for the Study of Religion, Nature & Culture. Online: http://www.religionand-nature.com/journal/index.htm/.

Larson, Gerald. "'Conceptual Resources' in South Asia for 'Environmental Ethics.'" In *Nature in Asian Traditions of Thought: Essays in Environmental Philosophy*, edited by J. Baird Callicott and Roger T. Ames, 267–77 and 325. SUNY Series in Philosophy and Biology. New York: State University of New York Press, 1989.

McCutcheon, Russell T. *Religion and the Domestication of Dissent: Or, How to Live in a Less Than Perfect Nation*. London: Equinox, 2005.

Meadow, Miranda. "Shadhiliyya Order." Online: http://www.pluralism.org/reports/view/134.

Nasr, Seyyed Hossein. "The Ecological Problem in Light of Sufism: The Conquest of Nature and the Teachings of Eastern Science." In *Sufi Essays*, edited by Seyyed Hossein Nasr, 152–63. 2nd ed. Albany: State University of New York Press, 1991.

Safi, Omid, editor. *Progressive Muslims: On Justice, Gender, and Pluralism*. Oxford: Oneworld, 2003.

Shadhiliyya Sufi Center. "Biography of Sidi Muhammad Saʿ id al-Jamal." Online: http://suficenter.org/index.php?option=com_content&view=article&id=32:biography-of-sidi-muhammad-said-al-jamal&catid=13:our-guide&Itemid=43.

Taylor, Bron Raymond. "Critical Perspectives on 'Religions of the World and Ecology.'" In *The Encyclopedia of Religion and Nature*, edited by Bron Raymond Taylor, 2:1375–76. 2 vols. London: Thoemmes Continuum, 2005.

———. "Religious Studies and Environmental Concern." In *The Encyclopedia of Religion and Nature*, edited by Bron Raymond Taylor, 2:1373–79. London: Thoemmes Continuum, 2005.

Tucker, Mary Evelyn. "Religion and Ecology: Survey of the Field." In *The Oxford Handbook of Religion and Ecology*, edited by Roger S. Gottlieb, 398–418. Oxford: Oxford University Press, 2006.

Webb, Gisela. "Sufism in America." In *America's Alternative Religions*, edited by Timothy Miller, 249–58. SUNY Series in Religious Studies. Albany: State University of New York Press, 1995.

Wescoat, James L. "From the Gardens of the Qurʾan to the 'Gardens' of Lahore." In *Islam and Ecology: A Bestowed Trust*, edited by Richard Foltz et al., 511–26. Religions of the World and Ecology. Cambridge: Harvard Divinity School, Center for the Study of World Religions, distributed by Harvard University Pres, 2003.

———. "The 'Right of Thirst' for Animals in Islamic Law: A Comparative Approach." *Environment and Planning D: Society and Space* 13 (1995) 637–54.

Weston, Anthony, and Jim Cheney. "Environmental Ethics as Environmental Etiquette." In *The Incompleat Eco-Philosopher: Essays from the Edge of Environmental Ethics*, edited by Anthony Weston, 65–88. Albany: State University of New York Press, 2009.

5

Opening the Language of Religion and Ecology

Viable Spaces for Transformative Politics

Whitney A. Bauman

Monotheism is a myth that grounds particular identity
in universal transcendence.[1]

Nature, a transcendental term in a material mask, stands at the
end of a potentially infinite series of other terms that collapse into it,
otherwise known as a metonymic list.[2]

The field of "Religion and Ecology" or "Religion and Nature" is prone
to a double-dose of foundationalism. On the one hand, there is nature
as foundation: what is Natural, Right, or Good is dictated by "material-
istic," scientific experts. Their collection of facts about the natural world
provides a transcendent space, Nature, which dictates the way things
are and in many cases *ought* to be. Some Religion and Ecology scholars,
along with other environmentalists and philosophers, share this tendency to treat nature as a foundation, and often suggest that humanity needs

1. Schwartz, *Curse of Cain*, 16.
2. Morton, *Ecology without Nature*, 14.

to adapt the ways in which we live, act, and think based on the information coming from ecology, physics, biology, genetics, neuroscience, etc. However, if that foundation is upset by paradigm shifts or phase-changes in hypotheses (Lakatos),[3] then Religion and Ecology has a second option for maintaining epistemological foundationalism through the religious: in the face of the Scientific Revolution, for instance, we see a rise in "Sola Scriptura," fideism, and pietism and away from the Book of Nature. This is also the classical reaction of literalism/fundamentalism that arises in response to Darwin's theory of evolution, which upset the Christianized version of Aristotelian teleology.

In other words, uncertainty in one realm (science or religion), has the potential to lead toward striving for a certain, transcendent foundation for our knowledge of the world in the other realm (religion or science, respectively). So, in eco-religious scholarship, both religion and science can become the space for transcendent knowledge claims, whether through "internal" (as is often the case with foundational religious claims) or "external" (as is often the case with foundational claims in science) processes. "Extreme externality . . . and extreme internality . . . wind up in the same place,"[4] which is a transcendent no-place.

Despite engagement with ever more sophisticated "post-" theories of "religion" and "nature," literature in Religion and Ecology still often participates in this two-sided foundationalism, relying on a transcendent "no space" for either subjective or objective assertions. Currently, this often takes the shape of arguing that religions ought to re(con)form to the scientific information regarding environmental crises, and thus re-organize around an affirmation of what is "natural." In this way, as Žižek has noted, science now plays the role of providing certainty and hope where religion once did: "The paradox effectively is that, today, science provides security which was once guaranteed by religion, and, in a curious inversion, religion is one of the possible places from which one can develop critical doubts about contemporary society."[5] In other words, "natural" sciences today seek to provide us with the certainty that there is indeed a "nature" to be saved, and with the hope that technological advances will get us there. The basic assumption of the scientific approach to "nature" is that the right information will affect a change

3. Lakatos, *For and Against Method*, 103–5.

4. Morton, *Ecology without Nature*, 132.

5. S. Žižek, *In Defense of Lost Causes*, 446.

in human behaviors accordingly. The basic message to religions is that they must conform or face further isolation from the realm of "expert" discourse.[6]

Among the many problems with this Enlightenment mentality are the facts that information does not necessarily affect change and that information about "nature" is always changing, always in flux. There is no one "nature" to return to or to save. Furthermore, the understanding of nature as something to be understood, as Sean Hargens and Michael Zimmerman point out, only takes into account the externality of life and disregards the internality of life. Hargens and Zimmerman argue for an "Integral Ecology," in which: "We cannot reduce our subjective and intersubjective dimensions to exterior objects. Interiors must be interpreted on their own terms."[7] Romantic and Modern ideas of "nature" are problematized by the ways global climate change affects nature, by recent discussions of postnaturalism,[8] and by the inability of most science to take the interior seriously (rather than trying to reduce it to exterior/material). Will the pendulum of certainty now swing back toward the side of religion, to some sort of pietistic truth dependent only upon faith and tradition? Must we oscillate between locating certainty on one side of the false dualisms of ideal/material, culture/nature, and/or epistemology/ontology?

There is another option: post-foundational thinking that embraces radical immanence in both religion and nature. Many models of such post-foundational thinking are emerging. For example, religious studies scholars and theologians such as Wentzel van Huyssteen, Catherine Keller, Gordon Kaufman, Ivone Gebara, Mark Taylor, and Thomas Tweed

6. On "expert discourse" see Bruno Latour, *Politics of Nature*. Interestingly, according to the hubris of some popular materialists, such as Richard Dawkins and Bill Maher, religions are basically so destructive to the planet that they must be destroyed or overcome; the rationalization of the world must be completed; the materialization of life must move forward if the environmental crisis is to be thwarted. Both Dawkins in *God Delusion*, and Bill Maher in his movie *Religulous* (2008) represent the fundamentalism of the "scientific materialism" that is supposed to supplant dogmatic, irrational religion.

7. Hargens and Zimmerman, *Integral Ecology*. Though some of the implications of Wilber's Integral Theory I cannot follow, and noting that there is no facile dualism between internal and external, I do agree that there is some sort of call for taking "interior" dimensions of all life (from atoms to humans and other organisms) seriously.

8. See e.g., Latour, *Politics of Nature*; Morton, *Ecology without Nature*; and Haraway, *When Species Meet*.

have all developed post-foundational understandings of religion.[9] On the "nature" side of the spectrum, we have many post-foundational understandings of the *Natura naturans* tradition (that is, active nature or "nature naturing") such as found in the works of Donna Haraway, Bruno Latour, Gayatri Spivak, and Deleuze and Guattari.[10] This chapter analyzes the move away from transcendent foundations and toward a radical immanence among scholars of religion and the natural world, and then argues that these moves provide us with a politically viable way forward in environmental ethics, philosophy, and theology as it seeks to address planetary problems. Inspired by Catherine Keller, Laurel Kearns, and Timothy Morton, I seek to develop a view of Religion and Ecology that acknowledges that all knowledge rests on changing "grounds" as opposed to stable, transcendent foundations.[11] From within changing grounds, it is impossible to see, feel, touch, and reason beyond the eco-social terrains that we inhabit at any given time, and it is useless to seek what is transcendentally "Nature" and what is transcendentally "Right." Rather, our thinking, reasoning, and ethical deliberations always already contain uncertainty based upon both the present perspective from which we think, feel, and act, and non-existent future emergent possibilities. The ethical weight of our actions are only fully determined in retrospect, thus we always act (already) from a somewhat agnostic perspective. When we deny this by filling what is mysterious with transcendent certainty, we cut ourselves off from the human and earth others in our living present. This is a form of eco-social violence.[12]

Thus, I argue that only when religious and philosophical reflection, as well as our scientific knowledge, becomes *viably agnostic* will our

9. See, eg: Van Huysteen, *Essays in Postfoundationalist Theology*; Keller, *Face of the Deep*; and Keller and Kearns, *Ecospirit*; Kaufman, *In Face of Mystery*; and Kaufman, *In the Beginning—Creativity*; Gebara, *Longing for Running Water*; Tweed, *Crossing and Dwelling*: Taylor, *After God*; and Lodge and Hamlin, *Religion and the New Ecology*.

10. Haraway, *When Species Meet*; Latour, *Politics of Nature*; Spivak, *Death of a Discipline*; Deleuze and Guattari, *A Thousand Plateaus*. Due mainly to space considerations, I limit myself here to specific thinkers rather than concepts. I could have examined the concepts of Non-Equilibrium Thermodynamics, Emergence, Chaos and Complexity, etc., but this is done elsewhere and by most of the people I reference here. Furthermore, comparing the philosophical aspects of both "religion" and "nature" using specific theorists keep the focus on the production of both "religion" and "nature."

11. Keller and Kearns, *Ecospirit*; Morton, *Ecology without Nature*.

12. Val Plumwood describes this process as "backgrounding" others in her book *Environmental Culture*.

understandings of nature as *natura naturans* become grounded, open toward the ever-changing grounds from and on which we all persist. "Truth is not to be found in correspondence—either between the word and the world in the case of science, or between the original and the copy in the case of religion—but in taking up again the task of *continuing* the flow, of elongating the cascade of mediations one step further."[13] In this way, the future of all life becomes radically open toward here-to-fore impossible possibilities, and thus discernment of how we ought to become in the natural-cultural worlds we inhabit becomes political.

A Historical Detour

Divisions between religion and nature or religion and science or epistemology and ontology have been anachronistically projected onto western thought prior to the Scientific Revolution and Reformation. However, before these shifts, there was no space to separate these phenomena: there was one cosmos, even if it was a hierarchical "chain of being." With the space provided by the Reformation and the Scientific Revolution came the birth of epistemology outside of a Catholic understanding, a space that would become "the secular." The problem of how to relate these two sides of reality together has been at the forefront of philosophical and religious investigations ever since.[14] However, just as the scientific revolution of the 15th/16th centuries led to a rereading of reality, and the evolutionary revolution of the 19th century led to re-readings of reality, so now, the ecological revolution brought most recently to awareness through the problem of global climate change gives us another chance to re-read reality. Two aspects of that rereading are the view of nature as active and a verb, and the fact that globalization changes epistemological claims.

Carolyn Merchant has described the Scientific Revolution as "the death of nature," noting that it was at this time that the world outside of humanity became a dead object, upon which active, living human beings could reflect. This shaped the course of intellectual and technological pursuit in the West for centuries, and through globalization has shaped the rest of the world, but it is not a reasonable view of the contemporary

13. Latour, "Thou Shalt Not Freeze Frame," 46.

14. For an outstanding analysis of this process, see Dupre, *Passage to Modernity*. Cf. Merchant, *Death of Nature*; and Taylor, *Secular Age*.

world. Global climate change, for instance, is an undeniable reminder that scientific knowledge and manipulation cannot contain the future of nature, and that we humans are indeed a part of nature. In other words, despite all of our actions and predictions, humans still remain a part (and not in control) of the future of nature.[15] Nature, whatever else it is, can no longer serve as the "given" Universal for relative cultural claims; it is an active, politically viable principle again. As Žižek argues, "What usually served as the recourse to Wisdom (basic trust in the background coordinates of our world) [i.e., Nature] is now *the* source of danger."[16] The foundational claim of western sciences and theologies—that Nature is stable, reliable, uniform, and knowable, and that creation is *for* human beings, respectively—is challenged by a future that is most certainly different and perhaps disastrous for the human species. This means that our actions in the present cannot be predicated based on past assumptions: time is open rather than closed by Reason or God. As Hannah Arendt notes, there is always some amount of uncertainty in any action and this is also true for the rest of the natural world.[17]

As global climate change and recent developments in scientific thought about nature have shifted our understandings away from stable foundations, so the process of globalization has shifted our understandings of the status of claims about meaning and value. One effect of the phenomena commonly referred to as globalization is that our "universal" value claims finally unfold as contextual. Most extant world religions and philosophical systems arose during a time (the axial age) when "universal" knowledge did not include widespread knowledge of the diversity of human peoples on the planet and of the ecological systems and species of the planet. Ignorance of diversity is impossible in the world shaped by colonization, scientific cataloguing, mass communication, and transportation; different and sometimes conflicting knowledge claims can be explored too easily. This is often referred to as the "space-time crunch": The speed of and access to information and the exponential growth in the space-time of the universe means that universal claims are much harder to justify. This results in a form of contextuality where universalism becomes more akin to uniqueness. From this perspective, "universal

---

15. This is most famously argued by Horkheimer and Adorno, *Dialectic of the Enlightenment*.

16. Žižek, *In Defense of Lost Causes*, 445.

17. Arendt, *The Human Condition*.

claims" are understood contextually: they are universal because they are representative of a specific, contextual eco-social place, people, and time-period.[18] Their uniqueness (as part of the ongoing process of universal expansion and geo-evolution) becomes the point at which they can be universalized as the "only" knowledge claims of their kind. Furthermore, this type of contextual-universal does not mean that value and knowledge claims do not matter to human and earth others. The local and global are not separate; contextual-universals arise out of specific contexts but return to affect many others. Continuing to try to write a contextually-specific knowledge claim across the whole globe (Universalism) leads to something like the globalization of free-market economics: One economic system, smuggling in its culture, forces itself upon the face of the whole planet. This leads to something like necrophilia, because colonizing the world with a transcendent idea or system of economics actually kills the diversity of life on the planet.

I am not arguing that any given idea is inherently wrong, but rather that ideas should be used more like scalpels than machetes. Confronting a world of many human and earth "others" requires precision rather than brute force. One idea does not fit all of life. Jean Luc Nancy writes of this dilemma as the problem of choosing between globalization (Universalizing through brute force) and world-formation (connecting with human and earth-others through dialogues in recognition and respect of differences).[19] Gayatri Spivak offers a similar choice between "the globe" and "the planetary."[20] Both of their analyses have implications for re-reading "religion" and "ecology/nature" as post-foundational categories.

Here I must ward-off easy dismissal of the task of post-foundational thinking: a contextual-universal does not amount to relativism. Relative claims pay no attention to context, but rather isolate subjects from histories of nature-cultures; they amount to solipsism. In other words, relativistic and universal claims make the same mistake: they force into the background the contexts out of which our meaning-making activities emerge. Might there then be a better model for thinking with nature and religion in this contemporary era of globalization and global climate

18. This contextual-universal is akin to what Sandra Harding identifies as "strong objectivity"; see Harding, *Is Science Multicultural?* 124–45.

19. Nancy, *Creation of the World.*

20. Spivak, *Death of a Discipline*, esp. chap. 3.

change? A model that navigates between outdated understandings of Universalism and its solipsistic child Relativism? A model that navigates between the extreme pendulum swings of scientific and religious certainty and leaves a space open for a radically new future?

Below I explore various "post-" understandings of nature in hopes that they will lead to contextual and thus politically transformative forms of knowing and acting. In a word, these are understandings of nature and religion as political. Religion, here, will be viewed as an emergent aspect of the human, natural world and as a process of worlding. Furthermore, religion is important because it functions in our cultures, economics, politics, and environments.[21] No matter how many evangelical atheists try to wipe religion away, there will always be at least historical traces of religions in our lives, shaping our continuing struggles to make meaning out of our lives. Religion, or re-reading/re-linking, is something that we as humans do. Whether or not calling it religious as such, at the heart of religious reflection and religious phenomena is the desire and need to make meaning out of our lives. In this sense, religion, even if it is as I suggest cultural-historical-ecological projection, is still meaning-full in and to the world around us. This is an attempt, then, then to take the world seriously without a transcendent foundation in nature, or religion without a transcendent foundation in Revelation. In the end, I argue, these postfoundational forms of "religion" and "nature" provide spaces for transformative politics.

Natura Naturans without Foundations: Taking the Unknown Seriously

Ursula Goodenough writes: "The continuation of life reaches around, grabs its own tail, and forms a sacred circle that requires no further justification, no Creator, no super-ordinate meaning of meaning, no purpose other than that the continuation continue until the sun collapses or the final meteor collides."[22] With the exception that I hope the circle is more like an open rhizome that can move in any direction, this is the active sense of nature that I aim to capture. What is essential to this understanding of nature is taking the unknown in our experiential

21. Durkheim, *Elementary Forms of Religious Life*.
22. Goodenough, *Sacred Depths of Nature*, 171.

horizons seriously.[23] A recent collection of essays entitled *The Virtue of Ignorance* in fact suggests this approach in environmental ethics.[24] We can only hear, see, touch, taste, smell, and think so far into the past and into the future before our senses are overcome by uncertainty. Beyond that is the unknown. Unfortunately, environmental ethics (whether religious or not) tends to fill that unknown space with a reified concept of what is "Natural" or "Unnatural." Whether it is through conserving or preserving wilderness areas, dividing the urban from the rural, making humans and technology somehow unnatural, or even suggesting that the current climate change is unnatural, these claims claim too much. Most often they separate humans, culture, and the mind from the rest of the natural world in some way. These foundational understandings of "nature" are indeed killing life, including but not limited to human life. Through these foundational understandings, ideas about what is natural and what is human are disconnected from the rest of the natural world and then subsequently imposed upon both. Under suffocating certainty about what is and is not "nature," many entities suffer the violence of conformity.[25] We need to relearn the virtue of un-knowing in regards to "nature." As the Talking Heads suggests in the title of one of their albums, we need to stop making sense.

This process of unknowing is not foreign to western traditions which include apophatic, negative, and post-colonial traditions within their histories of religious reflection. Unfortunately, these traditions have been overshadowed by a tendency toward certainty in religious reflection, which has led to violence against "otherness," "darkness," and to the rest of the natural world. Unknowing, deconstructing, apophasis, and learned ignorance are all methods for opening up living spaces for thinking anew. These methods can enable us to break out of suffocating certainties housed in transcendent foundations such as nature,

---

23. In one sense, I am merely highlighting the problem of the "quest for certainty" that John Dewey outlines in his Gifford lectures of the same title: *The Quest for Certainty*.

24. Vitek and Jackson, *Virtues of Ignorance*.

25. Perhaps a good parallel is the gender roles that feminists and queer theorists have brought to light. Certain, essential understandings of what "man/male" and "woman/female" are, have led to violence toward many human bodies. More broadly, this is why Foucault's genealogies are so important: they uncover the political processes through which ideas or assertions become habits, norms, simply "givens." This "cutting off from" and "certainty" is also part of what Teresa Brennan defines as the "foundational fantasy" of independence. See her book *Exhausting Modernity*.

revelation, and reason, and meet others anew in our evolving eco-social contexts. In these open spaces, perhaps best described as ecotones for emerging planetary identities, discourse about Religion and Ecology becomes transformative politics. Following, then, are some viable ways forward in thinking about what "nature" and "religion" might mean beyond foundations.

Deleuze and Guattari: Rhizomatic Thought and Radical Immanence

In *A Thousand Plateaus* Deleuze and Guattari posit "the rhizome" as metaphor for thinking in contra-distinction to teleological, arboreal thinking.[26] The importance of this metaphor goes beyond the challenge to teleology, however, and suggests that epistemology and ontology are and always have been epistem-ontology. That is, they are never separate, one is never transcendent to the other and thus neither can be used as a foundation. We exist in the mix, always already, and there are no ultimate origins or ends that serve as foundations for how we ought to proceed. Idealisms that attempt to impose epistemes on the world, and Materialisms that attempt to reduce the world both make the mistake of assuming that epistemology and ontology can be separated. The move toward rhizomatic thinking suggests that epistemology and ontology are always already implied by each other.

Rhizomatic thinking suggests that there are many creative offshoots and trajectories that can be explored, what Deleuze and Guattari refer to as "lines of flight". Some may be viable, others may be less so, but meaning and value are found in the process of always working from within and as a part of *natura naturans*. Because the future is open toward many different directions, one path doesn't have to define the way forward (or sideways). Depending on where one stands, there may be multiple futures worth working towards simultaneously. The point is that rhizomatic thought opens us up to the evolving eco-social contexts of which we are a part rather than suggesting a transcendent origin and telos for all of creation. In this sense, organisms, assemblages of bio-history and techno-nature, are not formed externally, but are rather formed from capacities that arise from the very process of interacting. Reality, material and ideal, is emergent. Identities are emergent and not pre-conceived.

---

26. Deleuze and Guattari, *A Thousand Plateaus*, 3–28.

"In a Deleuzian ontology resemblance and identity must be treated not as fundamental but as derivative concepts."[27]

The problem with thinking that relies on transcendent foundations is precisely that identities are seen as essential rather than as emergent. Such stable identities must be reinforced through a realm that transcends the material-flux of everyday experience. Whether through Forms, God, or Nature, this transcendent realm takes identity out of context with others and then imposes an order and stability where there is none. Purpose, value, and meaning become about returning things/entities to a pre-conceived balanced order. It is this ordering that serves as foundation (origin and End) for all life. It is this ordering that precisely cuts evolving nature-cultures off from eco-social context, thereby reifying a slice of time as that which is Right, Good, and/or Natural. Rhizomatic thinking is an exercise in keeping our thoughts and senses open toward the moving stream of life rather than damming up life into preconceived concepts. In the rhizomatic process, meaning and value becomes something that we do, not something we find in the pre-made, transcendent realm of "nature" or "revelation." In fact, for Deleuze and Guattari, transcendence is the major culprit of contemporary eco-social ills. Hence, they call for radical immanence.

As noted already, transcendence reifies identities and allows for the categorization of all life. In a world of radical immanence, identities are always becoming. Because there is no "outside" against which life can be judged, becoming is open to many possibilities. Deleuze and Guattari write of humans becoming plant, animal, and mineral; a post-human world is possible and not necessarily a bad thing if we are indeed becoming with other planetary creatures. "There is nothing outside being in relation to which being might be."[28] This radical immanence refocuses our attention both on the current context of becoming and on a future that is radically open. Inherent to this understanding of radical immanence and emergent becomings is a kind of respect for biodiversity, multi-perspectivalism, and democracy: "The fewer the life forms available for becoming other, the fewer the trajectories available for creative transformation."[29] In a world where neither "nature" nor "religion" is transcendent, they become loci for a democratic process of discernment

27. DeLanda, "Ecology and Realist Ontology," 39.
28. Hallward, *Deleuze and the Philosophy of Creation*, 15.
29. Bogue, "A Thousand Ecologies," 54.

regarding future becomings. The unknown future takes shape in the present in a radically creative and transformative way.

This is akin to what Gordon Kaufman suggests in his book *In the Beginning . . . Creativity*. For Kaufman, teleology and a personal God that backs up teleology lead to violence toward human and earth others and prevent human beings from feeling at home in the world. For him, rather, God should be thought of as Creativity. Rather than a thing, and reflection on that thing, then, theology and religious reflection become reflection on the very processes that enable creativity throughout the whole spectrum of life. For Kaufman, these reflections are bio-historically located as specific human projections for which we can take responsibility. Furthermore, he takes ultimate certainty as precisely problematic for the earth. Rather, at the edges of our knowing we should place mystery rather than certainty in the form of an Omni-God (robust theisms) or a Nothing (robust atheisms). In this way, religion becomes a process of fostering the further creative-destructive evolution of life on our planet. Religion returns us to our context, to the living present, rather than sealing us off from the rest of life in ultimate origins or ends. As Bruno Latour notes, in this way "religion . . . does everything to constantly redirect attention by systematically breaking the will to go away, to ignore, to be indifferent, blasé, bored."[30] Religious language and experiences should break open our reified concepts and senses, exposing us to the present moment of creative possibilities; religion should be about motion rather than arrival or rest. In other words, it is similar to what Latour identifies as "the collective."

Latour's Collective: Democracies of Creative Transformations

In Bruno Latour's *The Politics of Nature*, he argues that the opposition between nature and culture prevent any real environmental politics. Rather, nature is already preformed and culture must conform to it. Thus, he argues that we should rid ourselves of this binary altogether and in its place talk about "the collective." The collective is, for lack of better term and knowing that it is one he would not use, nature-culture in process: from destabilizing to re-stabilizing and destabilizing again, *ad infinitum*. In this model, there is no recourse to foundations, only the recognition that we live amidst evolving life-systems. For Latour, this is

30. Latour, "Thou Shalt Not Freeze Frame," 36.

the only way that nature can become again part of the political process, as active participant.

The import here for the Religion and Ecology discourse is that there is never a secure place, a transcendent space, from which to impose an ethic on the world. Rather, these emerge in the continuing collecting, destabilizing, and re-collecting process of the collective. As Donna Haraway notes, "Abstractions, which require our best calculation, mathematics, reasons, are built in order to be able to break down so that richer and more responsive inventions, speculations, and proposia—worlding—can go on."[31] Knowledge-making in the collective is inherently ethical and becomes a process of ongoing political dialogue with human and earth others. As Timothy Morton suggests, "This is ultimate rationality: holding our mind open for the absolutely unknown that is to come."[32]

For Catherine Keller, this is the model for *doing* religious reflection as well. Rather than, again, suggesting that religion makes certain a pure origin, pure self-identity, or pure end, religion is about opening onto the world.[33] Amidst this uncertainty lies the recognition that knowledge is always already "faith in" rather than "certainty of." Furthermore, all our reflection (religious and otherwise) emerges from socio-ecological-historical-shifting grounds rather than foundations. In other words, we don't create *ex nihilo* the world of nature with culture and language, nor does nature create ex nihilo culture and identity; rather all of these things co-create the present and we find ourselves as active participants in the mix. Again, religious thought becomes political, something for which we can take responsibility. Religious concepts and understandings collect and make meanings, but also destabilize extant meanings in order to continuously re-read evolving life.

This postfoundational understanding of religion and religious language is also shared by Mark Taylor. He writes, "Religion is an emergent, complex, adaptive network of symbols, myths and rituals that, on the one hand, figure schemata of feeling, thinking and acting in ways that lend life meaning and purpose and, on the other, disrupt, dislocate every stabilizing structure."[34] A further example is found in Thomas Tweed's

---

31. Haraway, *When Species Meet*, 93.

32. Morton, *Ecology Without Nature*, 205.

33. Respectively, *Face of the Deep*; *From a Broken Web*; *Apocalypse Now and Then*.

34. Originally found in Mark Taylor, *After God*. Here quotes in: Mark Taylor, "Refiguring Religion," 110.

understanding of religion in *Crossing and Dwelling*, in which religious "theories are positioned representations of a changing *terrain* by an itinerant cartographer."[35] Again, this changing understanding of the function of religion and religious language implies that postfoundational understandings of religion provide transformative spaces for politics. Furthermore, religious language, far from being a source of secure identity, is that which destabilizes boundaries between self/other, humans/earth-others, nature/technology.

Donna Haraway's Cyborg Ontology: Technology as Part of Emerging Planetary Identities

Donna Haraway has been outspoken about the problematic separation of nature and culture and puts the two together in evolving nature-cultures. For Haraway, we always already exist as natural-cultural creatures. Again, there is no pure foundation from which to move the rest of the world. She goes on to challenge the dualisms that result from the nature-culture split in her discussion of a cyborg ontology.[36] In a cyborg ontology nature, culture, humans, animals, technology, material, thought, and energy all exist always and already together; the division between nature and technology is questioned alongside the division between humanity and nature. This is an important challenge for environmentalists, who often tend towards Luddite thinking. It is also an important challenge specific to Religion and Ecology, because it helps to "earth" religious reflection; it reminds us that religious thought and religious practice are a part of the cyborg reality within which we exist. Thus, we should treat religions as an aspect of our worlds that help *matter* the planet. Religious ideas and rituals, as meaning-making practices, can be seen as a technology that shapes the world around us. They manipulate the world through structuring human-human, human-other animal, and human-earth relations. Religion, here, becomes in part an arm of environmental history.

Perhaps then, Religion and Ecology should begin to look more closely at how religions have been shaped by and shaped the rest of the world around them. Much of what has happened within the field has been geared toward apologetics, retrieval, re-construction, or rejection

35. Tweed, *Crossing and Dwelling*, 13.
36. Haraway, *Simians, Cyborgs, and Women*, 127–48.

of religion(s) and/or religious assumptions as either supportive of good environmental habits or supportive of destructive habits. This is good work, but what I am suggesting is a deeper assessment of how these religious traditions move from the "virtual" to the "material" worlds we live in. In other words, we must examine how religious traditions have mattered bodies and landscapes around us. This would be, in part, an assertion that landscape is life-scape not only for indigenous communities, but for all human communities. Max Weber's seminal work in what I would call "religious environmental history" provides a good historical root for this type of analysis.[37] Carolyn Merchant and Roderick Nash (among others) use the type of analysis that I am suggesting here as well. These scholars/authors show how religious values, concepts, and traditions materialize and shape the landscapes around us. On the flipside, we also need more scholarship like the work of Daniel Hillel and Theodore Hiebert, who reveal how environments shape religious traditions. In other words, how are specific religions or meaning-making practices shaped by the landscapes out of which they emerge?[38]

Another important component of what this means is that humans are always in a state of becoming. Phil Hefner writes of human becoming towards technology,[39] and Deleuze and Guattari (as mentioned before) write of human becoming mineral, plant, and animal. The important points Haraway, Hefner, Deleuze and Guattari share is that identities are ever-changing, exist as a result of changing assemblages with others, and are thus not stable. The past 500 years of technological and scientific development, colonization, globalization and now climate change have forever changed humanity: at each step new "others" come into contact. There is no nature or paradise to return to, but only an unknown future to move toward. In the face of this, holding on to certainty exacerbates the social and ecological ills that we know all to well. "Growing complexity, uncertainty, and insecurity create the desire for simplicity, certainty, and security, which leads to foundationalism on the left and the right . . . Every such flight from the present deepens the dangers we face."[40]

---

37. Weber, *The Protestant Ethic and the Spirit of Capitalism.*

38. Merchant, *Reinventing Eden*; Nash, *Wilderness and the American Mind*. Cf. Hillel, *The Natural History of the Bible*; Hiebert, *The Yahwist's Landscape.*

39. Hefner, *Technology and Human Becoming.*

40. Taylor, "Refiguring Religion," 118.

This process of human becoming with the rest of the natural world (including technology) may indeed suggest a post-human future but it also suggests a planetary future. Whatever else it may mean to be religious, scientific, human, plant, mineral, animal, or machine, it at least means that all identities stabilize and change within the planet that we call Earth. Our planetary identities are, of course, housed in a larger cosmic process, yet all that we know of this larger cosmic process is from within our planetary perspectives. We always already read the cosmos with the textual lens of the earth. The planetary context of our becoming human is described by Gayatri Spivak in *Death of a Discipline*.

Gayatri Spivak's Planetarity: Transformative Politics for the Earth

In *Death of a Discipline*, Spivak argues for a "planetary" vision of the world to overwrite that of the "global." For Spivak, the global vision imposes sameness everywhere, whereas a planetary vision pays deep attentions to the emergent diversities of thought, matter, ecosystems, and cultures that help to make up the world. Spivak's planetary vision is one that is post-colonial and of the earth rather than above the earth. What is important here for the Religion and Ecology discourse is that religions, re-linking's or re-readings, are multiple and *of* the earth. There is no need for a common denominator in multi-religious reflection, but rather the recognition that religions help to co-create the worlds in which we live, and for better and/or worse help to make up the planet on which we all (humans and non) live.

Catherine Keller takes up this idea of "planetary creation" in her work. From her perspective, creation is pluri-singular, spiraling, and origami-like. There is no Archimedean point that can move the world. Religion at its best is poetics and persuasion, a re-linking of life toward "common grounds" but never an imposition of one way of thinking as "global."[41] Another religious studies scholar that should be mentioned here is Anne Primavesi. Her work with the Gaia metaphor and "creation as gift" find resonance with Spivak's notion of planetarity. Creation is not foundation, but rather the gift of cosmic, geo, and historical evolution. Levels of life emerge out of others and none can be reduced to the other. There is no foundation, but rather the ongoing gift that we participate in

41. See, e.g., *Face of the Deep*; and Keller, *God and Power*.

and give to the rest of the earth and future generations.[42] Again, we have here understandings of thought and matter as post-foundational *and* open toward an unknown future. Having suggested *some* of the emerging connections between postfoundational discourse on both "religion" and "nature", I now turn toward some concluding remarks on how the discourse of "Religion and Ecology" can provide the open spaces needed for a transformative and planetary politics.

Religion and Ecology: The Spaces of Transformative, Planetary Politics

Nature without foundations becomes political. As Bruno Latour suggests, at this point in our evolving identities, humans must act as spokespersons for the life that is non-human. This is not to say that humans dictate the order of the rest of the natural world, but rather to recognize that inter-species communication, much less communication between different levels of reality, is always based upon our locatedness in the natural-cultural worlds as human beings (and even within that large category, our perspectives are located based upon class, race, gender, sexuality, etc.). In this context, it is worth carefully studying the efforts of Donna Haraway, Mark Bekoff, and others, to develop more fully inter-species communication, and efforts in Artificial Intelligence to develop more fully communication between humans and machines.

These efforts will no doubt change the role of humans as "spokesperson" in the future. However, at this point in time of our planetary development, the best we can do is to speak with/ on behalf of (rather than for) the rest of the natural-technological world. Deep attention toward the creative-continual processes of life that we are a part of means that spokespersons can never assume foundational authority. Rather, persuasive visions for how we want to live within the rest of the natural world should be debated on the stage of politics. How we become human with plants, minerals, other animals, technology, becomes a matter of persuasion based upon the best information we have and upon the most aesthetically and morally pleasing visions of the future that we are becoming toward.

Unhitching scientific information about nature from what is universally Nature and paying more attention to the politics and production

---

42. Primavesi, *Gaia's Gift*.

of scientific information may lead toward understandings of evolving nature-cultures that re-place human identities within the rest of the natural world. In other words, Nature no longer serves as the stable basis of our species or gender identities (biology, genetics, evolution, zoology), nor as the stable basis of our minds (Neuroscience), nor as the stable basis for our secure location between nature and technology (chemistry, physics, etc.). Information from science is no longer justification for what is and is not Natural; rather, information from the natural sciences is to be taken into deliberations for how we want to become as planetary becomings. This type of deliberation is at heart about meaning making.

Foundational understandings of religion often come up in contemporary political discourse, especially in the United States. Discussions around gay marriage, abortion, stem cell research, euthanasia, and even environmental degradation often end with dueling transcendent foundations touted as religious faith or belief. This is precisely the opposite of what religious discourse and inquiry should be about according to a post-foundational understanding. Rather than stabilizing one's own beliefs and identity in some transcendent foundation, religious language, concepts, and beliefs should return one to the ever-changing, complex eco-social present precisely to upset reified understandings and further the ongoing process of planetary becoming. The "re" of religion suggests that whatever else religion is/does, it disrupts structures of meaning, habits, ways of being in the world in attempts to re-read and/or re-link life. This rereading and relinking is similar to the emergent assemblages of Deleuze and Guattari, to the ongoing collective of Bruno Latour. This is how religion functions in a post-foundational context.

What would happen if both "nature" and "religion" were politicized? I argue for at least three tenants of a future for Religion and Ecology in the public sphere. First, nature is political/active. Conversations cannot be ended by appeals to what is "natural" or "unnatural"; this should be inadmissible in courts of law, and unacceptable in political debates. Rather than this foundational language, we should speak of our own preferences and argue for them in conversations. Conversations always already imply the willingness to be changed in dialogue. Foundational claims do not allow for argument or conversation; they cut the self off from the other and reify both. Sean Hargens and Michael Zimmerman have a wonderful illustration of how this might look in their book *Integral Ecology.*

Imagine a juniper in a forest with a number of sentient beings perceiving the tree: an ant, a blue jay, a mule deer, a . . . lumber-jack, a . . . backpacker, and a . . . scientist doing fieldwork. Now, as each individual 'looks' at the tree, they all enact a different tree. The ant feels the rough bark as it travels the scent trail leading to sugary sap. The blue jay experiences the tree as a source of insects to take care of its midday hunger. The mule deer sees the tree as protective shade from which to observe the nearby meadow. The lumberjack sees 1,200 board feet. The backpacker sees the intrin-sic value of the tree. The scientist sees the evolutionary trajectory of the tree as it struggles with this year's drought cycle . . . In short, there simply is no such thing as 'one tree'! Rather, there are different layers of trees enacted by each perceiver and the evolv-ing consciousness associated with it.[43]

A foundationalist would argue that there is only "one tree," while a post-foundationalist understands the multi-perspectives of what a tree is. The multiple views do not degrade the individual nature of the tree anymore than they degrade an individual human subject who defines him/her self as earthling, animal, human, parent, child, brother/sister, teacher, friend, lover, etc. Different eco-social contexts may demand that some perspectives be weighted more heavily than others, but never that a given perspective is invalid. What is called for is a pragmatist understanding of truth, information, and knowledge claims where "the reality-appearance distinction" is replaced "with the distinction between the more useful and the less useful."[44]

Second, humans are part of nature naturing. Exceptionalism is alive and well in much ecological discourse (religious and otherwise): humans are separated from the rest of the world as caretakers, stewards, or responsible for managing the rest of life on the planet. This language, again, serves to subvert the rest of nature as political and active. On the one hand, we must act as spokespersons and with the realization that we can never fully know what is best for a bird, or a river, or an atmosphere. However, this does not mean that we are not just as much an emergent part of ongoing creation.

This second point may seem obvious to many environmentally minded-thinkers, but a small experiment that I perform in almost all of my classes, and in almost every public lecture I give having to do with

43. Hargens and Zimmerman, *Integral Ecology*, 180.
44. Rorty, *Philosophy and Social Hope*, xxii.

"religion and the environment" suggests otherwise. The experiment involves asking the class to: "Close your eyes and imagine 'Nature'. Now, tell me what you thought of." The students often shout out words such as: birds, a mountain, the ocean, etc. When I ask how many of them imagined humans, usually only one or two people (if any) raise their hands. In a sense, the major aim of a postfoundational approach to "nature" and "religion" is to increase the number of people who imagine humans in the experiment.

Third, the unique aspect of human nature-naturing is the cultural/religious/ideal realm. Just because we are not exceptional, does not mean we are not unique; rather it means we are unique like all other systems, species, molecules, and individuals in nature. As humans, we have been gifted for better or worse with a unique capacity for imagining a world, making meaning out of the world, and taking responsibility for moving towards those imagined, meaning-full existences. We are not responsible for the future of the whole planet, but we are responsible for our interactions with human and earth "others." The worlds we want to live in and argue for rely more on persuasion in the political sphere than on recourse to any certain way that the world "Is." In fact, the aim of this third premise is no more than a recognition that claims about "nature" and "religion" have always been political and transformative (for better or worse); the political nature has just been put in the background by power relations, traditions, and habit. In a sense, we have been denying responsibility for our unique, meaning-making capacities. Denying the processes through which we co-construct religious meanings and scientific information denies the very freedom that we so often claim as a species "above the fray." Through acknowledging that humans as nature-naturing are meaning-making creatures, humans are returned to the rest of the natural world and given the freedom to evolve toward planetary identities. In this way, meaning-making creatures might help create an open space for the emergence of new planetary relations and identities.

Bibliography

Arendt, Hannah. *The Human Condition.* 2nd ed. Chicago: University of Chicago Press, 1998.

Bogue, Ronald. "A Thousand Ecologies." In *Deleuze Guattari & Ecology,* edited by Bernd Herzogenrath, 42–56. Basingstoke, UK: Palgrave Macmillan, 2009.

Brennan, Teresa. *Exhausting Modernity: Grounds for a New Economy*. London: Routledge, 2000.

Dawkins, Richard. *The God Delusion*. London: Bantam, 2006.

DeLanda, Manuel. "Ecology and Realist Ontology," in *Deleuze Guattari & Ecology*, edited by Bernd Herzogenrath, 23–41. Basingstoke, UK: Palgrave Macmillan, 2009.

Deleuze, Gilles, and Felix Guattari. *A Thousand Plateaus: Capitalism and Schizophrenia*. Minneapolis: University of Minnesota Press, 1987.

Dewey, John. *The Quest for Certainty: A Study of the Relation of Knowledge and Action*. Gifford Lectures 1929. New York: Putnam, 1960.

Dupre, Louis. *Passage to Modernity: An Essay on the Hermeneutics of Nature and Culture*. New Haven: Yale University Press, 1993.

Durkheim, Emile. *The Elementary Forms of Religious Life*. Translated by Carol Cosman. Abridged with an introduction and notes by Mark S. Cladis. Oxford World's Classics. Oxford: Oxford University Press, 2001.

Esbjörn-Hargens, Sean, and Michael Zimmerman. *Integral Ecology: Uniting Multiple Perspectives on the Natural World*. Boston: Integral, 2009.

Gebara, Ivone. *Longing for Running Water: Ecofeminism and Liberation*. Translated by David Molineaux. Minneapolis: Fortress, 1999.

Goodenough, Ursula. *The Sacred Depths of Nature*. New York: Oxford University Press, 1998.

Hallward, Peter. *Out of This World: Deleuze and the Philosophy of Creation*. London: Verso, 2006.

Harding, Sandra. *Is Science Multicultural? Postcolonialisms, Feminisms, and Epistemologies*. Race, Gender, and Science. Bloomington: Indiana University Press, 1998.

Haraway, Donna J. *When Species Meet*. Posthumanities 3. Minneapolis: University of Minnesota Press, 2008.

———. *Simians, Cyborgs and Women: The Reinvention of Nature*. New York: Routledge, 1991.

Hefner, Philip. *Technology and Human Becoming*. Facets. Minneapolis: Fortress, 2003.

Hiebert, Theodore. *The Yahwist's Landscape: Nature and Religion in Early Israel*. New York: Oxford University Press, 1996.

Hillel, Daniel. *The Natural History of the Bible: An Environmental Explanation of the Hebrew Scriptures*. New York: Columbia University Press, 2007.

Horkheimer, Max, and Theodor W. Adorno. *Dialectic of the Enlightenment: Philosophical Fragments*. Edited by Gunzelin Schmid Noerr. Translated by Edmund Jephcott. Cultural Memory in the Present. Stanford, CA: Stanford University Press, 2002, ed.

Kaufman, Gordon D. *In the Beginning—Creativity*. Minneapolis: Fortress, 2004.

Keller, Catherine. *God and Power: Counter-Apocalyptic Journeys*. Minneapolis: Fortress, 2005.

———. *Face of the Deep: A Theology of Becoming*. London: Routledge, 2003.

———. *Apocalypse Now and Then: A Feminist Guide to the End of the World*. Boston: Beacon, 1996.

———. *From a Broken Web: Separation, Sexism, and Self*. Boston: Beacon, 1988.

Keller, Catherine, and Laurel Kearns, editors. *Ecospirit: Religions and Philosophies for the Earth*. Transdisciplinary Theological Colloquia. New York: Fordham University Press, 2007.

Lakatos, Imre, Paul Feyerabend. *For and against Method: Including Lakatos's Lectures on Scientific Method and the Lakatos-Feyerabend Correspondence*. Edited with an introduction by Matteo Motterlini. Chicago: University of Chicago Press, 1999.

Latour, Bruno. "Thou Shalt Not Freeze Frame." In *Science, Religion, and the Human Experience*, edited by James D. Proctor, 27–48. Oxford: Oxford University Press, 2005.

———. *The Politics of Nature: How to Bring the Sciences into Democracy*. Translated by Catherine Porter. Cambridge: Harvard University Press, 2004.

Lodge, David, and Christopher Hamlin, editors. *Religion and the New Ecology: Environmental Responsibility in a World in Flux*. Notre Dame: University of Notre Dame Press, 2006.

Merchant, Carolyn. *Reinventing Eden: The Fate of Nature in Western Culture*. New York: Routledge, 2004.

———. *The Death of Nature: Women, Ecology, and the Scientific Revolution*. New York: HarperSanFrancisco, 1993.

Morton, Timothy. *Ecology without Nature: Rethinking Environmental Aesthetics*. Cambridge: Harvard University Press, 2007.

Nancy, Jean-Luc. *The Creation of the World, Or, Globalization*. Translated and with an introduction by François Raffoul and David Pettigrew. SUNY Series in Contemporary French Thought. Albany: State University of New York Press, 2007.

Plumwood, Val. *Environmental Culture: The Ecological Crisis of Reason*. London: Routledge, 2002.

Primavesi, Anne. *Gaia's Gift: Earth, Ourselves, and God after Copernicus*. London: Routledge, 2003.

Rorty, Richard. *Philosophy and Social Hope*. New York: Penguin, 1999.

Schwartz, Regina M. *The Curse of Cain: The Violent Legacy of Monotheism*. Chicago: University of Chicago Press, 1997.

Spivak, Gayatri. *The Death of a Discipline*. Wellek Library Lectures in Critical Theory. New York: Columbia University Press, 2003.

Taylor, Charles. *A Secular Age*. Cambridge: Harvard University Press, 2007.

Taylor, Mark C. *After God*. Religion and Postmodernism. Chicago: University of Chicago Press, 2007.

———. "Refiguring Religion." *Journal of the American Academy of Religion* 77 (2009) 105–19.

Tweed, Thomas A. *Crossing and Dwelling: A Theory of Religion*. Cambridge: Harvard University Press, 2007.

Van Huyssteen, Wentzel. *Essays in Postfoundationalist Theology*. Grand Rapids: Eerdmans, 1997.

Vitek, Bill, and Wes Jackson, editors. *The Virtues of Ignorance: Complexity, Sustainability, and the Limits of Knowledge*. Culture of the Land. Lexington: University Press of Kentucky, 2008.

Weber, Max. *The Protestant Ethic and the Spirit of Capitalism*. Routledge Classics. London: Routledge, 2001.

Žižek, Slavoj. *In Defense of Lost Causes*. London: Verso, 2008.

6

Feminist, Gender, and Sexuality Studies in Religion and Ecology

Where We Have Been, Where We Are Now, and Where We Might Go[1]

Tovis Page

"Gender," writes historian Virginia Scharff, "the bundle of habits and expectations and behaviors that organizes people and things according to ideas about the consequences of sexed bodies, is a crucial, deep, and far-reaching human medium through which we encounter nature."[2] This insight and its correlation—that mechanisms of regulating social relations, such as gender, are mediated in part through human interactions with nature—have proved rich stimuli for productive work across a range of academic fields and have gained particular saliency over the past few decades in light of increasingly urgent ecological concerns.

---

1. Two introductory acknowledgments are in order. 1) I first assessed the state of gender analysis in the field of Religion and Ecology in an article published in the *Journal for the Study of Religion, Nature and Culture* in 2007. While my core perceptions remain the same, the current piece has a different emphasis as well as several expanded sections. See Page, "Has Ecofeminism Cornered the Market?" 2) I would like to thank Whitney Bauman for his assistance with this chapter. I benefited from his editorial comments on the text as a whole and am especially grateful for his contributions to the final section on "queering" the field.

2. Scharff, *Seeing Nature*, xiii.

Feminists—particularly *eco*feminists—have interrogated the relations between gender and nature in order to expose the dynamics of male domination and ecological exploitation.

From the start, feminist and gender analysis has played an important role in the evolving field of Religion and Ecology. The early engagement of ecological concerns by feminist theologians—starting with Rosemary Radford Ruether's *New Woman, New Earth* in 1975—helped lay the groundwork for the subsequent development of this growing interdisciplinary field. Feminist and gender analysis is thus an important part of the land we inherit as scholars of Religion and Ecology. This chapter reviews and assesses feminist and gender studies in the field of Religion and Ecology to date, evaluating analytical trends, highlighting recent developments, and pointing to future directions.

The Inherited Land of Religion, Ecology, and Feminist/Gender Studies

The majority of extant work on gender in the field of Religion and Ecology is: 1) rooted in Christian theology; and 2) advances an ecofeminist perspective. A political standpoint as well as a diverse body of theory, ecofeminism can be defined by the core contention that the degradation of women and the degradation of the natural world—and thus feminism and environmentalism—are linked. The origins of ecofeminism are commonly indexed by the first appearance of the term in French feminist Francoise d'Eaubonne's *Ecofeminisme ou la Mort* (1974), and—in the United States—the confluence of the women's liberation, peace, antinuclear, and environmental movements of the 1970s and 80s.

Indicating widespread recognition of ecofeminism's importance within the Religion and Ecology field, many overview texts and anthologies include articles or even entire sections on ecofeminism.[3] Most of

3. These include Carroll et al., *Greening of Faith*; Foltz, *Worldviews*; Gottleib, *Oxford Handbook*; Gottleib, *This Sacred Earth*; Kearns and Keller, *Ecospirit*; Kinsley, *Ecology and Religion*; Taylor, *Encyclopedia*; Tucker and Grim, *Worldviews and Ecology*. Overviews and anthologies of Religion and Ecology from the perspective of a single religious tradition have likewise included ecofeminist perspectives. These include Foltz et al., *Islam and Ecology*; Hessel and Ruether, *Christianity and Ecology*; Tucker and Berthrong, *Confucianism and Ecology*. Anthologies of Christian ecological theology in particular tend to include articles on ecofeminism, such as Hallman, *Ecotheology*; Hessel, *Theology for Earth Community*.

these articles pertain to Christian ecofeminist theology and, to a lesser but still notable extent, post-Christian (eco)feminist spirituality. Over the past few decades, several anthologies on ecofeminism and religion have appeared, in addition to numerous monographs addressing and variously articulating Christian ecofeminist theology.[4] Euro-American practitioners and scholars of nontraditional feminist and earth-based spiritualities have also published articles and books that attend directly to the intersections between spirituality, gender, and the environment.[5] While a few scholars have addressed ecofeminism specifically or the intersections between religion, gender, and the environment more generally from non-Christian and non-Western perspectives, they are far outnumbered by those working in (or reacting to) Western Christian contexts.[6]

Ecofeminist scholars have contributed numerous insights and methodological approaches to the Religion and Ecology field. They have critically analyzed aspects of Western religion and culture that have historically legitimized the joint degradation of women (as well as non-elite males) and the natural world, especially conceptual frameworks of hierarchical dualism. They have proposed alternatives to dominant Western cultural ideals and theological models—for example, valuing interconnection and embodiment over autonomy and transcendence

---

4. Adams, *Ecofeminism and the Sacred*; Dietrich, *New Thing on Earth*; Eaton, *Introducing Ecofeminist Theologies*; Eaton and Lorentzen, *Ecofeminism and Globalization*; Gebara, *Longing for Running Water*; Gray, *Green Paradise Lost*; Grey, *Sacred Longings*; Halkes, *New Creation*; Johnson, *Women, Earth, and Creator Spirit*; Keller, *Apocalypse*; Keller, *Broken Web*; Keller, *Face of the Deep*; Low and Tremayne, *Women as Sacred Custodians*; MacKinnon and McIntyre, *Readings*; Primavesi, *Apocalypse to Genesis*; Rae, *Women, the Earth, the Divine*; Ress, *Ecofeminism in Latin America*; Ruether, *Gaia and God*; Ruether, *Integrating Ecofeminism*; Ruether, *Women Healing Earth*. Although not explicitly ecofeminist, Sallie McFague's works are frequently categorized among ecofeminist theological texts. See, for example, McFague, *Body of God*. Karen Baker-Fletcher's *Sisters of Dust* can be classified as an "ecowomanist" text, as it subscribes to womanism instead of feminism. Finally, many of the articles in the early interdisciplinary ecofeminist anthologies also address religion and spirituality. See Diamond and Orenstein, *Reweaving the World*; Plant, *Healing the Wounds*.

5. Christ, *Rebirth of the Goddess*; Eisler, *Chalice and the Blade*; Eller, *Lap of the Goddess*; Plaskow and Christ, *Weaving the Visions*; Sjöö and Mor, *Great Cosmic Mother*; Spretnak, *Politics of Women's Spirituality*.

6. For example, Vandana Shiva has written about ecofeminism from the perspective of Hindu and tribal women in India, and Wan-Li Ho has done so with respect to Buddhist women in Taiwan. Shiva, *Staying Alive*; Ho, "Environmental Protection." While many of the essays in Eaton and Lorentzen, *Ecofeminism and Globalization* and Ruether, *Women Healing Earth* reflect non-Western perspectives, most of them are Christian.

and imaging the divine as immanent in nature and/or as "feminine." Ecofeminist scholars in religion have highlighted ecoreligious actors (particularly women) and activities overlooked in malestream accounts of environmental action. And they have refused to separate social justice and ecological concerns, providing important correctives to ecological theories and theologies that universalize about the human species' relationship with nature rather than attending to structural inequalities that render some groups of people more susceptible to (and often less responsible for) environmental destruction than others.

Because most ecofeminist work in the field of religion is theological, Heather Eaton's evaluative summary of ecofeminist theology—presented with some variation in "Ecological-Feminist Theology" (1996) and *Introducing Ecofeminist Theologies* (2005)—is the most comprehensive review of the study of religion, gender, and ecology to date. Eaton identifies six common types of ecofeminist theology: theoretical or historical analyses of culture (Ruether and Elizabeth Dodson Gray); systematic theological reinterpretation (Elizabeth Johnson, Catherine Keller, and Anne Primavesi); scriptural studies (Primavesi, Carol Robb, and Anne Clifford); liberation theology (Ivone Gebara, Aruna Gnanadason, Mary Grey, and others); multicultural and multireligious perspectives (edited volumes by Carol Adams, Ruether, and Eaton and Lois Lorentzen); and ecofeminist spiritualities (Charlene Spretnak, Carol Christ, Starhawk, and others).[7] Critiquing the tendency among Euro-American ecofeminist theorists and theologians to focus on the cultural-symbolic rather than the material realm, Eaton argues that only liberationist approaches—especially those from the global South—have the potential to effectively address the myriad concrete social and ecological challenges facing us today. "Northern ecofeminism," she warns, "can fall prey to cultural escapism, illusions, and irresponsibility with an excessive emphasis on theory and a failure to attend to the world. This renders ecofeminist theology not only powerless to face the real issues it is addressing, but worse still, can find itself indirectly participating in the destruction of the world while creating beautiful theories about alternative futures."[8]

7. Eaton, "Ecological-Feminist Theology." She provides an updated version of this organizational schema in *Introducing Ecofeminist Theologies*, 74–88, but I prefer the original.

8. Eaton, *Introducing Ecofeminist Theologies*, 122.

Eaton's assessment signals an important developmental stage in ecofeminist theology: not only has it become popular and diverse enough to merit internal categorization and an introductory monograph of its own, but it has entered a new phase of reflexivity and critique. While ecofeminism has been a topic of contestation and debate outside the field of religion since the early 1990s,[9] it has only recently generated significant critique within religious and theological studies. Such critique poses a number of challenges to ecofeminist theory and theology, challenges that promise to push the study of religion, gender, and ecology in important new directions.

Areas of Current and Future Growth

Eaton's criticism of the tendency of Northern ecofeminists to focus on cultural-symbolic instead of material connections between women and nature (and between social and ecological forms of exploitation) points to several related problems, some of which scholars of religion have begun to address and some of which remain unmet. Since these and other problems addressed below present challenges for continued research, they might be better described as opportunities for growth. Although there are myriad directions in which this relatively young area of study might go, I address several that I find especially important. I group these new directions into two main clusters: the first group stems from the prevailing idealism within ecofeminist theology, and the second relates to the ways in which the analytical category of gender is conceptualized and applied in the field of Religion and Ecology. Together, these suggestions push in two directions, directions that I see as complementary instead of contradictory: the first calls for more *"on the ground"* work, and the second encourages greater engagement with recent *theoretical* trends in feminist, gender, and sexuality studies. Rather than claiming that a "lived religion" or practice-based approach is more important than theory (or vice versa), I contend that these are two necessary and mutually illuminating moves for future scholarship emerging from the nexus of religion, gender, and ecology. I call these two complementary moves "grounding ideals" and "destabilizing identities," respectively.

9. See, for example, social ecologist Janet Biehl's harsh critique of ecofeminism in *Rethinking Ecofeminist Politics.*

Grounding Ideals

Eaton's critique of the cultural-symbolic focus of Euro-American eco-feminist theologians—a focus I see as characteristic of extant work in ecofeminist theology more generally—leads to the first cluster of opportunities. Ecofeminist theologians share with ecofeminist theorists in other fields a strongly idealist tendency—that is, a tendency to assume that ideas, conceptual schemas, and thought patterns drive behavior, social formations, and socio-cultural change. Feminist critics from the social sciences identified this idealism relatively early in the development of ecofeminism. In 1992, feminist economist Bina Agarwal wrote: "[T]he connection between the domination of women and that of nature is basically seen [by ecofeminists] as ideological, as rooted in a system of ideas and representations, values and beliefs, that places women and the non-human world hierarchically below men. And it calls upon women and men to conceptualize themselves, and their relationships to one another and to the nonhuman world, in non-hierarchical ways."[10] One year later, feminist geographer and environmentalist Joni Seager criticized the idealism within ecofeminism as well, arguing that many ecofeminists adopt a "think-your-way-out-of-oppression stance" in which socio-political change is attributed almost exclusively to a change of consciousness.[11]

This idealist tendency has been strongly evident among ecofeminist scholars of religion, due in part to the disproportionate number of ecofeminist theologians—and corresponding dearth of ecofeminist ethnographers and historians—in the field to date. While there is no reason why theologians cannot use ethnographic and historical methods in their work, few ecofeminist theologians have yet done so.[12] Instead, they have often relied on more speculative methods akin to philosophy and have focused almost exclusively on religious modes of thought.

10. Agarwal, "Gender and Environment Debate," 120.

11. Seager, *Earth Follies*, 248.

12. To the extent that ecofeminist theologians have engaged in *historical* analysis, they have focused on the history of ideas, narrated extremely broadly to cover large sweeps of time and space. See, for example, Ruether, *New Woman, New Earth*, 186–214; and *Gaia & God*. Besides Mary Ress, few ecofeminist theologians draw seriously on *ethnographic* methods. See Ress, *Ecofeminism in Latin America*. That an ethnographic approach could bear fruit is evidenced by feminist theologian Mary McClintock Fulkerson's effective incorporation of ethnography into her feminist theological work suggests that an ethnographic approach could bear fruit for ecofeminist theologians as well. See Fulkerson, *Changing the Subject*.

To be fair, ecofeminist theologians are hardly alone in exhibiting this tendency. As Anna Peterson notes, Western theology, philosophy, and ethics in general have long followed an idealist logic that privileges the conceptual over the practical and assumes that "the right theories will lead automatically to effective forms of practice."[13] Along these same lines, Bron Taylor and others have argued that the field of Religion and Ecology itself reflects this idealist legacy. The most common approach to the study of Religion and Ecology to date consists of critically assessing religious traditions—often understood primarily as *worldviews* (instead of ways of life, for example)—according to ecological criteria, critiquing ideas and concepts that justify environmental degradation, and proposing eco-friendly alternatives.[14]

Similarly, ecofeminist writings in the field of religion often express the idealistic notion that replacing patriarchal and anthropocentric symbols and worldviews with feminist and ecological alternatives could affect a "change of consciousness" capable of transforming society to desired ends. Elizabeth Dodson Gray's early ecofeminist theological work is a classic example. "The problem of patriarchy is conceptual," she writes. "Patriarchy has erroneously conceptualized and mythed 'man's place' in the universe and thus—by the illusion of domination it legitimates—it endangers the entire planet." The key to transforming social and ecological relations, Gray concludes, lies in transforming individual and collective conceptions of humanity and its interrelations with the rest of nature.[15] Subsequent ecofeminist works in religion have likewise

13. Peterson, "Talking the Walk," 52.

14. This approach is evident, for example, in the World Religions and Ecology series edited by Mary Evelyn Tucker and John Grim and published by Harvard University Press. In focusing on the conceptual aspects of religion as driving human ecological behavior, scholars working in this vein affirm Lynn White Jr.'s early and influential contention that both the cause and the solution to the ecological crisis lie in religious conceptions of the role of humans in the world. Claiming that actions are determined by beliefs, White wrote: "What people do about their ecology depends on what they think about themselves in relation to things around them. Human ecology is deeply conditioned by beliefs about our nature and destiny—that is, by religion." (White, "Historical Roots," 30). For Bron Taylor's critical assessment of this approach to the study of Religion and Ecology, see Taylor, "Religious Studies." On the different approaches represented on the one hand by Tucker and Grim of the Forum on Religion and Ecology and on the other by Bron Taylor of the International Society for the Study of Religion, Nature, and Culture, see Jenkins, "After Lynn White."

15. Gray, *Green Paradise Lost*, ix.

focused on the conceptual as both the basis of, and the solution to, eco-social ills.[16]

Even ecofeminist theologians with Marxist/socialist or liberationist leanings, who aim to take particular circumstances, material conditions, and socio-economic structures seriously, often end up focusing on the conceptual realm as the main avenue for eco-social transformation. Ruether is a prime example. While she emphasizes the mutually constitutive relationship between ideologies and socioeconomic structures, Ruether stresses the conceptual more than the empirical or material in her work, aiming to effect *metanoia*—a change of consciousness—first and foremost. "A healed relation to each other and to the earth . . . calls for a new consciousness, a new symbolic culture and spirituality," she writes. "We need to transform our inner psyches and the way we symbolize the interrelations of men and women, humans and earth, humans and the divine, the divine and the earth. Ecological healing is a theological and psychic-spiritual process."[17] Likewise, Ivone Gebara, a Brazilian ecofeminist liberation theologian, writes: "There is a connection—one that is not always visible—between certain religious doctrines and the destruction of the ecosystem. And because this is so, to change these doctrines is to open a path towards resurrection, toward social and ecological justice."[18] While this kind of method has yielded significant insights as well as promising theological proposals, and although important connections exist between ideas, attitudes, and actions, the disproportionate emphasis on ideology has led to some unfortunate consequences in ecofeminist theology.

Because it focuses on ideas themselves and not on the various concrete circumstances in which ideas form, mutate, and take effect *differently*, this kind of approach often produces generic and universalizing

16. See, for example, Halkes, *New Creation*; Johnson, *Women, Earth, and Creator Spirit*; Keller, *Broken Web*; Keller, *Face of the Deep*; McFague, *Body of God*; Primavesi, *Apocalypse to Genesis*.

17. Ruether, *Gaia & God*, 4. While she goes on to say that concrete ecojustice work must accompany the *metanoia* process, her focus remains on the conceptual and symbolic. Ruether's most recent book on ecofeminism, *Integrating Ecofeminism*, attempts to remedy this earlier stance to some degree by insisting on the complex and ambivalent relationship between the worldview of a given society and its actual ecosocial track record. Yet she continues to identify religions with *worldviews* and argues that, as such, they are key to understanding and rectifying contemporary eco-social ills. The way we *think*, she continues to suggest, is the crux of the problem. Ruether, *Integrating Ecofeminism*, 47, 131.

18. Gebara, *Longing for Running Water*, 6.

claims (for example, that women are associated with nature and men with culture, that women possess special ecological knowledge due to their biological or social functions, and that non-dualistic worldviews correspond to socially and ecologically benign behaviors). Ecofeminist scholars in the field of religion have often taken concepts, symbols, and discourses pertaining to gender and the environment out of context, both in evaluating them from an ecofeminist perspective and in proposing ecofeminist alternatives. This is most often the case with historically dominant conceptions from the Judeo-Christian tradition (such as the doctrine of the Fall, the paradigm of hierarchy, the image of a transcendent male deity, and the idea of apocalypse), which are analyzed in the abstract.[19] In addition to critically assessing mainstream Judeo-Christian ideas out of specific contexts in which they are interpreted and used in different ways, ecofeminists also at times take *alternative* ideas, concepts, and symbols out of context as well, suggesting that various kinds of non-Western, ancient, or indigenous beliefs, principles, or symbols can be used for ecofeminist ends.[20] Such an approach assumes that concepts, symbols, and discourses possess inherent, fixed meanings and have predictable effects regardless of when, where, how, or why they are used.

Even when ecofeminists explicitly aim to take context into account, as Ivone Gebara does with poor, urban women in Latin America or several others have done with the Chipko women of the Indian Himalayas, these contexts tend to quickly fade from view as principles, ideas, symbols, and theological concepts take center stage.[21] Often specific contexts and communities serve only as orientation points for the theologian or theorist, providing a community of accountability and criteria for evaluation, but not themselves coming under examination. In their concrete, material specificities, these communities and contexts remain largely invisible to the reader, and the opportunity to examine the complex and sometimes contradictory relationship between normative ideas

19. So many ecofeminist theological texts critique patriarchal Christian symbols, concepts, and doctrines in the abstract that it would be unwieldy to cite specific cases.

20. See, for example, Kyung, "Ecology, Feminism"; Riley, "Ecology Is a Sistah's Issue"; Nyajeka, "Shona Women." For critiques of Euro-American ecofeminist utilization of Native American spirituality in this regard, see Gaard, "Ecofeminism and Native American Cultures"; Smith, "Ecofeminism through an Anticolonial Framework."

21. Gebara, *Longing for Running Water*; Gnanadason, "Toward a Feminist Eco-Theology"; Shiva, *Staying Alive*.

and everyday practices—as well as the coexistence of *multiple* norms and ideas—is lost.

In her most recent book on ecofeminism, *Integrating Ecofeminism, Globalization, and World Religions* (2005), Ruether makes some of these same critiques with respect to the 1996–1998 Harvard conferences and subsequent book series on world religions and ecology, but she does not extend her critique to ecofeminist theology.[22] Two other books, however, do. The decontextualized and universalizing aspects of ecofeminism are precisely the problems taken up in two important edited volumes that open new paths in the study of religion, gender, and ecology: Alaine Low and Soraya Tremayne's *Women as Sacred Custodians of the Earth?* (2001) and Eaton and Lorentzen's *Ecofeminism and Globalization* (2003). The essays in these collections test some of the core contentions of ecofeminism by examining the intersections between religion, gender, and the environment in particular contexts and concrete situations from around the world. The context-specific case studies reveal not only that ecofeminist claims apply in some circumstances but not in others, but also that ideas do not necessarily drive behavior in a direct, unilateral, or singular way.

As geographer Yi-Fu Tuan argued as early as 1968, religious beliefs concerning nature do not determine ecological behavior, or even necessarily shape it in a predictable or significant fashion.[23] Several anthropologists and scholars of Asian religions and cultures have since further shown that ideas do not always translate directly into practice—seemingly eco-friendly concepts and pro-woman symbols (such as earth goddesses and non-dualistic worldviews) sometimes coincide with misogynistic and environmentally destructive behavior.[24] Thus we cannot simply assume that adopting ecofeminist principles and theologies will generate more socially just and environmentally sustainable structures and practices. While most ecofeminist theologians writing today would likely agree with this statement, the overweening emphasis on the power of the conceptual in so much ecofeminist work necessitates making it more explicit. Doing so may help further the incipient shift from

22. Ruether, *Integrating Ecofeminism*, 45–129.

23. Tuan, "Discrepancies."

24. See Agarwal, "Gender and Environment"; Alley, "Idioms of Degeneracy"; Jackson, "Trouble with Anti-Dualism"; Li, "Cross-Cultural Critique"; Nagarajan, "Soil as the Goddess"; Narayanan, "One Tree." See also Ruether, *Goddesses*.

constructing ideals out of contexts to constructing ideals and practices from and for contexts.

Conversely, we also need to question whether androcentric and hierarchical worldviews always and everywhere lead to eco-socially destructive practices. While this is certainly true in many—if not most—instances, the correlation cannot simply be assumed and asserted, but must instead be empirically investigated in myriad concrete cases. For instance, important analytical work remains to be done on the theologies and practices of contemporary conservative religious groups, such as segments of the Roman Catholic and evangelical Protestant communities, who endorse environmental protection while adhering to traditional views on sex and gender. My own research on the (formerly) Roman Catholic lay women's community at Grailville in Loveland, Ohio, shows that "bad" ideas from a feminist ecological perspective sometimes coexist with "good" behavior. At Grailville in the 1940s and 50s, the ideas that women are more "natural" than men and therefore properly subordinate or less free and that humans are the capstone of creation coexisted with nontraditional gender roles and ecologically sustainable living practices.[25]

These sorts of findings suggest that not only concepts, ideas, and beliefs, but also the concrete practices of particular people and communities need to be analyzed and theorized with respect to the intersections between religion, gender, and ecology. As Peterson writes, acknowledging that people's actions do not necessarily follow their ideas "does not mean there is no relationship between changing practices and changing knowledge, language, and values. This relationship, however, entails complex, unpredictable, and open-ended mutual interactions, rather than the straightforward linear influencing we would desire."[26] While the essays in *Women as Sacred Custodians of the Earth?* and *Ecofeminism and Globalization* provide important first steps in moving towards more empirically grounded, critical, and contextualized interrogations into the intersections between religion, gender, and ecology, more sustained work in this vein remains to be done. The very format of the edited volume (the present one included)—long popular among ecofeminists for its ability to showcase a diversity of voices and perspectives—precludes the kind of in-depth, context-specific investigation advocated here.[27]

25. Page, "Problem of the Land."

26. Peterson, "Talking the Walk," 52.

27. Ecofeminist anthologies and edited volumes include Adams, *Ecofeminism and the Sacred*; Gaard, *Ecofeminism*; Diamond and Orenstein, *Reweaving the World*; Ruether,

More recent monographs by scholars of religion Rebecca Kneale Gould (*At Home in Nature* 2005) and Sarah McFarland Taylor (*Green Sisters* 2007) exemplify what sustained historical and ethnographic work along the lines outlined above might look like. Although neither Gould nor Taylor take gender as their central analytical lens or primary theoretical concern, both attend to gender as it relates to religion and nature in particular communities and specific historical-cultural contexts. In addition, both look closely at religious and cultural practices that help to constitute and contest cultural norms, social identities, and values pertaining to gender and the environment, thereby offering refreshing new perspectives on the dynamic interplay between behavior and belief.[28] The study of religion, gender, and ecology would be greatly enriched by similar book-length works, especially those in which gender plays a more central analytical role.

Destabilizing Identities

A second set of opportunities for growth pertains to the way in which the analytical category of gender itself is understood and applied in Religion and Ecology studies. Whereas the former section argues for more grounded scholarship, this section calls for more theoretical scrutiny, especially with respect to the foundational categories of the religion, gender, and ecology subfield. Most analyses of gender in the study of Religion and Ecology to date treat gender either as homologous with sex (rooted in biology) or—more often—as the cultural meanings and social norms mapped onto biological sex. While the former approach sees both sex and gender as stemming from "nature" and therefore as relatively impermeable to the vicissitudes of history and culture, the latter distinguishes between "natural" sex (male and female) and "cultural" gender (masculinity and femininity) in order to challenge restrictive gender norms as socially produced, variable, and open to change. Both of these approaches focus on the *products* of gender—especially women, but also the various cultural norms applied to women and men—and maintain a framework of binary sexual difference that both reflects and

---

Women Healing Earth; Warren, *Ecological Feminism*; Warren, *Ecofeminism*; Plant, *Healing the Wounds*.

28. Gould, *At Home in Nature*; Taylor, *Green Sisters*.

reinforces what LGBTQ (lesbian, gay, bisexual, transgender, and queer) theorists refer to as "compulsory heterosexuality."[29]

By contrast, poststructuralist approaches to gender—which are indebted to Michel Foucault's three-volume analysis of sex and sexuality in Western culture, *The History of Sexuality*—question the biological nature of sex itself. Poststructuralist gender theorists tend to see gender as a *productive cultural process* that "creates" and then "naturalizes" the heteronormative male/female binary as universal and biologically fixed. As Judith Butler writes in her now classic text, *Gender Trouble* (1990): "Gender ought not to be conceived merely as the cultural inscription of meaning on a pregiven sex . . . gender must also designate the very apparatus of production whereby the sexes themselves are established. As a result, gender is not to culture as sex is to nature; gender is also the discursive/cultural means by which 'sexed nature' or 'a natural sex' is produced and established as 'prediscursive,' prior to culture, a politically neutral surface *on which* culture acts."[30] With the development of poststructuralist accounts of gender over the past two decades, gender can now refer to both the *products* of sexual differentiation—women and men and the various characteristics and roles attributed to them—and the *processes* of that differentiation. From this perspective, sex and gender interact with other means of marking social identity, such as ethnicity or race, that maintain their normative power through complex and repetitive practices and ideologies that make them seen "natural."

With the exception of Catherine Keller,[31] scholars of religion, gender, and ecology have not yet taken up this kind of poststructuralist approach to both gender and nature. But this approach offers myriad opportunities to think creatively about the religion-gender-nature nexus. Perhaps most importantly, it challenges the constructions of identity that form the basis of much past and present discourse on the topic. Instead of determinate, binary identity categories—man/woman, gay/straight, human/animal,

---

29. The concept of compulsory heterosexuality received its first real use in Adrienne Rich's influential pamphlet, "Compulsory Heterosexuality and Lesbian Existence." The concept implies that our social, cultural, and legal systems render heterosexuality compulsory: heterosexuality is essentially forced on individuals as the only acceptable ("normal") option. Under these conditions, individuals are assumed to be straight unless they come out of the closet. Rich, "Compulsory Heterosexuality."

30. Butler, *Gender Trouble*, 7.

31. Keller engages seriously, but not uncritically, with poststructuralist gender analysis. See, for example, *Apocalypse*, 224–71.

nature/culture—work in this vein produces more ambiguous, complex, and fluid notions. Donna Haraway's writing on cyborgs and companion species, for example, highlights the myriad ways in which entities conventionally categorized as fixed and mutually exclusive—such as animals, humans, and machines—not only change significantly over time, but also intertwine in substantial ways.[32] By transgressing the boundaries between nature-culture-technology, Haraway enables identity categories to become political rather than foundational. We should take "*pleasure in the confusion of boundaries*," she advises, and "*responsibility* [for] their construction."[33]

A poststructuralist understanding of gender opens up several promising new avenues of investigation for the study of religion, gender, and ecology. First, it brings into focus not only *ideologies and discourses* of gender, which feminists and ecofeminists have been analyzing for several decades, but also the myriad forms of *embodied practice* through which these ideologies and discourses take effect in concrete, material terms. The understanding of gender as "performative," pioneered by Butler and taken up by other feminist and queer theorists, calls attention to the various *acts* that produce the appearance of binary gender as "natural" and stable. In this view, gender—and identity in general—is not a substantive or ontological given, but rather the effect of certain (regulatory and compulsory) practices, certain ways of speaking and styling the body that constitute individuals as either "men" or "women." "The various acts of gender," writes Butler, "create the idea of gender, and without those acts, there would be no gender at all."[34] In light of this analytic, scholars of religion, gender, and ecology might begin to attend more closely to the ways in which religion contributes to processes of subject formation, not only through normative ideals and ideologies, but also through myriad forms of practice. How are gendered and ecological modes of subjectivity constituted in part through specific religious and cultural practices? This line of questioning brings under investigation a wide range of religious phenomena not commonly studied by ecofeminists: the gendered and ecological implications of various types of ritual, devotional, and everyday practice; of modes of dress and bodily comportment; and of pedagogical or disciplinary programs specifically

32. Haraway, *Simians, Cyborgs, and Women*; and Haraway, *When Species Meet*.
33. Haraway, "Cyborg Manifesto," 150.
34. Butler, *Gender Trouble*, 140.

geared towards shaping certain kinds of religious subjects (such as religious education and spiritual formation programs).

Second, a poststructuralist analysis of gender calls for more rigorous critical analysis of the nature/culture binary that feminists, environmentalists, and ecofeminists have so often reinscribed in their defenses of "women" and/or "nature." One way of interpreting poststructuralist critiques of sex and gender is that they aim not to do away with sex/gender categories altogether but rather to reveal the distinction between "nature" and "culture" that underlies them as discursively produced. Butler's claim that "sex . . . ha[s] been gender all along"[35] aims to block foundationalist appeals to the (heterosexed) body as simply "natural," outside of culture, and thus somehow removed from the dynamics of power, historical contingency, and change. Although critics of poststructuralism frequently interpret this kind of move as reducing everything to human culture (something that environmentalists, sensing the further colonization of nature, tend to resist), it is more accurate to say that this type of argument denies the ability of humans to directly *access* reality (or "nature") apart from the cultural apparatuses that enable apprehension in the first place. This demands recognition of the contingency of the categories we take for granted and rely upon in our scholarship and in our politics—namely, for ecofeminists, the categories "women" and "nature."[36]

Here ecofeminist theologians and scholars of religion might productively follow the lead of ecofeminist theorist Catriona Sandilands, who argues against an identity-based approach to ecofeminist politics and proposes instead an ecofeminist politics of radical democracy. Rather than further solidifying the categories "women" and "nature" and the binaries that constitute them, an ecofeminist politics of radical democracy emphasizes "performative affinities," provisional identities, strategic coalitions, public debate, openness, and futurity.[37] One outcome of this type of ecofeminist reflection is that categories of gender and nature—and, in the case of religious ecofeminism, religious truth claims—are viewed as co-constructed and fluid instead of as essential or foundational. At this point, most ecofeminist theorists have moved beyond the essentialist/

35. Ibid., 8.

36. Some Religion and Ecology scholars have addressed the problems of the nature/culture binary and have tried to reconceive the category of "nature" in light of postmodern theory, but few ecofeminist theologians have yet done so with respect to both "nature" *and* "women." For an example of the former, see Muraca, "Getting Over 'Nature.'"

37. Sandilands, *Good-Natured Feminist.*

constructivist debate surrounding sex and gender, and most ecofeminist theologians have a robust understanding of religious knowledge production that includes critiques of the relationship between power and knowledge. However, few ecofeminists have moved beyond some type of essentialist conception of nature as something that must be returned to, saved, or preserved. Ecofeminist theologians and scholars of religion are not alone in holding onto this Western and idealized understanding of nature, but they may be well-poised to lead the way in breaking down foundational conceptualizations of nature within the wider Religion and Ecology field. This "queering of nature," as we might call such a reworking of the category, is important for feminist, gender, and queer studies outside the field of religion as well, for without queering the concept of nature, sex and gender are always at risk of both reification and coercive regulation under the labels "natural" or "unnatural."

Finally and relatedly, a poststructualist theory of gender challenges the heteronormative basis of much feminist and ecofeminist theory and theology, thus opening the door for the potential queering of the study of religion, gender, and ecology itself. Scholars of Religion and Ecology (especially ecofeminist theologians) have analyzed religious perspectives on sexuality to some degree, but few have ventured much beyond the inherited land of heterosexuality.[38]

Ecofeminist theorist Greta Gaard started the process of bringing queer theory into dialogue with ecofeminism in her 1997 article, "Toward a Queer Ecofeminism." Drawing on both ecofeminist and queer theories, she writes: "The oppression of queers may be described . . . as the product of two mutually reinforcing dualisms: heterosexual/queer, and reason/the erotic."[39] These two interlocking dualisms likewise depend upon and reinforce other hierarchical binaries, Gaard argues, such as human/animal and masculine/feminine. Because compulsory heterosexuality entails the suppression of so-called "animal passions," for example, it contributes to human exceptionalism—the assumption that humans are separate from, and superior to, the rest of the natural world. Gaard further notes the contradictory way in which Western culture codes

38. Reflecting its focus on population, for example, the essays in Coward and Maguire, *Visions of a New Earth* focus exclusively on the reproductive aspects of sexuality. For examples of recent efforts *outside* the field of religion to broaden ecofeminist and environmental justice scholarship beyond the normative heterosexual purview, see Stein, *New Perspectives*.

39. Gaard, "Toward a Queer Ecofeminism," 118.

homosexuality with respect to nature. Maligned as "unnatural" (that is, as "*against* nature") in a heteronormative discourse that defines "natural" sex as procreative sex, homosexuality is simultaneously deemed too "*close* to nature" when characterized as somehow more bestial than heterosexuality. Why this contradictory use of "nature"? According to Gaard, "On the one hand, from a queer perspective, we learn that the dominant culture charges queers with transgressing the natural order, which in turn implies that nature is valued and must be obeyed. On the other hand, from an ecofeminist perspective, we learn that Western culture has constructed nature as a force that must be dominated if culture is to prevail. Bringing these perspectives together indicates that, in effect, the 'nature' queers are urged to comply with is none other than the dominant paradigm of heterosexuality."[40]

This equation of "nature" with "heterosexual," Gaard argues, parallels—and undergirds—the equation of "woman" with "mother" that feminists have so roundly deconstructed. A queer theoretical lens thus highlights the ways in which traditional gender roles are defined by the heterosexual imperative, which in turn grounds itself on a certain construction of nature—one characterized primarily by sexual reproduction. Yet recent work by biologists shows nature to be far from exclusively heterosexual. Bruce Bagemihl and Joan Roughgarden, for example, have documented extensive same-sex sexuality and gender variation in the natural world.[41] When scientific evidence of "evolution's rainbow" (Roughgarden's phrase) is taken into account, "nature" can no longer serve as the basis for heteronormativity because nature itself appears remarkably queer!

While several attempts have been made to articulate a "queer ecofeminism" and a "queer ecology" outside the study of religion,[42] few parallel efforts have yet been made in the field of Religion and Ecology. Both J. Michael Clark (*Beyond Our Ghettos* 1993) and Daniel Spencer (*Gay and Gaia* 1996) have articulated a gay ecological theology, and though

40. Ibid., 120–21.

41. Bagemihl, *Biological Exuberance*; Roughgarden, *Evolution's Rainbow*. Gaard cites several other earlier studies documenting the diversity of sexual practices in other species. See Gaard, "Toward a Queer Ecofeminism," 121.

42. Along with Gaard, Catriona Sandilands has sought to queer ecofeminist and ecological theory. Sandilands, "Mother Earth"; and Sandilands, "Desiring Nature." See also Mortimer-Sandilands, "Unnatural Passions?" In addition, several essays in Stein, *New Perspectives* bring LGBTQ issues directly into the study of environmental justice.

pioneering and informative, their approaches are firmly rooted in identity politics and manifest idealist tendencies of the sort outlined above.[43] Like many ecofeminist liberation theologians, both Clark and Spencer rely upon the identitarian logic of standpoint epistemology, arguing that lesbians and gay men have a special role to play in revisioning eco-social relations because of their experiences of oppression. Instead of shoring up a particular type of identity (in this case gay and lesbian identity), a poststructuralist queer approach would highlight the mechanisms through which sexual and gender identities are constituted, locating the political within processes of identity formation, not in their effects (that is, not in identities themselves).

Although she does not explicitly set out to articulate a queer ecofeminist theology, Catherine Keller does at least seem to step in this direction in *Face of the Deep,* and she does so from a non-identitarian perspective. Delineating a feminist *"tehomic* theology" of creation, Keller examines the links between homophobia and what she terms *"tehomophobia"* (fear of the watery deep, of chaos, of the primal abyss), and her constructive theological proposal at times appears notably queer.[44] While these texts by Clark, Spencer, and Keller are welcome initial explorations of new terrain, options abound for further queering ventures in Religion and Ecology.

By highlighting the potential of poststructuralist approaches to sexuality and gender studies in the field of Religion and Ecology, I do not mean to imply that this is the *only* productive approach or that it is problem-free. Poststructuralist theory is notoriously abstruse and speculative. It is most fruitful, in my estimation, when applied to concrete situations and particular communities.[45] But it also plays an important role in holding open a space for thinking beyond the boundaries of the present—a space without which we would remain locked into the identity politics of the day.

Of the many potential new paths to be explored in religion, gender, and ecology studies, the handful mentioned here—increased use of historical and ethnographic methods; more in-depth, context-specific, and practice-sensitive studies; greater critical attention to the complex and dynamic interplay between belief and behavior; increased utilization

43. Clark, *Beyond Our Ghettos*; Spencer, *Gay and Gaia.*
44. See Keller, *Face of the Deep,* 22–24, 61–63.
45. See, for example, Fulkerson, *Changing the Subject.*

of poststructuralist accounts of sex, gender, and identity; and efforts to queer the field—promise not only to further enrich the developing field of Religion and Ecology, but also to demonstrate the ongoing importance within this field of feminist and gender analysis.

Bibliography

Adams, Carol J., editor. *Ecofeminism and the Sacred*. New York: Continuum, 1994.

Agarwal, Bina. "The Gender and Environment Debate: Lessons from India." *Feminist Studies* 18 (1992) 119–58.

Alley, Kelly. "Idioms of Degeneracy: Assessing Ganga's Purity and Pollution." In *Purifying the Earthly Body of God: Religion and Ecology in Hindu India*, edited by Lance E. Nelson, 297–330. SUNY Series in Religious Studies. Albany: State University of New York Press, 1998.

Bagemihl, Bruce. *Biological Exuberance: Animal Homosexuality and Natural Diversity*. New York: St. Martin's, 1999.

Baker-Fletcher, Karen. *Sisters of Dust, Sisters of Spirit: Womanist Wordings on God*. Minneapolis: Fortress, 1998.

Biehl, Janet. *Rethinking Ecofeminist Politics*. Boston: South End, 1991.

Butler, Judith. *Gender Trouble: Feminism and the Subversion of Identity*. Thinking Gender Series. New York: Routledge, 1990.

Carroll, John E. et al., editors. *The Greening of Faith: God, the Environment, and the Good Life*. Hanover, NH: University Press of New England, 1997.

Christ, Carol. *Rebirth of the Goddess: Finding Meaning in Feminist Spirituality*. New York: Routledge, 1997.

Clark, J. Michael. *Beyond Our Ghettos: Gay Theology in Ecological Perspective*. Cleveland: Pilgrim, 1993.

Clifford, Anne. "Feminist Perspectives on Science: Implications for an Ecological Theology of Creation." *Journal of Feminist Studies in Religion* 8 (1992) 65–92.

Coward, Harold and Daniel C. Maguire, editors. *Visions of a New Earth: Religious Perspectives on Population, Consumption, and Ecology*. Albany: State University of New York Press, 2000.

Diamond, Irene, and Gloria Orenstein, editors. *Reweaving the World: The Emergence of Ecofeminism*. San Francisco: Sierra Club Books, 1990.

Dietrich, Gabriele. *A New Thing on Earth: Hopes and Fears Facing Feminist Theology (Theological Ruminations of a Feminist Activist)*. Delhi, India: ISPCK, 2001.

Eaton, Heather. "Ecological-Feminist Theology." In *Theology for Earth Community: A Field Guide*, edited by Dieter Hessel, 77–92. Ecology and Justice Series. Maryknoll, NY: Orbis, 1996.

———. *Introducing Ecofeminist Theologies*. Introductions in Feminist Theology 12. London: T. & T. Clark, 2005.

Eaton, Heather, and Lois Ann Lorentzen, editors. *Ecofeminism and Globalization: Exploring Culture, Context, and Religion*. Lanham, MD: Rowman & Littlefield, 2003.

Eisler, Riane. *The Chalice and the Blade: Our History, Our Future*. Cambridge: Harper & Row, 1987.

Eller, Cynthia. *Living in the Lap of the Goddess: The Feminist Spirituality Movement in America*. Boston: Beacon, 1995.

Foltz, Richard, editor. *Worldviews, Religion and the Environment: A Global Anthology*. Belmont, CA: Wadsworth, 2003.

Foltz, Richard, et al., editors. *Islam and Ecology: A Bestowed Trust*. Religions of the World and Ecology. Cambridge: Harvard Divinity School, Center for the Study of World Religions, distributed by Harvard University Press, 2003.

Fulkerson, Mary McClintock. *Changing the Subject: Women's Discourses and Feminist Theology*. Minneapolis: Fortress, 1994.

Gaard, Greta. "Ecofeminism and Native American Cultures: Pushing the Limits of Cultural Imperialism?" In *Ecofeminism: Women, Animals, Nature*, edited by Greta Gaard, 295–314. Ethics and Action. Philadelphia: Temple University Press, 1993.

———, editor. *Ecofeminism: Women, Animals, Nature*. Ethics and Action. Philadelphia: Temple University Press, 1993.

———. "Toward a Queer Ecofeminism." *Hypatia* 12 (1997) 114–37.

Gebara, Ivone. *Longing for Running Water: Ecofeminism and Liberation*. Minneapolis: Fortress, 1999.

Gnanadason, Aruna. "Toward a Feminist Eco-Theology for India." In *Women Healing Earth: Third World Women on Ecology, Feminism and Religion*, edited by Rosemary Radford Ruether, 74–81. Ecology and Justice Series. Maryknoll, NY: Orbis, 1996.

Gottlieb, Roger, editor. *Oxford Handbook of Religion and Ecology*. Oxford: Oxford University Press, 2006.

———, editor. *This Sacred Earth: Religion, Nature, Environment*. 2nd ed. New York: Routledge, 2004.

Gould, Rebecca Kneale. *At Home in Nature: Modern Homesteading and Spiritual Practice in America*. Berkeley: University of California Press, 2005.

Gray, Elizabeth Dodson. *Green Paradise Lost*. Wellesley, MA: Roundtable Press, 1981.

Grey, Mary. *Sacred Longings: The Ecological Spirit and Global Culture*. Minneapolis: Fortress, 2004.

Halkes, Catharina. *New Creation: Christian Feminism and the Renewal of the Earth*. Louisville: Westminster John Knox, 1991.

Hallman, David G., editor. *Ecotheology: Voices from South and North*. Maryknoll, NY: Orbis, 1994.

Haraway, Donna J. "A Cyborg Manifesto: Science, Technology, and Socialist-Feminism in the Late Twentieth Century." In *Simians, Cyborgs, and Women: The Reinvention of Nature*, 149–81. New York: Routledge, 1991.

———. *Simians, Cyborgs, and Women: The Reinvention of Nature*. New York: Routledge, 1991.

———. *When Species Meet*. Minnesota: University of Minnesota Press, 2008.

Hessel, Dieter, editor. *Theology for Earth Community*. Maryknoll, NY: Orbis, 1996.

Hessel, Dieter, and Rosemary Radford Ruether, editors. *Christianity and Ecology: Seeking the Well-Being of Earth and Humans*. Religions of the World and Ecology. Cambridge: Harvard Center for the Study of World Religions, distributed by Harvard University Press 2000.

Ho, Wan-Li. "Environmental Protection as Religious Action: The Case of Taiwanese Buddhist Women." In *Ecofeminism and Globalization: Exploring Culture, Context, and Religion*, edited by Heather Eaton and Lois Ann Lorentzen, 123–45. Lanham, MD: Rowman & Littlefield, 2003.

Jackson, Cecile. "Gender, Nature and Trouble with Anti-Dualism." In *Women as Sacred Custodians of the Earth? Women, Spirituality and the Environment*, edited by Alaine Low and Soraya Tremayne, 23–44. New York: Berghahn, 2001.

Jenkins, Willis. "After Lynn White: Religious Ethics and Environmental Problems." *Journal of Religious Ethics* 37 (2009) 283–309.

Johnson, Elizabeth. *Women, Earth, and Creator Spirit*. The Madeleva Lecture in Spirituality. New York: Paulist, 1993.

Kearns, Laurel, and Catherine Keller, eds. *Ecospirit: Religions and Philosophies for the Earth*. New York: Fordham University Press, 2007.

Keller, Catherine. *Apocalypse Now and Then: A Feminist Guide to the End of the World*. Boston: Beacon, 1996.

———. *Face of the Deep: A Theology of Becoming*. New York: Routledge, 2003.

———. *From a Broken Web: Separation, Sexism, and Self*. Boston: Beacon, 1993.

Kinsley, David R. *Ecology and Religion: Ecological Spirituality in Cross-Cultural Perspective*. Englewood Cliffs, NJ: Prentice Hall, 1995.

Kyung, Chung Hyun. "Ecology, Feminism, and African and Asian Spirituality." In *Ecotheology: Voices from South and North*, edited by David Hallman, 175–78. Geneva: WCC Publications, 1994.

Li, Huey-li. "A Cross-Cultural Critique of Ecofeminism." In *Ecofeminism: Women, Animals, Nature*, edited by Greta Gaard, 272–94. Philadelphia: Temple University Press, 1993.

Low, Alaine, and Soraya Tremayne, editors. *Women as Sacred Custodians of the Earth? Women, Spirituality and the Environment*. New York: Berghahn, 2001.

MacKinnon, Mary Heather, and Moni McIntyre, editors. *Readings in Ecology and Feminist Theology*. Kansas City: Sheed & Ward, 1995.

McFague, Sallie. *The Body of God: An Ecological Theology*. Minneapolis: Fortress, 1993.

Mortimer-Sandilands, Catriona. "Unnatural Passions? Notes Toward a Queer Ecology." *Invisible Culture* 9 (2005). Online: http://www.rochester.edu/in_visible_culture/Issue_9/sandilands.html/.

Muraca, Barbara. "Getting Over 'Nature': Modern Bifurcations, Postmodern Possibilities." In *Ecospirit: Religions and Philosophies for the Earth*, edited by Laurel Kearns and Catherine Keller, 156–77. Transdisciplinary Theological Colloquia. New York: Fordham University Press, 2007.

Nagarajan, Vijaya. "Soil as the Goddess Bhudevi in a Tamil Hindu Women's Ritual: The Kolam in India." In *Women as Sacred Custodians of the Earth? Women, Spirituality and the Environment*, edited by Alaine Low and Soraya Tremayne, 159–74. New York: Berghahn, 2001.

Narayanan, Vasudha. "'One Tree Is Equal to Ten Sons': Some Hindu Responses to the Problems of Ecology, Population, and Consumption." *Journal of the American Academy of Religion* 65 (1997) 291–332.

Nyajeka, Tumani Mutasa. "Shona Women and the Mutupo Principle." In *Women Healing Earth: Third World Women on Ecology, Feminism, and Religion*, edited by Rosemary Radford Ruether, 135–42. Ecology and Justice Series. Maryknoll, NY: Orbis, 1996.

Page, Tovis. "Has Ecofeminism Cornered the Market? Gender Analysis in the Study of Religion, Nature, and Culture." *Journal for the Study of Religion, Nature and Culture* 1 (2007) 293–319.

———. "The Problem of the Land Is the Problem of the Woman: A Genealogy of Ecofeminism at Grailville." PhD diss., Harvard University, 2008.

Peterson, Anna. "Talking the Walk: A Practice-Based Environmental Ethic as Grounds for Hope." In *Ecospirit: Religions and Philosophies for the Earth*, edited by Laurel Kearns and Catherine Keller, 45–62. Transdisciplinary Theological Colloquia. New York: Fordham University Press, 2007.

Plant, Judith, editor. *Healing the Wounds: The Promise of Ecofeminism*. Philadelphia: New Society, 1989.

Plaskow, Judith, and Carol Christ, editors. *Weaving the Visions: Patterns in Feminist Spirituality*. San Francisco: Harper & Row, 1989.

Primavesi, Anne. *From Apocalypse to Genesis: Ecology, Feminism and Christianity*. Minneapolis: Fortress, 1991.

Rae, Eleanor. *Women, the Earth, the Divine*. Maryknoll, NY: Orbis, 1994.

Ress, Mary. *Ecofeminism in Latin America*. Women from the Margins Series. Maryknoll, NY: Orbis, 2006.

Rich, Adrienne. *Compulsory Heterosexuality and Lesbian Existence*. London: Onlywomen, 1981.

Riley, Shamara Shantu. "Ecology Is a Sistah's Issue Too: The Politics of Emergent Afrocentric Ecowomanism." In *Ecofeminism and the Sacred*, edited by Carol J. Adams, 191–204. New York: Continuum, 1993.

Robb, Carol, and Carl Casebolt. *Covenant for a New Creation: Ethics, Religion, and Public Policy*. Maryknoll, NY: Orbis, 1991.

Roughgarden, Joan. *Evolution's Rainbow: Diversity, Gender, and Sexuality in Nature and People*. Berkeley: University of California Press, 2004.

Ruether, Rosemary Radford. *Gaia & God: An Ecofeminist Theology of Earth Healing*. San Francisco: HarperSanFrancisco, 1992.

———. *Goddesses and the Divine Feminine: A Western Religious History*. Berkeley: University of California Press, 2005.

———. *Integrating Ecofeminism, Globalization and World Religions*. Nature's Meaning. Lanham, MD: Rowman & Littlefield, 2005.

———. *New Woman, New Earth: Sexist Ideologies and Human Liberation*. Boston: Beacon, 1995.

———, editor. *Women Healing Earth: Third World Women on Ecology, Feminism, and Religion*. Ecology and Justice Series. Maryknoll, NY: Orbis, 1996.

Sandilands, Catriona. "Desiring Nature, Queering Ethics: Adventures in Erotogenic Environments." *Environmental Ethics* 23 (2001) 169–88.

———. *The Good-Natured Feminist: Ecofeminism and the Quest for Democracy*. Minneapolis: University of Minnesota Press, 1999.

———. "Mother Earth, the Cyborg, and the Queer: Ecofeminism and (More) Questions of Identity." *National Women's Studies Association Journal* 9 (1997) 18–40.

Scharff, Virginia J., editor. *Seeing Nature through Gender*. Lawrence: University of Kansas Press, 2003.

Seager, Joni. *Earth Follies: Coming to Feminist Terms with the Global Environmental Crisis*. New York: Routledge, 1993.

Shiva, Vandana. *Staying Alive: Women, Ecology, and Development*. London: Zed, 1989.

Sjöö, Monica, and Barbara Mor. *The Great Cosmic Mother: Rediscovering the Religion of the Earth*. San Francisco: Harper & Row, 1987.

Smith, Andy. "Ecofeminism through an Anticolonial Framework." In *Ecofeminism: Women, Culture, Nature*, edited by Karen J. Warren, 21–37. Bloomington: Indiana University Press, 1997.

Spencer, Daniel T. *Gay and Gaia: Ethics, Ecology, and the Erotic*. Cleveland: Pilgrim, 1996.

Spretnak, Charlene, editor. *The Politics of Women's Spirituality: Essays on the Rise of Spiritual Power within the Feminist Movement*. Garden City, NY: Anchor, 1982.

Stein, Rachel, editor. *New Perspectives on Environmental Justice: Gender, Sexuality, and Activism*. New Brunswick, NJ: Rutgers University Press, 2004.

Taylor, Bron Raymond et al., editors. *The Encyclopedia of Religion and Nature*. 2 vols. London: Thoemmes Continuum, 2005.

Taylor, Bron Raymond. "Religious Studies and Environmental Concern." In *The Encyclopedia of Religion and Nature*, edited by Bron Raymond Taylor, 2:1373–79. 2 vols. London: Thoemmes Continuum, 2005.

Taylor, Sarah McFarland. *Green Sisters: A Spiritual Ecology*. Cambridge: Harvard University Press, 2007.

Tuan, Yi Fu. "Discrepancies between Environmental Attitude and Behavior: Examples from Europe and China." *Canadian Geographer* 12 (1968) 176–91.

Tucker, Mary Evelyn, and John Berthrong, editors. *Confucianism and Ecology: The Interrelation of Heaven, Earth, and Humans*. Religions of the World and Ecology. Cambridge: Harvard Center for the Study of World Religions, distributed by Harvard University Press 1998.

Tucker, Mary Evelyn, and John A. Grim, editors. *Worldviews and Ecology: Religion, Philosophy and the Environment*. Ecology and Justice Series. Maryknoll, NY: Orbis, 1994.

Warren, Karen J., editor. *Ecofeminism: Women, Culture, Nature*. Bloomington: Indiana University Press, 1997.

———, editor. *Ecological Feminism*. Environmental Philosophies Series. New York: Routledge, 1994.

White, Lynn Jr. "The Historical Roots of Our Ecologic Crisis." In *Readings in Ecology and Feminist Theology*, edited by Mary Heather MacKinnon and Moni McIntyre, 25–35. Kansas City: Sheed & Ward, 1995.

7

Practically Natural

Religious Resources for Environmental Pragmatism[1]

LUCAS F. JOHNSTON AND SAMUEL SNYDER

While the boundary between the study of religion and philosophy can be blurred, there is often a strong distinction between environmental philosophers and scholars of religion concerned with environmental issues. This essay seeks to build bridges across this boundary by arguing that pragmatic philosophers and religion scholars have much to learn from one another. Using discussions of sustainability as our primary focus, we will present the insights of environmental philosophers who are working toward a pragmatist environmental ethic and develop an argument about the importance of religion to their project.

We propose three methodological moves that we believe will facilitate a robust discussion between philosophical pragmatists and scholars of religion and nature: (1) Attention to *experience* in general and religious experience in particular is a vital bridge between the *values* and *behaviors* that have received philosophical attention.[2] (2) Neither

1. Our thanks to the editors for their careful reading of the text and suggestions for improvement.

2. We use the term "religion and nature" to refer to the field of scholarship under discussion in this book, and the overlaps and distinctions between *religion and ecology* and *religion and nature* are discussed elsewhere in this volume. From a pragmatic perspective the term "nature" has greater heuristic value than "ecology" because it allows reflection on a broader range of phenomena. While both terms have their appeal

religious nor environmental communities should be understood as private or insular; rather both must be studied with special attention to the ways they communicate their narratives and beliefs beyond their own communities. (3) Philosophers and religious studies scholars alike must make the pragmatic move of studying religion with primary attention to its impacts upon society and the world. With these proposals, we advocate a move toward a more pragmatic study of religion and nature and a more sensitive study of religion among pragmatists.

The Philosophical Environmental Ethics Background

In part, environmental pragmatism emerged in reaction to a common theme in philosophical environmental ethics: the idea that values exert a causal influence on behaviors—that if humans get *values* right, practices will follow. Many of the early conversation among environmental ethicists involved debates regarding the importance of establishing a non-anthropocentric environmental ethic. Led by scholars such as Bryan Norton, environmental pragmatists challenged scholars who imagined this to be the primary ethical task. They suggested that the focus on generating a single ethic that could account for all moral quandaries faced by human societies was unhelpful, arguing instead that a non-anthropocentric ethic is just one rather narrow approach to formulating an environmental ethics, and that any uniform system is unlikely to be able to account for the variety of ethical perspectives evidenced in the general populace.

Related to this debate over non-anthropocentric ethics were other philosophical debates about the locus of value (does value inhere in particular entities or does it originate in the one evaluating value?), and whether ethical monism or pluralism is the superior approach. On the one hand, monists advocated bio-centric or eco-centric ethical theories that were imagined as guiding or significantly informing environmental behavior.[3] On the other hand, pluralists suggested that several different,

---

and their drawbacks, (e.g., nature is considered too vague and ill-defined by many environmental scientists), the religion and nature conversation has considered not only what is encompassed under the rubric of "environment" (what surrounds humans) or "ecology" (scientifically measurable interacting "systems"), but also questions of what is "natural" and what is not, and how these determinations are made.

3. P. Taylor, *Respect for Nature*; Callicott, "Animal Liberation"; Rolston, *Environmental Ethics*.

even competing theories of value related to nature should be considered.[4] Monist non-anthropocentrists, Norton contended, imagined their task too narrowly as "throwing fully formed theories and principles over the edge of the ivory tower, to be used as intellectual armaments by the currently outgunned environmental activists."[5]

Norton attempted an important bridge between these perspectives in *Toward Unity Among Environmentalists* (1991) when he suggested that, despite significant disagreements about the locus of value and the shapes of their respective ethical systems, anthropocentrists and non-anthropocentrists would in many cases ultimately concur on the proper policy processes and outcomes. Norton's point was based on his assumption that people do not perceive and negotiate real life moral quandaries first or foremost through the lens of an overarching ethical theory.

However, the preoccupation with the idea that theories of value (particularly metaphysical ones) are the primary shapers of environmental behaviors has persisted within environmental and religious studies. It is often traced to the historian Lynn White, Jr.'s claim that the Judeo-Christian worldview exhibited an elective affinity for particularly invasive agricultural technologies, buttressing the now-dominant "dominion" interpretation of the mandate in Genesis to subdue the earth.[6] White's thesis has been challenged, however. For example, James Proctor and Evan Berry have pointed out that inferring a causal relationship between broad social behaviors and individual religious beliefs is dubious.[7] In addition, recent studies indicate that although up to 80 percent of Americans express resonance with pro-environmental values, less than 20 percent of those concerned actually act upon those values.[8] If these surveys and scholars are accurate, then the idea that religious values determine ecological behaviors is suspect. It is this apparent gap between

4. See Weston, "Beyond Intrinsic Value"; Stone, "Moral Pluralism"; Light and Katz, *Environmental Pragmatism*; Wenz, "Minimal, Moderate, and Extreme Moral Pluralism"; Norton, *Searching for Sustainability*; and Light, "Callicott and Naess."

5. Norton, "Why I Am Not A Nonanthropocentrist," 345.

6. White, "Historical Roots," 1203–7. The idea that there is a Judeo-Christian worldview has been called into question, and important criticisms highlight that the idea that Christianity is the fulfillment of Jewish tradition derives from a particular and partisan Protestant interpretation of this history. We are aware of and generally in accord with such critiques, but we use the term here because it was used by the scholars that are the objects of our discussion.

7. Proctor and Berry, "Social Science on Religion and Nature," 1572–77.

8. Duke University, "Survey."

moral vision and practical action, and the flaccidity of environmental philosophy with regard to public policy, which fertilized the soil for the emergence of environmental pragmatism.

Environmental Pragmatism: An Overview

Given this context, it is possible to articulate more clearly what we mean when we refer to environmental pragmatism. Drawing on philosophical pragmatism, particularly the work of William James, Charles Sanders Peirce, and John Dewey, environmental pragmatists have maintained that many formulations of environmental ethics which depend upon bio-centric or eco-centric ethics are, as Ben Minteer put it, "too ontologically and epistemologically flawed to be philosophically persuasive, and that [non-anthropocentrism] is a politically ineffective and ultimately unnecessary position."[9] Although some self-styled environmental pragmatists such as Andrew Light suggest that they are *methodological* pragmatists, and only loosely related genealogically to American philosophical pragmatism, most concur that their focus is a sort of productive social therapy, whereby the terms of debate among various constituencies are clarified and held up for scrutiny in the public sphere. Driving these scholars is the perception that, while environmental philosophy emerged as a field of study around the early 1970s, it has produced few tangible results in terms of policy outcomes and sustainable cultural behaviors. For example, Light and Katz noted that "the intramural debates of environmental philosophers although interesting, provocative and complex, seem to have no real impact on the deliberations of environmental scientists, activists, and policy-makers."[10]

To move toward a minimal definition, Light and Katz offered four key modes of environmental pragmatism in the introduction to their edited volume *Environmental Pragmatism*:

1. Examinations into the connections between classical American philosophical pragmatism and environmental issues.

2. The articulation of practical strategies for bridging gaps between environmental theorists, policy analysts, activists, and the public;

9. Minteer, *The Landscape of Reform*, 180.
10. Light and Katz, *Environmental Pragmatism*, 1.

3. Theoretical investigations into the overlapping normative bases of specific environmental organizations and movements, for the purposes of providing grounds for the convergence of activists on policy choices; and among these theoretical debates,

4. General arguments for theoretical and meta-theoretical moral pluralism in environmental normative theory.[11]

In addition, environmental pragmatism, particularly the sort that is strongly influenced by the American philosophers who birthed it, is a *problem-centered* approach that begins with particularly recalcitrant public environmental problems (i.e., climate change, restoration of ecosystems, etc.), and moves toward generating the political structures that can solve them.[12]

All four of these aims are integrated in Bryan Norton's 2005 book, *Sustainability*, the most systematic and philosophically sophisticated expression of environmental pragmatism to date. Norton suggests that political and social processes should be guided by a philosophy of adaptive ecosystem management. Norton's grasp of the relevant literature across a range of disciplines is noteworthy and he has a gift for building productive bridges between them. For example, he makes use of the philosophy of adaptive management, pioneered by ecologists H. T. Odum and C.S. Holling (among others), with special attention to the role of hierarchy theory (derived from general systems theory) as understood by Holling.[13] These perspectives were joined with a pragmatic philosophical approach that focused on democratic processes.

But how does a problem-based and pluralistic political deliberation process include religious values? We now turn to this question, which has been given insufficient attention by scholars outside religious studies, in part because the definitions of religions exercised by those outside this discipline are, ironically, often more restrictive than those deployed by religious studies scholars.

11. Ibid, 5.

12. Norton, interview, June 29, 2009.

13. Many consider Howard T. Odum to be one of the primary contributors to the development of adaptive management. However, Norton argues that Odum was a systems ecologist, and while he paid attention to the social aspects of ecological problems, he was less attuned to political processes than was Holling (interview, June 29, 2009).

Sustainability, Pragmatism, and Religion

In his recent work, Norton applied his pragmatist approach to the contested idea of "sustainability." This is a challenge: When oil companies, international political bodies, the Sierra Club, radical environmentalist, and indigenous organizations all use sustainability (or some variation of it) to describe their agendas and goals, it is vitally important that there be more focused investigation into particular deployments of the term and the values these uses imply. It is the dizzying variety of different understandings of sustainability that prompted Norton to propose a constructive social science research program, one engaged in developing "a new kind of integrative social science."[14]

Norton recognized that pluralism inevitably leads to "a range of values from consumptive to transformative to spiritual."[15] He argued that "[sustainability's] meaning . . . is intimately tied to the values of the community that uses the term. This view is contrary of course, to that of economists and others who seek a 'purely descriptive' concept of sustainability."[16] Instead, Norton offered what he called a *schematic definition* of sustainability, which included as foci four categories of "sustainability values": 1) community-procedural values, 2) weak sustainability (economic) values, 3) risk-avoidance values, and 4) community identity values.[17] Such a schematic definition

> characterizes and relates the key components of a definition [of sustainability] while leaving specification of the substance of

14. Norton, *Sustainability*, 291.

15. Ibid, 373.

16. Ibid, 386. By "purely descriptive," Norton means a concept of sustainability that uses a universal formula to achieve sustainability in particular situations, by—to use one example from ecological economics—assigning contingent values to ecological entities, and summing the costs and benefits of preserving or exploiting them. Purely descriptive definitions of sustainability may be helpful in some cases, but for Norton they are inadequate in the long run since they do not attend to the other important types of values that he believes are essential for sustainability (Ibid, 379–99).

17. Ibid, 365–71. The first set of values is concerned primarily with the political processes that allow appropriate values to be vetted for community analysis and revision. The second attends to economic assessments of values, acknowledging their importance for both human well-being and political traction. The third refers to creating opportunities to increase social resilience when faced with both external and internal disruptions. Finally, community identity values are those embraced by particular communities of accountability and which they find to be central to what it means to belong to that particular community.

those components open. Speaking schematically, we can say that sustainability is *a relationship between generations such that the earlier generations fulfill their individual wants and needs so as not to destroy, or close off, important and valued options for future generations.*[18]

The categories above can include a plurality of values, Norton argued, including consumptive values, transformative and spiritual values and everything in between, allowing for their variation over space and time.[19] Thus, filling in the content of these categories with specific (and locally dependent) values is an exercise in solidifying the identity of a particular community and supervising their exchange relations.[20] In short, Norton views sustainability as an active, pragmatic, and comprehensive (politico-socio-economic) philosophy of adaptive management.

As political scientists Michael Kenny and James Meadowcroft have argued, "nearly all definitions [of sustainability] concede that it involves the re-orientation of the 'meta-objectives' of a given society—by raising questions about different possible social trajectories through which the society may move, and then by promoting some of these as more 'sustainable' than others."[21] Norton addressed the importance of these meta-objectives when he argued that "individual preferences and social values—as well as the institutions that shape them—must be considered, and modeled, as endogenous to the social process of environmental management."[22] But Norton also argued that commitments to risky partnerships (commitments to negotiate with others outside one's familiar communities) are *"independent of the particular beliefs and values of the participants."*[23] Drawing on the work of sociologist Jürgen Habermas, Norton further contended that his "discourse ethics promotes multilay-

18. Ibid, 386, italics in original.

19. Ibid, 373.

20. Given the definition of religion offered by David Chidester, Norton's notion of sustainability is doing religious work to the extent that it is forging community, shaping exchange relations and focusing desire (see Chidester, *Authentic Fakes*). It is important to note that we are not claiming, as Kevin Elliot has, that Norton's definition is in part "metaphysical" (Elliot, "Norton's Conception of Sustainability"). We believe he has adequately answered Smith's charge ("Politics and Epistemology"). Religion, as we define it here, need not imply the addition of a metaphysical layer of reality.

21. Kenny and Meadowcroft, *Planning Sustainability*, 4.

22. Norton, *Searching for Sustainability*, 409.

23. Norton, *Sustainability*, 285, italics his.

ered communication channels that are unshaken by substantive beliefs or personal values."[24]

Religious or spiritual values, Norton says, may be vetted within particular communities, but cannot be reliably translated into the language of democratic politics. Indeed, for Norton the whole point of a problem-focused approach is to ensure that such subjective metaphysical commitments are not the focus of public policies designed to appease the majority in democratic populations.[25]

This process-oriented, adaptive model is indeed helpful for viewing policy making as a series of "reflective" and "action" phases, where public discussion about community mores (the reflective phase) lays the groundwork for experimental action (the active phase), which leads to re-visitation of community goals. We agree that these developments in environmental philosophy are important and badly needed, and our work is in significant ways indebted to Norton and other moral pluralists. There are three points, however, where we think religion scholars can productively contribute to the research program imagined by the environmental pragmatists.

First, although *values* have been given much attention by environmental philosophers, and *behaviors* have been identified as following from or generating new values, relatively little attention has been paid to the psychological variable that might be termed *experience*. Peak experiences and other life events that are formative for the moral imagination are often framed in emotive or affective verbiage and related to others people and communities in the form of stories.

Second, such community-bound, highly affective stories are often pointed outward, transmitted to other constituencies, and when they are, they are usually understood as reflecting the core values of those who tell them by those outside their own community group. Although environmental pragmatists are consummate pluralists, at least some believe that the inclusion of such deeply affective and partisan stories within political processes is unproductive. If anything, this is indicative of the lack of attention to religion in environmental pragmatism—an avoidance which is not surprising given classical pragmatism's ambivalence toward religion.

24. Ibid, 288.

25. Norton, interview 3 January 2008.

This is related to a third consideration that has to do with the definition of religion employed for analytical purposes. In part, Norton assumed a definition of religion that is "Protestant" in spirit if not in name. That is, Norton endorsed the idea that religion is a private affair confined to the home and the home community. We would argue, however, that religion is also a set of values related to practices that help negotiate relationships with those both inside *and* outside particular communities. In what follows we will provide greater detail about these areas where we think pragmatism might benefit from greater attention to the religious dimensions of public life.

More Practical Environmental Pragmatism: Experience, Values and Their Transmission

Experience and Values

Although debates over values (Where is the locus of value? Should value be human-centered or not? Monist or pluralist? Preservative or restorative?) occupied most environmental ethics conversations for two decades, other works have asked what role particular behaviors might have on the formulation of values.[26] Robyn Eckersley, for example warned in her critiques of pragmatism's emphasis on methodology that pragmatists too often avoided or sidestepped the host of deep seated issues, values, or beliefs involved in environmental politics or conflict.[27] While certain practices may cultivate awareness of new environmental issues or particular ecological relationships, they do so because they engage particular cognitive mechanisms that attach emotion, and thus moral, meaning to particular experiences. This important variable, experience, has been under-scrutinized by many philosophers. This experiential variable should be added to the mix to form an experience/practice/values matrix.

Ben Minteer has also noted the scant attention to religion and religious values among environmental pragmatists.[28] Indeed, he implicated

26. Peterson, "Toward a Materialist Environmental Ethic."

27. Eckersly, "Environmental Pragmatism, Ecocentrism, and Desire," 53. Norton, for one, suggested that his work on sustainability assumed an already-engaged and proactively-adaptive political process (interview 29 June 2009). To be fair, Norton does not intend to mislead his readers about this, and indeed makes it clear throughout *Sustainability* that this is one of his guiding assumptions.

28. Minteer, "Pragmatism, Piety, and Environmental Ethics," 179–96.

himself in this neglect before articulating a means of embracing the role of religious values and experience in policy deliberation. Minteer's response was an exploration of Dewey's work, particularly Dewey's articulation of "natural piety." Simply described, natural piety refers to the formation of affective or spiritual values based on experiences in the natural world. This is a form of piety or faith that is not contingent upon traditional religious belief or practice. In his retrieval of Dewey, Minteer attempted to expand the scope of pragmatism to include a form of environmental ethics contingent upon humans' spiritual experiences with nature. In so doing, he argued that religious experiences in nature have the potential to foster an ethic of respect for nature. These religious experiences do not focus on brokering with divine agents, but instead are "directed at the enabling conditions of lived experience" in nature.[29]

Reflecting on the contemporary lack of engagement with nature among young people, Richard Louv's *Last Child in the Woods* (2005) discussed the loss of certain capacities in humans when deprived of experience with or in nature, and the human ecologist Paul Shepard explored similar themes beginning at least as early as the 1980s.[30] Shepard's argument was that the "human genome" evolved in the Pleistocene, and that affectively charged experiences in nature help to shape the cognitive machinery that humans now use to perceive the world. These parts of the human physiology and psyche are stunted when there is no engagement with natural stimuli. Moreover, when describing such (perhaps increasingly infrequent) encounters with non-human nature, most people are forced to draw upon religious or spiritual language, metaphor and imagery to describe the deeper affective portions of their experiences.

The bulk of one author's (Snyder's) research supports Eckersly's, Minteer's and Shepard's ideas, elucidating how nature-based experiences —such as hiking, hunting, or fishing—are often perceived as religious experiences facilitated by being-in-nature. Such religious experiences and practices can indeed create gateways to forms of more engaged environmental ethics and concern, including varieties of environmental activism from grassroots politics to ecological restoration.[31] Minteer has hinted at the importance that such generic nature reverence plays

29. Ibid, 186.

30. Louv, *Last Child in the Woods*; Shepard, *Nature and Madness* and *Coming Home to the Pleistocene*.

31. Snyder, "New Streams of Religion." See also Taylor, "Surfing into Spirituality."

in fomenting environmental attitudes and behaviors, but we also want to encourage him (and his philosophical kin) to expand his gaze a bit more to include world religions.

Drawing on Dewey, Minteer specifically resisted describing a spiritually-grounded ethic of the environment with reference to supernatural or transcendent divinities, and suggested that a spiritually-grounded ethic of the environment can emerge solely from experiences in and with the natural world.[32] So, he does not mention the variety of world religions, particularly those which are deity-dependant. In this, he ignored potentially important sources for successful environmental ethics. Research continues to reveal that religion can indeed be a strong and powerful component in the development of engaged and successful environmental ethics. Although worldwide membership in institutional religions is declining, by some accounts the eleven faiths typically referred to as the major global religions comprise approximately two thirds of the world's population, own around seven percent of the world's habitable land, and hold approximately six to eight percent of the global investment market. They are, therefore, an important ingredient in the quest for a sustainable global community.[33]

Oftentimes environmental pragmatists would prefer that when religious values are translated into the public sphere they be transmogrified into something more digestible for those who do not concur with their metaphysical presuppositions. They are right to worry about the inclusion of core values and deep beliefs in public deliberation, for religious language is often imprecise, subjective, and abstract. Certainly a diverse populous requires significant practice at translating religious language into effective public policy images, but there should be no doubt that this is already underway. Recent public debates about reproductive choices and the inclusion of evolutionary theory in teaching curricula clearly illustrate that religious messages and public image events carry public weight.[34] This entry of religion into the public sphere is inevitable as long

32. Minteer, "Pragmatism, Piety, and Environmental Ethics," 186.

33. Palmer and Findlay, *Faith in Conservation*, xi.

34. Ironically, by marginalizing strong religious statements and values from public deliberation, some environmental pragmatists have mimicked one of their favorite sparring partners, J. Baird Callicott. In *Earth's Insights* (1994), Callicott surveyed both global religions and traditional belief systems in search for common grounds for environmental ethics. In so doing, however, he concluded that religion-based environmental ethics would be much more convincing if they were shorn of their supernatural

as people are religious: It is no more possible or advisable to suggest that believers bracket or ignore the religious traditions that shape them than it would be to ask secular humanists to deny their concern with human well being during public negotiation.

What we are suggesting, then, is that there may be a logical incongruity when pluralists decide that everyone can come to the negotiating table while also dictating what sort of information is relevant for those participants to display and discuss in the public eye. The decision about what data is relevant should also be a matter of public deliberation. Norton and many other pragmatists would likely agree with us in this, so long as it is conceded that not *all* religious or spiritual discourse is equally relevant or helpful in solving particular environmental problems. Indeed, this is one area where religious studies scholars might help to generate a more productive, "reflective" phase in the formulation of public policy that addresses specific issues. By helping to note when particular belief systems or religious values are *maladaptive*, religion scholars can move policy-formulation process forward in helpful ways.

The Transmission of Values

The other author's (Johnston's) interview work with dozens of high level actors in various sustainability movements indicate that the urban planners Michael Kenny and James Meadowcroft are correct: nearly all definitions of sustainability envision a re-orientation of the "meta-objectives" of a society, whether it is a new ethic, an alternative anthropology, or a more holistic perception.[35]

---

tenets. Commenting on Christianity and Judaism specifically, he argued that "purged of [their] literal elements, the stewardship environmental ethic powerfully speaks to the present condition of the relationship of human beings to nature (Callicott, *Earth's Insights*, 23).

35. "New" and "alternative" are terms that advocates use to express what they feel is a new set of guiding principles and values that differ in significant ways from those held by the dominant culture. For examples of this language that range from counter-hegemonic social movements to mainstream development and international political institutions, see Sumner, *Sustainability and the Civil Commons*, 112; Hawken, *Blessed Unrest*; Goldsmith et al., *Blueprint for Survivial*, vi; Edwards, *The Sustainability Revolution*, 2; Golliher, "Ethical, Moral, and Religious," 446; International Union for the Conservation of Nature, *Caring for the Earth*, 9; World Bank, *Making the Sustainability Commitment*, xxv; WCED, *Our Common Future*, 1.

Norton's "community identity values" may be too limited to characterize what people mean when they talk about a new approach to ethics. To assume that the ripples of community values extend only within the bounds of a particular community misses the richly networked relationships among the various sectors of society. In many cases, insiders are pointing these agreed-upon community values outward to critique the larger culture and its social trajectory. Core values of communities are intentionally marketed outside their social boundaries for the purpose of forging partnerships and educating others about community values.

Religious language and stories can be and are used to translate core values and deep beliefs across diverse constituencies with differing value structures. Exposing the values at play in various definitions of sustainability becomes especially important in a pluralistic global context, where those who provide the funding and institutional support for sustainable development programs have in mind a concept of sustainability that is not only foreign but often unwelcome to those who are the "targets" of such development. For example, some conservation and development agencies assume that sustainable development requires engagement with the global market. In contrast, the idea of sustainability may be deployed by indigenous or other marginalized groups as a strategic term to resist incorporation into the global market and its attendant values.[36] The current "moral austerity" of environment-related policy making cannot be overcome without making these value foundations explicit.[37]

Indeed, the anthropologist Robin Wright has noted that in many cases, religiosity may either facilitate or hamper the success of sustainable development projects, depending on the resonance of such religiosity with the values of the granting or funding bodies. In these cases, religion is certainly an important factor in sustainability. Further, if most of the world's population does not draw significant boundaries between religious and political life, then democratic processes coupled with sustainable development schemes *must* allow reflection and public debate about the veracity and potential helpfulness of religious values in solving particular problems to produce viable, sustainable public policy.[38]

36. Wright, "Art of Being Crente"; and Trusty, *Politics of Representing Nature*.

37. Gilroy and Bowersox, eds. *The Moral Austerity of Environmental Decision Making*.

38. David Chidester notes that a now out of date guidebook for Christian missionaries put the number of "animistic" peoples on the planet, those who do not resonate with traditional Western categories and concepts, at roughly 40% (Chidester, "Animism," 78,

Indeed, several individuals from our case studies engaged in deliberation precisely *because* of their religious beliefs and values, not in spite of them.

In Norton's deliberative politics such commitments to risky partnerships (commitments to negotiate with others outside of one's own community) have nothing to do with "*the particular beliefs and values of the participants.*"[39] We believe Norton may have utilized an outdated and essentially private definition of religion to state his case. In addition, religious beliefs and practices are often important ingredients in political deliberation, and we hope to point to ways that social scientists and humanities scholars can help produce more effective policy solutions by vetting specific beliefs and practices in the public sphere and assessing their ability to address real world problems. During this reflective phase, while the "truth" of particular religious traditions is not at stake, religious practices and beliefs can and should be assessed according to their ability to effectively characterize and propose solutions to specific human (and particularly ecological) problems.

Rethinking Religion for a Constructive and Adaptive Social Science Research Program

In *A Common Faith* (1960), Dewey's approach to religion and religious experience (and he differentiates between them) suggested that religion and religious experience are possible without belief in or dependence upon the supernatural. Norton and Light are just two contemporary philosophers who likewise pursue a post-metaphysical approach to environmental ethics. Norton traced his post-metaphysical model to Jürgen Habermas, while Light argued that environmental pragmatism requires "making the kind of arguments that resonate with the moral intuitions that most people carry around with them on an everyday basis."[40]

Pragmatists would do well, however, to take note of current scholarship in religious studies. While those outside the field tend to view

study referenced from 1991). The anthropologist Darrell Posey suggests that, excluding urban populations, indigenous peoples could amount to 85% of the world's population (*Indigenous Knowledge and Ethics*). One publication from the IUCN, UNEP, and WWF put the number of indigenous peoples at about 200 million, or approximately 4% of the (then) global population (*Caring for the Earth*, 61).

39. Norton, *Sustainability*, 285.

40. Light, "Restoring Ecological Citizenship," 444.

religion as dependent upon belief in gods or deities, many in religious studies understand belief, faith, and the supernatural to be only a few aspects of religion.[41] Belief in supernatural beings has proven ineffective as a litmus test for religiosity in light of strong genealogical critiques of religion as a category.[42] While the term religion is now used across the globe, it does not always or even usually refer to supernatural agents and miracle occurrences that intervene in the natural order. Instead, religion should be imagined as strategically, intellectually, and socially useful in several contexts, for both Westerners and non-Westerners who have adapted the term as a means of explaining their life-ways to others. In fact, some religious studies scholars have adopted a methodology focused less on what people *believe* and more on what people *do* with their religious categories. Russell McCutcheon's response to an audience question at a conference is illustrative: following his presentation he was asked whether he meant that religion was "*also* social, biological, political, economic, and so on, or whether [McCutcheon] was saying that religion was *only* social, biological, political, economic, and so on." McCutcheon's answer: "Only. Next question?"[43]

McCutcheon may have been unduly provocative in his response, but his point is significant: for scholars of religion, analysis should focus not on supposed internal subjective states and beliefs but on the effects that these beliefs, values and practices have (through their believers) in the real world. According to this understanding, scholars of religion should attend to subjective states to the extent that they are affirmed by persons or communities rather than searching for an essentially religious facet of experience or thought abstracted from people in particular places.[44]

41. Chidester, *Authentic Fakes*; Hall, *Lived Religion*; Orsi, "Everyday Miracles."

42. Asad, *Genealogies of Religion*; Masuzawa, *The Invention of the World Religions*; Dubuison, *The Western Construction of Religion*; McCutcheon, *Manufacturing Religion*. See also Evan Berry's chapter in this volume.

43. McCutcheon, *Critics Not Caretakers*, x.

44. Cases where a priori metaphysical assumptions guide research might include earlier scholars such as Rudolph Otto, who suggested that religious experience was grounded in the perception of a *mysterium tremendum*, or Mircea Eliade, who argued that religion was a cultural phenomenon that reflected encounters with something objectively real in nature called *the sacred*. More recent examples might include scholars who claim that followers of this or that religion (say, Islam) would naturally behave in a particular fashion if they were *authentic* believers (say, authentic Muslims). McCutcheon's *Religion and the Domestication of Dissent* has provided an extended critique of overbroad and essentialist understandings of Islam following the attacks on the New York City World Trade Centers on September 11, 2001. Such essentialist claims

McCutcheon's response and research agenda can be related to a group of scholars who argue that the study of religion should be conceived as a "materialist phenomenology of religion."[45] Religion scholars David Hall, Robert Orsi, Thomas Tweed and others have advanced a methodology that allows for the investigation of affective states through empathetic observation or participation, but contextualizes these observations by attending to socio-political circumstances.[46]

But such religious production is not found only within the boundaries of the traditional "world" or "global" religions. For religion scholar Rebecca Gould's subjects, experiences in nature were sources of "meaning and authority" for both individuals and communities.[47] Her study of homesteading in the United States is similar in approach to the one Minteer articulated through Dewey's idea of "natural piety," which highlights a "sense of awe and meaningful appreciation of the natural world" through direct "religious" engagement with it.[48] While she might not consider herself a pragmatist, we believe that Gould's work is something that environmental pragmatists ought to consider as instructive. In such analyses a religious relationship with nature takes place beyond the walls of a mosque, synagogue, or church in the experiential spaces of nature.

Building a bounded definition of religion is less important than learning what it means for particular people in their places. Ludwig Wittgenstein (for one) has questioned whether providing a solid definition of any term is necessary for understanding:

> We are able to use the word "plant" in a way that gives rise to no misunderstanding, yet countless borderline cases can be constructed in which no one has yet decided whether something still falls under the concept "plant." Does this mean that the meaning of the word "plant" in all other cases is infected by uncertainty, so that it might be said we use the word without understanding it? Would a definition which bounded this concept on several sides make the meaning of the word clearer to us in *all* sentences?[49]

may tell more about those who imagine and endorse them than they do about those who are studied by looking through such lenses.

45. Orsi, "Everyday Miracles," 8.

46. Tweed has argued that this methodology is indebted to the work of philosophical pragmatism, notably that of Hilary Putnam (*Crossing and Dwelling*).

47. Gould, *At Home in Nature*, 4.

48. Minteer, "Pragmatism, Piety, and Environmental Ethics," 191.

49. Wittgenstein, *Philosophical Grammar*, 73.

Wittgenstein's answer, and ours, is "no." Many have used the term religion to refer to institutional manifestations of religion (those confined by buildings and traditions), as well as more commonplace and everyday experiences of affectively-grounded communion with others (even, as religion scholar David Chidester has, referring to baseball or live music performance).[50] In our understanding of religion, all of these uses of the term "count." As Saler put it, "if we deem admission to a group (as comprehended by the category religion) to be a matter of 'more or less' rather than a matter of 'yes or no,' then an argument can be made for admitting 'secular religions' and 'quasi-religions' as peripheral members."[51] Conceptualizing religion in this way, as a category that refers to overlapping attributes or family resemblances (first proposed by Wittgenstein), "facilitates going beyond religion [as synonymous with institutional practice and creed] and attending to 'the religious dimension' of much of human life."[52] If all of these varied sets of characteristics "count," from substantive definitions to functional ones, from subjectively-derived definitions to those that suggest religion is a product of society, it allows analysis of a wider range of social phenomena with a

50. Chidester, *Authentic Fakes.*

51. Saler, "Toward a Realistic," 230. Using the same theories that Saler utilized more than a decade earlier, anthropologist Jonathan Benthall argued that "Linguists have developed the idea of 'prototype semantics,' whereby the applicability of a word to a thing is not a matter of 'yes or no,' but rather of 'more or less.'" Further, he said that "these criteria may be graded" (Benthall, *Returning to Religion*, 21). If some aspects of human lives contain more religion-resembling features than others, we may find that "some religions, in a manner of speaking, are 'more religious' than others" (Saler, *Conceptualizing Religion*, xiv), though this "more" does not refer to a greater authenticity, but rather a closer resemblance to one or more prototypes of that category.

52. Saler, *Conceptualizing Religion*, 214; see also Saler, "Toward a Realistic," 230. Saler and Benthall, as well as religion scholars Manuel Vasquez and Bron Taylor, have utilized Wittgenstein's *family resemblances* model to analyze religion (Saler, "Toward a Realistic," 197; Benthall, *Returning to Religion*, 46–80; Vasquez, "Studying Religion in Motion"; Taylor, "Exploring Religion, Nature, and Culture," 15–17; Taylor, *Dark Green Religion*, 4–5). In *Conceptualizing Religion* Saler compares the virtues and pitfalls of both family resemblances (derived from linguistic philosophy), and polythetic classification (derived from biology), arguing that both tools would likely have what he calls a "practical convergence," producing similar results when applied to a term such as religion (Saler, *Conceptualizing Religion*, 170). In the end, however, the family resemblance model, coupled with "prototype theory" is Saler's preference. For criticisms of the family resemblance approach, see *Perspectives on Method and Theory in the Study of Religion: Adjunct Proceedings of the XVIIth Congress of the International Association for the History of Religions* (Geertz and McCutcheon, *Perspectives on Method and Theory*, 287–337).

religious studies lens than would otherwise be the case. It is possible, for example, to attend to the "religious dimension" of social movements while withholding judgment about where they fall on the "more to less religious" continuum. Envisioning religion as a pool of loosely related elements allows analysis of how the religious dimensions of social movements help to forge community, facilitate exchange, and focus desire.[53] Religion scholars should attend to this religious dimension wherever they find it, even (and perhaps especially) if it occurs outside the boundaries of what is considered typically religious. Given this expanded definition of religion, it is also our hope that scholars from other disciplines will be less shy about attempting to understand the complex ways in which religion also contributes to better understandings of their own fields of study.

If religion is intimately involved in creating community cohesion (and simultaneously bounding that community by excluding others), facilitating exchange relations, and focusing desire, the most productive analytical approach is to trace the material manifestations and public deployments of such inferences.[54] As the anthropologist Scott Atran and his co-authors put it,

> People's mental representations interact with other people's mental representations to the extent that those representations can be *physically transmitted in a public medium* . . . These public representations, in turn, are sequenced and channeled by ecological features of the external environment (including the social environment) that constrain psychophysical interactions between individuals.[55]

Cultural "things" like religion, then, are "distributions of [mental] representations in a human population, *ecological patterns of psychological things.*"[56] Understanding particular cultures, or in this case social movements, depends upon noting which representations appear to be the most

---

53. Chidester argued that something is doing religious work when it is "engaged in negotiating what it means to be human" (*Authenic Fakes*, 18), and shaping the public sphere by "forming community, focusing desire, and facilitating exchange" (5).

54. Anna Peterson ("Toward a Materialist") has argued for the merits of a materialist environmental ethic.

55. Atran, Medin, and Ross, "The Cultural Mind," 751.

56. Sperber, "The Modularity of Thought," 73.

"catching," the most persistent over time, and the best suited for navigating particular social and ecological problems.[57]

There exists the possibility for a productive reinforcement between environmental pragmatists and religion and nature scholars to generate a genuinely constructive, iterative and adaptive process of ecosystem management. Religion scholars can help environmental pragmatists to envision a broader and more productive reflective phase of the policy deliberation process. But it requires greater nuance in the use of terms typically left confined within particular disciplinary silos, and a greater willingness to practice vetting highly affective narratives in the public sphere. If ethics are to evolve from lived experience, as pragmatists would have it, and restoration, conservation and conflict resolution are to become effective spaces for public deliberations on societal values, then greater attention to experiential sources of core values and deep beliefs is required. If we accept Light's challenge and focus on the "empirical question of what morally motivates humans to change their attitudes, behaviors, and policy preferences toward those more supportive of long-term environmental sustainability," then it may be necessary to acknowledge that in many cases moral motivation derives from religious commitments (in the broad sense that religion has been defined here).[58] This is, in spirit at least, a pragmatist approach.

Bibliography

Albanese, Catherine. *America, Religion and Religions*. Belmont, CA: Wadsworth, 1999.
Asad, Talal. *Genealogies of Religion: Disciplines and Reasons of Power in Christianity and Islam*. Baltimore: Johns Hopkins University Press, 1993.
Atran, Scott et al. "The Cultural Mind: Environmental Decision Making and Cultural Modeling within and across Populations." *Psychological Review* 112 (2005) 744–76.
Benthall, Johnathan. *Returning to Religion: Why a Secular Age Is Haunted by Faith*. Library of Modern Religion 1. London: Tauris, 2008.
Callicott, J. Baird. "Animal Liberation: A Triangular Affair." *Environnemental Ethics* 2 (1980) 311–38.
———. *Earth's Insights: A Survey of Ecological Ethics from the Mediterranean to the Australian Outback*. Berkeley: University of California Press, 1994.
———. "Intrinsic Value, Quantum Theory, and Environmental Ethics." *Environmental Ethics* 7 (1985) 257–75.

57. Ibid, 54.
58. Light, "Restoring Ecological Citizenship," 446.

Chidester, David. *Authentic Fakes: Religion and American Popular Culture.* Berkeley: University of California Press, 2005.

———. "Animism" in *Encyclopedia of Religion and Nature*, edited by Bron Raymond Taylor et al., 1:78–81 London: Theommes Continuum, 2005,

Dewey, John. *A Common Faith.* A Yale Paperbound. New Haven: Yale University Press, 1960.

DeYoung, Raymond. "Changing Behavior and Making It Stick: The Conceptualization and Management of Conservation Behavior." *Environment and Behavior* 25 (1983) 485–505.

Dubuisson, Daniel. *The Western Construction of Religion: Myths, Knowledge, and Ideology.* Translated by William Sayers. Baltimore: Johns Hopkins University Press, 2003.

Duke University. "Survey: Why Pro-Environmental Values Don't Always Translate into Votes." Nicholas Institute for Environmental Policy Solutions, Duke University School of the Environment and Earth Sciences, Durham N.C. Online: http://www .dukenews.duke.edu/2005/09/nicholaspoll.html/.

Eckersley, Robyn. "Environmental Pragmatism, Ecocentrism, and Deliberative Democracy: Between Problem Solving and Fundamental Critique." In *Democracy and the Claims of Nature: Critical Perspectives for a New Century*, edited by Ben A. Minteer and Bob Pepperman Taylor, 49–70. Lanham, MD: Rowman and Littlefield, 2002.

Edwards, Anders. *The Sustainability Revolution: Portrait of a Paradigm Shift.* Gabriola Island, BC: New Society, 2005.

Elliott, Kevin. "Norton's Conception of Sustainability: Political, Not Metaphysical." *Environmental Ethics.* 29 (2007) 3–22.

Davison, Aidan. *Technology and the Contested Meanings of Sustainability.* Albany: State University of New York Press, 2000.

Geertz, Armin W., and Russell T. McCutcheon, with the assistance of Scott S. Elliott. *Perspectives on Method and Theory in the Study of Religion: Adjunct Proceedings of the XVII Congress of the National Association for the History of Religions.* Leiden: Brill, 2000.

Gillroy, John Martin, and Joe Bowersox, editors. *The Moral Austerity of Environmental Decision Making: Sustainability, Democracy, and Normative Argument in Policy and Law.* Durham: Duke University Press, 2002.

Goldsmith, Edward et al. *Blueprint for Survival.* Boston: Houghton Mifflin, 1972.

Golliher, Jeff. "Ethical, Moral and Religious Concerns." In *Cultural and Spiritual Values of Biodiversity*, edited by Darrell Posey, 437–48. Nairobi: United Nations Environment Programme, 1999.

Gould, Rebecca Kneale. *At Home in Nature: Modern Homesteading and Spiritual Practice.* Berkeley: University of California Press, 2005.

Hall, David D., editor. *Lived Religion: Toward a History of Practice.* Princeton: Princeton University Press, 1997.

Hawken, Paul. *Blessed Unrest: How the Largest Movement in the World Came into Being, and Why No One Saw It Coming.* New York: Viking, 2007.

International Union for the Conservation of Nature (IUCN). United Nations Environment Program (UNEP), and World Wide Fund for Nature (WWF). *Caring for the Earth: A Strategy for Sustainable Living.* Gland, Switzerland: World Conservation Centre 1991.

Kenny, Michael, and James Meadowcroft, editors. *Planning Sustainability.* London: Routledge, 1999.

Kollmus, Anja, and Julian Agyeman. "Mind the Gap: Why Do People Act Environmentally and What Are the barriers to Pro-environmental Behavior?" *Environmental Education and Research* 8 (2003) 239–60.

Light, Andrew. "Callicott and Naess on Moral Pluralism." In *Environmental Ethics: An Anthology*, edited by Andrew Light and Holmes Rolston III, 229–47. Blackwell Philosophy Anthologies 19. Malden, MA: Blackwell, 2003.

———. "Restoring Ecological Citizenship." In *Democracy and the Claims of Nature: Critical Perspectives for a New Century*, edited by Ben Minteer and Bob Pepperman Taylor, 153 –72. Lanham, MD: Rowman and Littlefield, 2002.

———. "Callicott and Naess on Pluralism." *Inquiry* 39 (1996) 273–94.

Light, Andrew, and Avner De-Shalit. "Introduction: Environmental Ethics—Whose Philosophy? Which Practice?" in *Moral and Political Reasoning in Environmental Practice*, edited by Andrew Light and Avner De-Shalit, 1–27. Cambridge: MIT Press, 2003.

Light, Andrew, and Eric Katz, editors. *Environmental Pragmatism*. London: Routledge, 1996.

Louv, Richard. *Last Child In the Woods: Saving Our Children from Nature-Deficit Disorder*. Chapel Hill, NC: Algonquin, 2005.

Masuzawa, Tomoko. *The Invention of World Religions, Or, How European Universalism Was Preserved in the Language of Pluralism*. Chicago: University of Chicago Press, 2005.

McCutcheon, Russell T. *Critics Not Caretakers: Redescribing the Public Study of Religion*. SUNY Series, Issues in the Study of Religion. Albany: State University of New York Press, 2001.

———. *Manufacturing Religion: The Discourse on Sui Generis Religion and the Politics of Nostalgia*. New York: Oxford University Press, 1997.

———. *Religion and the Domestication of Dissent, or, How to Live in a Less Than Perfect Nation*. Religion in Culture. London: Equinox, 2005.

Minteer, Ben A. *The Landscape of Reform: Civic Pragmatism and Environmental Thought in America*. Cambridge: MIT Press, 2006.

———. "Pragmatism, Piety, and Environmental Ethics." *Worldviews: Global Religions, Culture, and Ecology* 12:2–3 (2008) 179–96.

Minteer, Ben A., and Bob Pepperman Taylor. *Democracy and the Claims of Nature: Critical Perspectives for a New Century*. Lanham, MD: Rowman and Littlefield, 2002.

Norton, Bryan. "Politics and Epistemology: Inclusion and Controversy in Adaptive Management Processes." *Environmental Ethics* 29 (2007) 299–306.

———. *Searching for Sustainability: Interdisciplinary Essays on the Philosophy of Conservation Biology*. Cambridge Studies in Philosophy and Biology. Cambridge: Cambridge University Press, 2003.

———. *Sustainability: A Philosophy of Adaptive Ecosystem Management*. Chicago: University of Chicago Press, 2005.

———. *Toward Unity among Environmentalists*. New York: Oxford University Press, 1991.

———. "Why I Am Not a Nonanthropocentrist: Callicott and the Failure of Monistic Inheretism." *Environmental Ethics* 17 (1995) 341–60.

Orsi, Robert. "Everyday Miracles: The Study of Lived Religion." In *Lived Religion in America: Toward a History of Practice*, edited by David D. Hall, 3–21. Princeton: Princeton University Press, 1997.

Palmer, Martin, with Victoria Finlay. *Faith in Conservation: New Approaches to Religions and the Environment*. Directions in Development. Washington DC: The World Bank, 2003.

Peterson, Anna L. *Seeds of the Kingdom: Utopian Communities in the Americas*. Oxford: Oxford University Press, 2005.

———. "Toward a Materialist Environmental Ethic." *Environmental Ethics* 28 (2006) 375–94.

Posey, Darrell Addison. *Indigenous Knowledge and Ethics: A Darrell Posey Reader*. Studies in Environmental Anthropology 10. New York: Routledge, 2004.

Proctor, James D., and Evan Berry. "Social Science on Religion and Nature." In *Encyclopedia of Religion and Nature*, edited by Bron Raymond Taylor et al., 2:1572–77. London: Thoemmes Continuum, 2005.

Rolston, III, Holmes. *Environmental Ethics: Duties to and Values in the Natural World*. Ethics and Action. Philadelphia: Temple University Press, 1986.

Saler, Benson. *Conceptualizing Religion: Immanent Anthropologists, Transcendent Natives, and Unbounded Categories*. Studies in the History of Religions 56. Leiden, Netherlands: Brill, 1993.

———. "Toward a Realistic and Relevant 'Science of Religion.'" *Method & Theory in the Study of Religion* 16 (2004) 205–33.

Shepard, Paul. *Coming Home to the Pleistocene*. Edited by Florence R. Shepard. Washington, DC: Island, 1998.

———. *Nature and Madness*. Athens: University of Georgia Press, 1982.

Snyder, Samuel. "New Streams of Religion: Fly-Fishing as Lived Religion of Nature." *Journal of the American Academy of Religion* 75 (2007) 896–922.

Sperber, Dan. "Anthropology and Psychology: Towards an Epidemiology of Representations." *Man* 20 (1985) 73–89.

———. "The Modularity of Thought and the Epidemiology of Representations." In *Mapping the Mind: Domain Specificity in Cognition and Culture*, edited by Lawrence A. Hirschfeld and Susan A. Gelman, 39–67. Cambridge: Cambridge University Press, 1994.

Stone, Christopher D. "Moral Pluralism and the Course of Environmental Ethics." *Environmental Ethics* 10 (1988), 139–54.

Sumner, Jennifer. *Sustainability and the Civil Commons: Rural Communities in the Age of Globalization*. Toronto: University of Toronto Press, 2005.

Taylor, Bron Raymond. *Dark Green Religion: Nature Spirituality and the Planetary Future*. Berkeley: University of California Press, 2010.

——— et al., editors. *Encyclopedia of Religion and Nature*. 2 vols. London: Thoemmes Continuum, 2005.

———. "Exploring Religion, Nature and Culture—Introducing the Journal for the Study of Religion, Nature and Culture." *Journal for the Study of Religion, Nature and Culture* 1 (2007) 5–24.

———. "Surfing Into Spirituality and a New, Aquatic Nature Religion. *Journal of the American Academy of Religion,* 75 (2007) 923–95.

Taylor, Paul W. *Respect for Nature: A Theory of Environmental Ethics*. Studies in Moral, Political, and Legal Philosophy. Princeton: Princeton University Press, 1986.

Taylor, Sarah McFarland. *Green Sisters: A Spiritual Ecology*. Cambridge: Harvard University Press, 2007.

Trusty, Teresa. "The Politics of Representing Nature, Culture, and Conservation in Northwestern Bolivia." PhD diss., University of Washington, 2009.

Tweed, Thomas A. *Crossing and Dwelling: A Theory of Religion.* Oxford: Oxford University Press, 2006.

Vasquez, Manuel. "Studying Religion in Motion: A Networks Approach." *Method & Theory in the Study of Religion* 20 (2008) 151–84.

Wenz, Peter S. "Minimal, Moderate, and Extreme Moral Pluralism." *Environmental Ethics* 15 (1993) 61–74.

Weston, Anthony. "Beyond Intrinsic Value: Pragmatism in Environmental Ethics." *Environmental Ethics* 7 (1985) 321–39.

White, Lynn, Jr. "The Historical Roots of Our Ecologic Crisis." *Science* 155 (1967) 1203–7.

Wittgenstein, Ludwig. *Philosophical Grammar.* Edited by Rush Rhees. Translated by Anthony Kenny. Berkeley: University of California Press, 1974.

World Bank. *Making Sustainable Commitments: An Environment Strategy for the World Bank.* Washington DC: World Bank, 2001.

World Commission on Environment and Development (WCED). *Our Common Future.* Oxford: Oxford University Press, 1987.

Wright, Robin. "The Art of Being *Crente*: The Baniwa Protestant Ethic and the Spirit of Sustainable Development." *Identities: Global Studies in Culture and Power* 16 (2009) 202–26.

8

How Does It Feel to be an Environmental Problem?

Studying Religion and Ecology in the African Diaspora[1]

ELONDA CLAY

African Americans developed what in modern terms might be regarded an environmental ethos long before the environmental justice movement, before the civil rights movement, and before they were emancipated and had citizenship rights conferred upon them.

—Mart A. Stewart[2]

We inherit colonial habits along with degraded habitats . . . Again and again, catastrophe generates public demands for protection and renovation, followed by a new cycle of oblivion and ruthless exploitation.

—David Lowenthal[3]

1. The author would like to thank her parents, Rhonda L. Smith, Joseph L. Smith, and Melvin Clay, along with Dr. Jennifer L. Baldwin, and the editors for their assistance and feedback.
2. Stewart, in *To Love the Wind and the Rain*, 17.
3. Lowenthal, "Empires and Ecologies: Reflections," 232.

"Do we have any reason to believe that the culture most responsible
for the ecological crisis will also provide the moral and intellectual
resources for the earth's liberation? . . . I have a deep suspicion about
the theological and ethical values of white culture and religion."

—James Cone[4]

"We have wanted all our lives to know that Earth, who has somehow
obtained human beings as her custodians, was also capable of creating
humans who could minister to her needs, and the needs of her creation.
We are the ones."

—Alice Walker[5]

In *The Souls of Black Folk*, W. E. B. Du Bois posits that the unasked
question directed towards blacks during the post-emancipation era was
"How does it feel to be a problem?" DuBois continues to be renowned
for his term, "the problem of the color-line."[6] The color-line refers to
those practices and ideas involving racial/ethnic difference that result
in the maintenance of hierarchical social ordering and asymmetrical
power relations among human groups. Philosopher and Du Bois scholar
Nahum Chandler notes, "The problem of the negro in America was
long understood within the African American intellectual community
in the United States as a fundamental part of the question of colonialism and its aftermath."[7] This chapter posits the question, "How does it
feel to be an environmental problem?" in order to investigate current
postcolonial, post-industrial contexts and the implications of their aftermath—ecologically and socially—as well as to challenge thinking that
reproduces constructions of race and environmental degradation solely
as a problem for people of color. Throughout this essay, I question how
and why black bodies become a problem in the discourse of Religion
and Ecology. Put another way, how did the phrase "environmental racism" become a signifier and substitute for people of African descent
as religious and environmental agents in much of Religion and Ecology
literature?

4. Cone, "Whose Earth Is It Anyway?" 31.
5. Walker, *We Are the Ones.*
6. Du Bois, *The Souls of Black Folk,* 37, 34.
7. Chandler, "W. E .B. Du Bois as a Problem for Thought," 44.

The study of African diasporic religious traditions[8] in the United States and their ecological perspectives has long been connected to the historical beginnings of the environmental justice movement in the early 1980's. Yet to limit the discussion of religious and environmental themes among African Diaspora peoples to environmental racism and justice oversimplifies the complex cultural and communal contexts in which Blacks experience nature and live out their environmental ethos. My aim is to explore theoretical and methodological issues related to the study of Religion and Ecology in the African Diaspora. By breaking with some thematic and conceptual limitations of previous scholarship and building upon the legacies of environmental justice, religious studies, Religion and Ecology/Nature, and ecocriticism, I hope to open up new directions for future research.

I begin by reviewing popular anthologies, journals, and encyclopedias in Religion and Ecology/Religion and Nature, noting that this field tends to conflate the African Diaspora with the category of environmental racism and that the actual religions of the African Diaspora religions are only marginally incorporated into the religious and environmental histories of the Americas. As a response and corrective, I assert that a 'world religions' approach to the African Diaspora is inadequate and suggest that the broader interdisciplinary framework of religion and globalization is better suited to analyze diasporic religions.

My next task is to contextualize and historicize the study of the African Diaspora religions by arguing that our historic horizons begin not with environmental racism and activism, but with the analytical concept of diaspora and the Black Atlantic diaspora to the Americas.

8. For this essay, the phrases 'African diasporic religious traditions,' 'black religions' and 'African American religions' are used synonymously. Although the terms do not completely equate in light of popular and disciplinary usage, I see sufficient overlap in the terms to take this liberty. African diasporic religious traditions are also known as African-derived religions and New World African religions. I situate US North American black traditions within a hemispheric perspective of the Americas, although they are indisputably transcultural and have multiple forms and trajectories. African Americans are not limited to US-born black citizens, and the term as used here encompasses the entire American hemisphere, thus giving preference to an inclusive yet heterogeneous view of blacks from South, Central, and North America, the Caribbean, as well as more recent African immigrants to the United States. I use the terms 'black' and 'African American' interchangeably; however, the term 'black' may also reference peoples of African descent globally, including African and African Diaspora peoples such as Afro-Brazilians, Afro-Cubans, Haitians, Black British, Afro-Caribbeans, Dominicans, and Afro–Latin Americans or global peoples who self-identify politically as black.

The concept of transcultural ecological knowledge is offered to describe dynamic aspects of cultural contact and exchange, adaptive practices, and intergenerational transmissions of knowledge, taking into account the ecological interventions and unpredictable landscape transformations that result from these processes.

Throughout the chapter, three emergent themes for the study of the African Diaspora in Religion and Ecology are highlighted: the intersections of nature and race; the diversity of transatlantic Black identities and intra-diasporic religious pluralism;[9] and the possibilities and limitations of inheriting environmental racism as a proxy for the study of African American religions and ecology. Building on these themes, I conclude with recommendations for further study.

Marginality and Conflation of African Diaspora Religions within Religion and Ecology

The relatively rare attention to the categories "black religions", "African American religions", or "African Diaspora religions" within popular anthologies and edited volumes on Religion and Ecology reflects what historian of religion Charles Long has described as the invisibility of black religion in American religious history. Long asserts that many of the approaches in the study of American religions and non-Christian religions have rendered the religious reality of non-Europeans to a state of invisibility or addenda because religion is defined either as revealed Christianity and its institutions or as civil religion; thus functioning to justify the history of European immigrants.[10] Gaps in teaching resources are also evident in the neglect of African diasporic religions or black environmental thought as viable topics in many Religion and Ecology and Environmental Ethics syllabi.[11]

---

9. Of course, this chapter itself does not fully escape the US-centrism that is common in the field of Religion and Ecology; however, I recognize the need to expand research agendas to reflect other global geographies of religion.

10. Long, *Significations*, 162.

11. This statement reflects syllabi on the Religion and Ecology and environmental ethics from four syllabi project websites: The *AAR Syllabus Project*—Religion and Ecology, The *Forum on Religion and Ecology* syllabi page, *Wabash Center Internet Guide to Religion*: Religious Thought—Environmental Ethics—Religious Aspects, and the *Environmental Ethics Syllabus Project*, edited by Robert Hood.

When one reads the journals *Worldviews: Global Religions, Culture, and Ecology*, *Ecotheology*, and *Journal of Religion, Nature, and Culture*, the phrase "African American" is notably rare, and little evidence can be found of research concerning the African Diaspora. "Racism" and "environmental justice" are far more common, but these are not adequate substitutes for the study of diasporic religions and their environmental praxis.[12]

One need only consider the titles and content of the ten volume Religions of the World and Ecology series, edited by Mary Evelyn Tucker and John Grim to illustrate this point further.[13] While African Indigenous religions are included in the volume on 'Indigenous Traditions' and African American religious thought is represented in the 'Christianity and Ecology' volume, there are no chapters devoted to Religion and Ecology in the African Diaspora as it is more broadly conceived. Contributors Williams and Miller-Travis focus on public policy concerns and environmental justice praxis respectively, while Kalu focuses on development, environmental degradation, and indigenous African worldviews. Similarly, in Tucker's 2003 book *Worldly Wonder: Religions Enter into Their Ecological Phase*, religious pluralism, diversity, and multiculturalism are celebrated, but diasporic religions are absent from the dialogue. In Tucker's book, environmental racism is the only snapshot taken of Black life.

The edited volumes *This Sacred Earth*, edited by Roger S. Gottlieb; *Worldviews, Religion, and Ecology*, edited by Richard C. Foltz; and *Ecospirit* edited by Laurel Kearns and Catherine Keller include US African American scholars and address issues of environmental racism and ecological justice; however, these books do not delve deeply into the implications of the colonial origins of the analytical category of 'religion' and

12. Sadly, African American religions are not the only traditions treated marginally in Religion and Ecology. Mexican and Latin American religious traditions, for example, are also frequently missed in the Western/Indigenous and North/South geographical dichotomies. Although geographers like Toledo and Bartera-Bassols have contributed extensive research on ethnoecological practices, cosmological frameworks, and biodiversity among indigenous rural communities in Mexico, very little research has been done on what is happening to Mesoamerican ethnoecology and religious practices in the midst of contemporary labor migrations to the United States; estimated to represent over eleven million immigrants (Bartera-Bassols and Toledo, "Ethnoecology of the Yucatec Maya," 9–41).

13. See the Religions of the World and Ecology series edited by Mary Evelyn Tucker and John A. Grim.

the imperial practices of power that were part and parcel of the study of indigenous and diasporic African peoples. Other anthologies, such as *To Love the Wind and the Rain: African American Environmental History* edited by Dianne D. Glave and Mark Stoll; and *Restoring the Connection to the Natural World: Essays on the African American Environmental Imagination,* edited by Sylvia Mayer, do an excellent job of excavating African American environmental history and deconstructing social constructions of nature and race. In these cases, however, religion is ancillary to the main historical emphasis of these books and the study of African American religions is limited to the historical role of black Protestants in environmental activism. Lastly, encyclopedias and overviews of Religion and Ecology, such as Bron Taylor's *Encyclopedia of Religion, Nature, and Culture*; and Roger S. Gottlieb's *Oxford Handbook of Religion and Ecology* include essays on African diasporic religions, yet there are few cross-references between African Indigenous and African Diaspora religions.[14]

The limited attention to African diasporic religions and their conflations with environmental racism reveal unresolved interpretive issues, which primarily take two forms. In the first form, environmental racism becomes that which represents all black experiences and knowledge of the environment. In the second form, U.S. black churches become that which represents all expressions of African diasporic religiosities. Race becomes the silent partner for both of these conflations, as social constructions of race and the collective actions and conditions of racialized peoples are key components of American understandings of religions, environments, and nature. These conflations are predicated on a shortsighted view of environmental history, religious history in the Americas, and the legacies of complex, often contradictory race relations; resulting in the reduction of African American cultural relationships with the environment to either the environmental justice movement or to ecosystems of victimization and violence.

Several correctives are available to future research. One is to redirect research by asking: "How do race, religion, and environmentalism intersect currently and historically? How do religions respond to racial oppression and structural racism and mobilize for sustainability in politically progressive ways?" This calls for scholars to interrogate the meanings and political dynamics of racism in a globalized, 'colorblind,'

14. See Jenkins, "Religion and Ecology: A Review Essay," 7.

post-civil rights era.[15] Another corrective is to recognize environmental degradation as one of several forms of environmental injustice.[16] Geographer Laura Pulido, based on data from her research on urban development in Southern California, draws the conclusion that the historical processes of suburbanization and decentralization as means of securing white privilege are less obvious forms of racism.[17] Similarly, environmentalist and Islamic scholar Asghar Ali recognizes differential exposure to environmental racism among racial/ethnic groups, yet advocates shared responsibility to dismantle environmental injustice. Ali further explains, "Justice means that racism should not be conflated with other categories and thus made obscure and invisible but that it should be openly discussed with the full participation of all."[18]

Religion and Ecology needs to maintain caution against overdependence on outmoded epistemic foundations deeply rooted in nineteenth century evolutionist studies for the academic study of Indigenous cultures (formerly described as 'primitive' and 'emotional') and African Diasporic cultures (formerly described as 'deviant and inferior' or 'innately religious'). Religious scholars Talal Asad, Sam Gill, Tomoko Masuzawa, and Russell T. McCutcheon have each discussed the history and politics of the analytical categories 'religion' and 'world religion' in relation to the imposed emic perspectives, power relations, and social hierarchies implicitly contained within Western religious classification systems. Many African Diasporic religions, because of their unique social forms, may not demonstrate the universalized comparative features of social movements designated as 'world religions' and so often become marginalized or ignored within religious scholarship.

Thus, the 'world religions' approach to Religion and Ecology leaves much to be desired for the study of the African Diaspora. Approaches that assume cultural variations and encompass an understanding of complexity related to religious traditions practiced in different geographical contexts are more helpful for the study of diasporic religions, transnational identities and belongings, and multiple heritages. These approaches are characterized by caution and limitation; as anthropologist Steven

15. Winant, "Teaching Race and Racism in the Twenty-First Century," 14–22.

16. Bullard, "Environmental Justice Challenges," 34–35.

17. Pulido, "Rethinking Environmental Racism," 12–40.

18. Ali, "Conceptual Framework for Environmental Justice," 51–52.

Vertovec reminds us, no one framework can completely address our endeavors to examine, interpret, and re-imagine religion and diaspora.[19]

Diaspora, Ecology, and Africans in the Making of the Americas

One of the first questions concerning African American religions and ecology should be: "What happens to ecological knowledge and religious practices in migrations and diasporas?" The theoretical framework of diaspora has been employed for several decades to describe the dispersal and displacement of diverse African populations from Africa during the four centuries of the transatlantic slave trade. The word diaspora itself, traditionally associated with Jewish dispersions, is defined as "the means to scatter over or spread."[20]

In the forced migrations of Africans from the fifteenth to the nineteenth centuries, Africans became involuntary migrant populations to the Americas and the Caribbean. As migrants, African populations adapted their ecological practices to their new local biodiversity by revising their understanding of nature through (a) transported landscapes[21] (b) their own exploration and observation of the climate and environment and application of prior ecological knowledge, (c) their interactions and exchanges (including alliances, conflicts, intermarriages, and sexual violence) with indigenous Amerindian peoples and Europeans, (d) new knowledge they acquired as enslaved or indentured persons while doing coerced agrarian labor on plantations for the production of cash crops, and (e) their negotiation and survival of dominant, often anti-African social structures. Because of the dangerous risks these forced immigrants faced in trying to preserve their indigenous knowledge, many practices were covertly disguised or practiced "underground" in order to avoid violent persecution from slave owners or government officers.[22]

---

19. Vertovec, "Religion and Diaspora," 275–304.

20. Cohen's *Global Diaspora*; and Evans and Braziel's *Theorizing Diaspora* offer deeper analyses of diaspora as a theoretical framework.

21. Transported landscapes refer to those local forms of plant and animal life or local methods that were transported to different places by native peoples; or specimens transported by colonists, missionaries, scientists, and others back to European countries and to Britain. See Blair, "Transported Landscapes," 85–112.

22. Stewart, *Three Eyes for the Journey*, 92, 169.

While the history of settler impact on the ecologies of the Americas, India, Australia, and Africa have been well researched, the substantial impact of diasporic Africans on the environments of the 'New World' has been largely ignored. As descendants of the African Diaspora, blacks have inherited sociopolitical situations as well as cultural and oral traditions that often inform their current ecological attitudes and practices. Similar to indigenous Amerindian peoples, much of what was known by indigenous African peoples was transmitted inter-generationally through oral tradition and religious practices such as initiation rituals, seasonal celebrations, nature-based livelihoods, plant knowledge, and folk medicine. That knowledge has undergone innumerable transformations due to chattel slavery, ecological imperialism, anti-African and Afro-phobic attitudes of European settlers, industrialization, and urbanization.

It is important to recognize that the settler colonies of the New World were not just landscapes of domination; they were also landscapes of resistance and survival. The landscape legacies of Africans in the Americas have only recently been researched in ways that challenge inaccurate historical narratives. Recent research from cultural geographers Judith Carney and Robert A. Voeks reveals that diasporic Africans transformed the landscapes of the Americas not only for plantation agrarian economy, but also for self-sufficiency, survival, resistance, and identity.[23] European settlers often did not possess the agricultural knowledge to successfully cultivate and harvest crops such as rice and other staples. African migrants' prior sophisticated knowledge of rice cultivation gave them the capacity to contribute far more than brawn to the development of plantation societies in the Americas.[24] Transformed landscapes provided subsistence and resulted in the continuation of many of the foodways among Africans in the Americas.[25] Crops of African origin, such as peanuts (originally from Brazil and Peru and transported again during the Diaspora), coffee, okra, yams, black-eyed peas, pumpkins, sesame, watermelon, cucumbers, eggplant, and many others traveled with enslaved Africans over the Atlantic and have become foods that

23. Carney and Voeks, "Landscape Legacies of the African Diaspora," 139–52.

24. Littlefield, *Rice and Slaves*, 80.

25. The degree to which European settler societies relied on the agricultural expertise of forced African immigrants for the cultivation of cash crops such as rice and indigo indicates that African peoples with advanced agricultural knowledge and skills were highly sought.

many Americans now eat and enjoy.[26] Knowledge of the medicinal and ritual value of plants was also an important aspect of continuing African Indigenous religious practices.

For the most part, consideration of non-Western ecological knowledge is placed into the category of traditional ecological knowledge (TEK), which implies a systematic approach to understanding and interacting with one's environment based on cultural and practical applications built up over time and generations. TEK is often interrelated with indigenous traditions (spirituality, cosmology, and ethical principles), lifeways, and livelihoods. Activities such as land management, cultural understandings of landscapes and habitats, uses of natural resources, the transfer of intergenerational knowledge orally or through apprenticeship, medicinal uses of plants, and skills related to agriculture, horticulture, fishing, and wildlife are all associated with TEK. This approach to interacting with nature has been of particular interests in recent years to scholars because of its contributions to sustainable development and insights into natural processes and ecosystems. While once romanticized as the solution to Western disregard for and exploitation of nature, TEK has in more recent years received a more nuanced and multilayered treatment by researchers.

Studies of TEK tend to assume that indigenous populations have not been displaced or migrated to other continents in thousands of years, while they do recognize that indigenous peoples have experienced major changes due to processes of globalization, such as colonialism and modernization. Of course, not all peoples are so stable, and the insights of a diasporic culture do not fit neatly into the category of TEK. So, I offer the concept 'transcultural ecological knowledge' as a means to describe the interweaving of transposed adaptive practices that occur in the midst of migrations, diasporas, and flows of human-nature interactions. Transcultural ecological knowledge or TCEK, is the cumulative potential and practical knowledge of groups that currently or historically have been dispersed from an original homeland, displaced from one geographic area to another, or deterritorialized and have adapted and acquired additional knowledge that is then applied to alter or understand their secondary environment.

My use of the term "transcultural" relates the complexities of cultural plurality and exchange, including the power dynamics of such an

26. Harris, "Same Boat, Different Stops," 169–82.

exchange. Transculturation, a term introduced by Cuban anthropologist Fernando Ortiz speaks to the experiences of migrants as one that reflects not only a one-way conversion and deculturation, but as a multidirectional process of cultural adaptation. Some aspects of the second culture are only partially adopted, strategically performed in certain situations, or even resisted. Meant to counter the term "acculturation" as introduced by Polish anthropologist Malinowski, transculturation denotes not the replacement of one culture by another, but the creation of a third distinct culture, one in which traces of the two previous cultures (the newly evolving and the displaced primary) are maintained.[27] For Ortiz, the term transculturation was essential to understanding the history of Cuba and the Americas.

Analyzing the African Diaspora to the Americas with an attention to transculturation and power reveals that there is an active, not passive, contestation of culture, meaning and identity among peoples subjected to forced migration, slavery, coerced conversion, colonization, and ecological imperialism. Transcultural ecological knowledges are subjugated environmental epistemologies that merit serious attention from scholars of religion and environmental practitioners because they occupy and negotiate the spaces in-between indigenous and Western in Religion and Ecology discourse. Their presence reminds us that ecological perspectives and religious practices are not always respecters of nation-state boundaries or neat taxonomies.

The question of what happened to traditional African ecological knowledge during and after the African Diaspora to the Americas resulting from the trans-Atlantic slave trade has far reaching implications for traditional cultures and sustainable practices today, in part because global diasporas due to labor and economic shifts, wars, ecological degradation, and other reasons are on the rise. The complexities of displacement, migration, deterritorialization, transnational identities, and hybridity are an ongoing and recurring theoretical and practical challenge for Religion and Ecology.

How, then, should Religion and Ecology/Nature conceptualize and work with cultural traditions? Transcultural ecological knowledges bring to the fore the challenges and paradoxes real-world cultural and social practices pose for the field's idealist presuppositions, a point that has been poignantly argued by Sponsel (2005), Taylor (2005), and

27. Ortiz, *Contrapunteo cubano del tabaco y del azúcar,* 96–97.

Kalland (2005). Religion is more than beliefs and values, transcendence and essence; religion is also embodied knowledge that is situated in networks of 'relations, practices, and space/place'—both external and internal to religions.[28] Anthropologist and conservationist Michele Cocks has argued that culture "must be understood as a dynamic process of transcultural exchange with constant re-articulations of tradition resulting in the persistence of certain cultural practices amongst any group of people."[29] Persistent patterns of human practices are far more resilient than we'd like to admit; often involving destructive, constructive, and ambiguous performances of power, survival, and resistance. Potential solutions to the ecological crisis are therefore not solely dependent on moral and spiritual reform; solutions are also dependent on social and cross-cultural relationships. This somber reality accentuates the need for scholars and practitioners to exercise reflexivity within their research and community work.

Transatlantic Black Religious and Cultural Identities

The diversity of transatlantic Black religious traditions and the heterogeneity of black populations living within and traveling back and forth between various homelands and host lands creates "persistent tensions between the global and the local" and brings our attention to the spatiality of religion in addition to the multiple geographical contexts of religions.[30] In light of the complexity and contradictions of multiple and mixed historical diasporic encounters, a broadly inclusive and non-essentialist approach to black culture and religion is necessary. African diasporic religions require a nuanced research methodology that takes intra-diasporic religious pluralism and cultural difference, past and present degrees of translocalism, and conflicts and distinctions internal to transatlantic Black communities into consideration.

Black religion should not simply be conflated with black Christianity or even institutional religious forms. Furthermore, the functions and meanings that ritual, material culture, folk religion, popular religion, sacred space, divination or conjure, modes of religious expression such as dance, music, and new media play in the religiosity of African Americans,

---

28. Ivakhiv, "Religion, Nature and Culture: Theorizing the Field," 47–57.

29. Cocks, "Biocultural Diversity," 195.

30. Stump, *Geography of Religion*.

whether or not they are institutionally affiliated, reveals levels of diverse practices and locations of religion. Transnational Black immigrants living in the United States usually create their own sacred spaces to maintain a sense of shared culture, although some choose to express their religiosity with US racial/ethnic religious communities or join multicultural ones. Religious community itself can be an essential means by which immigrants navigate racial and cultural boundaries in the United States, especially as immigrants begin to encounter the combination of geographies of race and belonging and racializing processes expressed in different U.S. regions.[31]

The religious landscape of black communities is vast and multilayered. Although many diasporic Africans self-identify as Christian, there are also persons that identify with a variety of other faiths, including but not limited to Islam, Judaism, Buddhism, the Yoruba-Orisha tradition, Candomblé, Vodou, Santeria, and non-institutional forms such as black folk religion, nature-based spirituality, metaphysical traditions, civil religion, and postmodern religiosities. Changes in the transcontinental and transatlantic religious landscapes are also bringing about intensified global encounters *between* transatlantic Black religious and racial/ethnic groups. The United States, as a site of converging and overlapping diasporas and migrations, is the dwelling place of African diasporic communities from Europe, Canada, Mexico, Central America, South America, and the Caribbean as well as U.S. born African American communities. Not to be neglected is the growing presence of African-born immigrants within the United States or Africans of the New Diaspora. The interactions between African Indigenous and African Diaspora religions are not fixed or stuck in the past; diasporas are created by their homelands as much as they are creators of their homelands.[32]

Diasporic foodways, organic farming, and food access are a priority for several African diasporic religious groups.[33] Muslim African Americans, Black Hebrew Israelites, and Rastafari have dietary laws that have led them to choose alternative food supply sources—including food co-ops, cooperative agriculture and faith-based organic farming—in order to avoid the genetically modified and processed foods sold in many

31. Johnson, *Diaspora Conversions*, 2007.

32. Matory, *Black Atlantic Religion*, 16.

33. The data presented in this paragraph is the result of the author's participant observation and informal interviews at several sites within US African American communities in Chicago, Illinois, and Atlanta, Georgia.

grocery stores. The fruits and vegetables grown on their farms are sometimes made available to non-members in urban communities at a low cost as a way to foster good community relations and offset the negative impact of living in urban areas. Muslim African Americans groups in particular have been very outspoken in their rejection of cloned meats and genetically modified foods, and have actively supported black farmers in their land right struggles. With a more entrepreneurial response to desires for healthy living that focuses on vegetarian prepared "soul food," the Black Hebrew Israelites have established restaurants in several U.S. cities with large black populations. Broadly speaking, many African Americans have nutrition and wellness concerns that come out of a cultural view that health and disease are directly related to environmental factors and food intake.

The interrelationship between U.S. African American religious and civic environmentalism also becomes more apparent at the local level. For example, grassroots environmental justice organizations such as the Chicago-based non-profits Blacks In Green, The Center for Urban Transformation, and Faith In Place often count a 'faith base' of religious persons as active members. These advocates and activists participate in diverse faiths. Some religious groups have a long history of local involvement in environmental justice, for example Black Catholics and the Knights of Peter Claver[34] and the Nation of Islam.[35] Concurrently, environmental organizations like Green For All, GreenFaith, and Sustainable South Bronx also partner with other faith-based organizations to address local, regional, national, and global environmental concerns. Interorganizational cooperation and cross-institutional volunteerism for the purpose of mobilization for environmental activism are often overlooked in discussions on African American religious environmentalism.

The Limitations and Possibilities of Inheriting Environmental Racism for the Study of African Diasporic Religions

"How can we inherit that which did not belong to our ancestors?"
—Olabiyi B. Yai[36]

---

34. Washington, "'We've Come This Far by Faith,'" 195–208.
35. Akom, "Cities as Battlefields," 711–30.
36. Yai, "African Diasporan Concepts and Practice," 253.

Many Religion and Ecology scholars from various racial, ethnic and class backgrounds have built the foundation for the study of black religions and ecology on the themes of environmental racism and ecological justice. This has opened up spaces in the academy and in the public sphere upon which environmental abuses and concerns could be confronted, research could be conducted, and solutions sought in blighted and exploited communities through environmental activism. Themes of liberation and acts of ecological justice have enabled African Americans and people of many faiths and cultures to re-imagine their relationships to nature, humans, and animals; empowering many to work towards a just and sustainable future. However, this foundation has created other factors that narrow and essentialize what it means to be black and marginalize some forms and traditions of black religious practice. It has left blacks from multiple locales with a religious diversity and vitality that has been mediated through the lenses of dominant Western culture, nineteenth century evolutionist or romanticist theories of religion, and US Black Protestantism.

On the one hand, environmental racism and the struggle for ecological justice are imposed inheritances. They are the result of centuries of patterned exploitation of land, natural resources, and human labor as well as the result of Christian complicity with slavery and racism, ecological imperialism, and government-sanctioned expropriation of lands inhabited by cultural and racial/ethnic "Others." On the other hand, because of the deep history of slavery and segregation, specifically in the United States, environmental injustice has been a historic factor in the shaping of black environmental attitudes and values that are both sustainable and non-sustainable. Environmental racism remains a structural and existential component of black life. Racism is not, however, the totalizing defining cornerstone of African diasporic religious practices or cultural engagements with nature.

The "embodied embedded memory of slavery";[37] including the internal contradictions of white Christian complicity with slavery and segregation, ongoing racist practices, and the ethical disparities of daily intercultural encounters, have been a source of tension in racial relations and a catalyst for reimagining black life religiously, ideologically, and politically. When the weight of the entanglement of race, religion and imperialism became increasingly more urgent during the 1960's,

37. Harding, "E a Senzala: Slavery, Women, and Embodied Knowledge," 12.

as manifested in the rhetoric of the Civil Rights movement, the Black Power movement, and the Black Arts movement, U.S. North American blacks chose a variety of responses. The continuum of responses to negotiations of transatlantic Black identities and belongings, what I call the intra-diasporic dilemma, has included re-interpretations of Christian thought that reject Eurocentrism; the re-Africanizing of collective community rituals and festivals; converting to other faiths such as Islam, Judaism, Buddhism; practicing New World African religions; Black Humanism; cultivating cultural nationalism and Afrocentric thought, out of which emerged the popular ritual celebration Kwaanza; relying on black folk traditions and creative arts; alternative spirituality; multiple belonging; new religious movements; civil religion; and participating in racial justice institutions that address economic, political, and social issues and affirm racial/ethnic identity. None of these responses are new; they are re-articulations and innovations that our ancestors imparted for survival, agency, wisdom, well-being, and joy. They are all positions of historical and potential politicization of environmental concerns.

Are there still grounds for optimism without the reduction of all black environmental experiences and knowledge to environmental racism? One way forward is to search for common ground somewhere between saving polar bears and struggles for clean air. This means creating a strategic middle ground between subaltern environmentalism (the environmental justice movement) and mainstream environmentalism.[38] Historic interests, such as conservation and nature preservation, need to be balanced with the inclusion of other interests, such as toxic work and living conditions, poverty, and urban environmental concerns. Progressive politics within religious environmentalism will require new patterns of cultural encounter and interaction based on inconvenient truths, respect, and reciprocity. Less hierarchical forms of organization could assist in creating spaces for democratic forms of decision-making that include groups which have been previously marginalized. Finally, by freeing ourselves from the fore-mentioned conflations and binaries, we may better confront both racism and exploitation and pursue more effective strategies for environmental sustainability and biocultural diversity.

The "greening" of our traditions also calls for a rethinking, re-reading, and re-embodiment of the ethics and politics of religious environmentalism. There are cross-cultural barriers in the way of building

38. Pulido, *Environmentalisn and Economic Justice*, 209.

sustainable communities and cultivating interfaith environmental mobilization. The question of whether or not whites can betray their own color and class privilege in their daily dealings with people of color and genuinely incorporate anti-racism politics into their eco-theological and ethical identities is still unanswered. Some scholars have worked hard to meet this challenge while others have remained silent.[39] Conversely, the question of whether or not blacks will view the environmental crisis as solely a "white man's burden," as a strategy for whites to avoid racial difference and secure privilege, or as a mere distraction from the struggle against racial injustice is also still unanswered. Some blacks engage in the type of cross-cultural coalition building that can bring more cultural diversity to established predominately-white environmental organizations while others choose the increased autonomy of maintaining their own grassroots organizations. The right to environmental self-determination and the pursuit of higher levels of interreligious and minority membership in already-established networks are not mutually exclusive strategies for environmental justice praxis.

Recommendations for Further Study

Understudied Religious Traditions and Ecology

Essays concerning African diasporic traditions and ecology included in Religion and Ecology anthologies thus far have been sparse, mostly normative and constructive, and predominantly Protestant Christian. Questions of conceptual frameworks, strategies, and methodologies in the study of Religion and Ecology in the African Diaspora remain mostly underdeveloped. Representative essays from Black liberation theology and Womanist religious thought are commendable starting points; however, they are only part of the whole to be explored on the subject. Other Christian traditions (Catholic, Spiritualist, Evangelical, or Pentecostal) are ripe for further exploration. Moreover, Islam, Judaism, Buddhism, pragmatist philosophy, Black Humanism, and African diasporic religions also provide perspectives that take ecology and reciprocity and reverence of the Earth seriously. Spiritual practices among diasporic peoples, such as contemplation with nature, being in the moment, deep

39. Cone, "Whose Earth Is It, Anyway?" 30. For a similar argument, see also Gottlieb, "Religious Environmentalism in Action," 467–509.

breathing, fishing, gardening, animal companionship, and prayer often reveal pragmatic environmental principles and sustainable practices. Music, religious visual culture, dance, folklore, film/media, and material culture provide significant entry points for research. Natural sacred places, such as lakes, rivers, woodlands, mountains, parks, gardens, and even farms are sites that shape racial and cultural identity.

Further study of black women and religion in the context of the African Diaspora will substantially advance understandings of gender and environmental justice, but also of religion and transcultural ecological knowledges more broadly. Everyday religious and ecological practices, rituals, performances, and negotiations of power related to race/ethnicity, religion, class, sexuality, nationality, citizenship, age, and geography are factors that influence the shape of black women's participation in religious environmentalism and the extent to which religious and ecological knowledge are effectively transmitted inter-generationally. In many African Diaspora communities, women have traditionally functioned as cultural bearers of knowledge, a role that has been defended by both conservative and progressive ideologies. The study of women's ways of networking and organizing for community work, within and across nation-state borders and racial/ethnic identities, could potentially illuminate pathways from local environmental activism to more formal transnational environmental politics.

Environmental Advocacy in African American Communities

Resources for ecological practice are already available within African diasporic cultures, so that an overarching effort towards transformative practice may not need to focus on the greening and reforming of African American religious traditions. Culturally conscious efforts towards environmental literacy and advocacy could focus on recovering and reinventing cultural heritage, invigorating intergenerational storytelling and knowledge sharing, and broadening conceptual boundaries for nature-based forms of religiosity. By enhancing existing relationships between religious and civic environmentalism and creating spaces for marginalized voices, untapped potential for environmental advocacy and collaboration can be more fully developed.

Methodology and Methods

"Religion" and "ecology" as concepts are not ahistorical or value-neutral. Historical ecology and African Diaspora studies are valuable in assessing how place, diaspora, and migration relate to changes in ecological knowledge, creative innovation in rituals, and landscape transformation. The insider/outsider problem must be reconsidered in light of religious scholars projecting their own ideological positions, research interests, and intercultural assumptions onto black people, black faiths, and black environmentalisms. African Diaspora traditions and environmental practices should be studied as convergences and emergences and for the meanings they have for their participants, not as imitations of Euro-American religious traditions or oversimplified syncretisms, and not as if their forms automatically correspond with Western theological categories.[40]

Case studies, spatial and temporal analyses that take transtemporal and translocative actions into account,[41] and oral histories are potentially fruitful methods of investigation. Qualitative methods also offer a means to illuminate the voice and meanings of religious participants and derive analytical categories from Black Atlantic diaspora groups as much as possible rather than impose empirical categories. Systems approaches, such as ecology of religion, geography of religion, or spiritual ecology, may be better research methodologies than religious environmentalism for the study of some African Diaspora religions, such as Rastafari in Jamaica, who view landscapes as sacred sites and practice deep ecology.

In drawing from the theories and methods from multiple disciplines, I have argued in this essay that Religion and Ecology has much to learn from further engagement with African diasporic traditions. The mix of continuities and discontinuities of traveling and transformed African religions and indigenous ecological practices is not an isolated case by any means; all religions and ecologies experience change, mutability, and multiformity. Does the inclusion of diasporic religions, transnational identities, and transcultural ecological knowledge into Religion and Ecology discourse challenge traditional sensibilities concerning the 'religious' and assumptions of single locale, non-hybrid environmental thought and practices? I hope so. Our future engagement in dialogues

40. Fauset, *Black Gods of the Metropolis*; Washington, *Black Sects and Cults*; Long, *Significations*; West and Glaude, *African American Religious Thought*.

41. Tweed, *Our Lady of the Exile*, 95.

concerning the study of Religion and Ecology in the African Diaspora may assist all of us in turning up new soil on old ground.

Bibliography

Akom, A. A. "Cities as Battlefields: Understanding How the Nation of Islam Impacts on Civic Engagement, Environmental Racism, and Community Development in a Low Income Neighborhood." *International Journal of Qualitative Studies in Education* 20 (2007) 711–30.

Ali, Asghar. "A Conceptual Framework for Environmental Justice based on Shared but Differentiated Responsibilities." In *Global Citizenship and Environmental Justice*, edited by Tony Shallcross and John Robinson, 41–77. At the Interface / Probling the Boundaries 17. Amsterdam: Rodopi, 2006.

Asad, Talal. *Genealogies of Religion: Discipline and Reasons of Power in Christianity and Islam.* Baltimore: Johns Hopkins University Press, 1993.

Bartera-Bassols, Narciso, and Victor M. Toledo. "Ethnoecology of the Yucatec Maya: Symbolism, Knowledge and Management of Natural Resources." *Journal of Latin American Geography* 4 (2005) 9–41.

Bhattacharyya, Gargi et al. *Race and Power: Global Racism in the Twenty-First Century.* London: Routledge, 2002.

Blair, Ruth. "'Transported Landscapes' Reflections on Empire and the Environment in the Pacific." In *Five Emus to the King of Siam: Environment and Empire*, edited by Helen Tiffin, 85–112. Cross/Cultures 92. Amsterdam: Rodopi, 2007.

Bullard, Robert D. "Environmental Justice Challenges at Home and Abroad." In *Global Ethics and Environment*, edited by Nicholas Low, 33–41. London: Routledge, 1999.

Carney, Judith A., and Robert A. Voeks. "The Landscape Legacies of the African Diaspora in Brazil." *Progress in Human Geography* 27 (2003) 139–52.

Chandler, Nahum D. "The Figure of W. E. B. Du Bois as a Problem for Thought." *CR: The New Centennial Review* 6, (2002) 29–55.

———. "Of Exorbitance: The Problem of the Negro as a Problem for Thought." *Criticism* 50 (2008) 345–410.

Cocks, Michelle. "Biocultural Diversity: Moving beyond the Realm of 'Indigenous' and 'Local' People." *Human Ecology* 34 (2006) 185–200.

Cohen, Robin. *Global Diasporas: An Introduction.* Global Diasporas. Seattle: University of Washington Press, 1997.

Cone, James H. "Whose Earth Is It, Anyway?" In *Earth Habitat: Eco-Injustice and the Church's Response*, edited by Dieter Hessel and Larry Rasmussen, 23–32. Minneapolis: Fortress, 2001.

Du Bois, W. E. B. *The Souls of Black Folk.* 1903. Boston: Bedford Books, 1997

Fauset, Arthur Huff. *Black Gods of the Metropolis: Negro Religious Cults of the Urban North.* Philadelphia: University of Pennsylvania Press, 2002.

Foltz, Richard C., editor. *Worldviews, Religion, and Ecology: A Global Anthology.* Belmont, CA: Wadsworth, 2003.

Gabriel, Satyananda. "The Continuing Significance of Race: An Overdeterminist Approach to Racism." *Rethinking Marxism: A Journal of Economics, Culture & Society* 3:3 (1990) 65–78.

Gill, Sam. "The Academic Study of Religion." *Journal of the American Academy of Religion* 62 (1994) 965–75.

Glave, Diane D., and Mark Stoll, editors. *To Love the Wind and the Rain: African Americans and Environmental History.* Pittsburgh: University of Pittsburgh Press, 2006.

Gottlieb, Roger S. "Religious Environmentalism in Action." In *The Oxford Handbook of Religion and Ecology,* edited by Roger S. Gottlieb, 467–509. Oxford: Oxford University Press, 2006.

———, editor. *This Sacred Earth: Religion, Nature, Environment.* 2nd ed. New York: Routledge, 2004.

Harding, Rachel E. "E a Senzala: Slavery, Women, and Embodied Knowledge in Afro-Brazilian Candomblé." In *Women and Religion in the African Diaspora: Knowledge, Power, and Performance,* edited by R. Marie Griffith and Barbara Diane Savage, 3–18. Lived Religions. Baltimore: John Hopkins University Press, 2006.

Harris, Jessica B. "Same Boat, Different Stops: An African Atlantic Culinary Journey." In *African Roots/American Cultures: Africa in the Creation of the Americas,* edited by Shelia S. Walker, 169-182. Lanham, MD: Rowman & Littlefield, 2001.

Hucks, Tracey E. "'I Smoothed the Way, I Opened Doors': Women in the Yoruba-Orisha Tradition of Trinidad." In *Women and Religion in the African Diaspora: Knowledge, Power, and Performance,* edited by R. Marie Griffith and Barbara Diane Savage, 19–36. Lived Religions. Baltimore: John Hopkins University Press, 2006.

Ivakhiv, Adrian. "Religion, Nature and Culture: Theorizing the Field." *Journal for the Study of Religion, Nature, and Culture* 1 (2007) 47–57.

Jenkins, Willis. "Religion and Ecology: A Review Essay on the Field." *Journal of the American Academy of Religion* (2009) 1–11.

Johnson, Paul Christopher. *Diaspora Conversions: Black Carib Religion and the Recovery of Africa.* Berkeley: University of California Press, 2007.

Kalland, Arne. "The Religious Environmentalism Paradigm." In *Encyclopedia of Religion and Nature,* edited by Bron Raymond Tayor et al., 2:1367–71. London: Thoemmes Continuum, 2005.

Kearns, Laurel, afnd Catherine Keller. *Ecospirit: Religions and Philosophies for the Earth.* Transdisciplinary Theological Colloquia. New York: Fordham University Press, 2007.

Littlefield, Daniel C. *Rice and Slaves: Ethnicity and the Slave Trade in Colonial South Carolina.* Urbana: University of Illinois Press, 1991.

Long, Charles H. *Significations: Signs, Symbols, and Images in the Interpretation of Religion.* Minneapolis: Fortress, 1986.

Lowenthal, David. "Empires and Ecologies: Reflections on Environmental History." In *Ecology and Empire: Environmental History of Settler Societies,* edited by Tom Griffiths and Libby Robin, 229–35. Seattle: University of Washington Press, 1997.

Lucal, Betsy. "Oppression and Privilege: Toward a Relational Conceptualization of Race." *Teaching Sociology* 24 (1996) 245–55.

Masuzawa, Tomoko. *The Invention of World Religions: Or, How European Universalism Was Preserved in the Language of Pluralism.* Chicago: University of Chicago Press, 2005.

Matory, J. Lorand. *Black Atlantic Religion: Tradition, Transnationalism, and Matriarchy in the Afro-Brazilian Candomblé.* Princeton: Princeton University Press, 2005.

Mayer, Sylvia, editor. *Restoring the Connection to the Natural World: Essays on the African American Environmental Imagination.* Hamburge: LIT 2003.

Nesheim, Ingrid et al. "What Happens to Traditional Knowledge and Use of Natural Resources When People Migrate?" *Human Ecology* 34 (2006) 99–131.

Ortiz, Fernando. *Contrapunteo cubano del tabaco y del azúcar.* Caracas: Biblioteca Ayacucho, 1978.

Pulido, Laura. *Environmentalisn and Economic Justice: Two Chicano Struggles in the Southwest.* Society, Environment, and Place. Tuscon: University of Arizona Press, 1996.

———. "Rethinking Environmental Racism: White Privilege and Urban Development in Southern California." *Annals of the Association of American Geographers* 90 (2000) 12–40.

Raboteau, Albert J. "Response to Papers on: 'Survival, Resistance, and Transmission: New Historiographical and Methodological Perspectives for the Study of Slave Religion.'" *The North Star* 8 (2005). Online: http://www.princeton.edu/~jweisenf/northstar/volume8/raboteau.html.

Sansone, Livio et al. *Africa, Brazil, and the Construction of Trans-Atlantic Black Identities.* Trenton: Africa World, 2008.

Smith, Kimberly K. *African American Environmental Thought: Foundations.* American Political Thought. Lawrence: University Press of Kansas, 2007.

Sponsel, Leslie. "Spiritual Ecology: Towards an Overview in Anthropology and Beyond." *Annual Conference for the American Anthropological Association.* Washington DC, 2005.

Stewart, Dianne. *Three Eyes for the Journey: African Dimensions of the Jamaican Religious Experience.* Oxford: Oxford University Press, 2005.

Stewart, Mart A. "Slavery and African American Environmentalism." In *To Love the Wind and the Rain: African Americans and Environmental History,* edited by Diane D. Glave and Mark Stoll, 9–20. Pittsburgh: University of Pittsburgh Press, 2006.

Stuckey, P. Sterling. "Through the Prism of Folklore: The Black Ethos in Slavery." *The Massachusetts Review* (1968) 417–37.

Stump, Roger W. *Geography of Religion: Faith, Place, and Space.* Lanham, MD: Rowman & Littlefield, 2008.

Taylor, Bron Raymond et al., editors. *The Encyclopedia of Religion and Nature.* 2 vols. London: Thoemmes Continuum, 2005.

Tucker, Mary Evelyn, with Judith Berling. *Worldly Wonder: Religions Enter Their Ecological Phase.* The Second Master Hsüan Hua Memorial Lecture Chicago: Open Court, 2003.

Tucker, Mary Evelyn, and John A. Grim. *Religions of the World and Ecology.* 10 vols. Boston: Harvard University Press, 1997–2004.

Tweed, Thomas A. *Our Lady of the Exile: Diasporic Religion at a Cuban Catholic Shrine in Miami.* Religion in America Series. Oxford: Oxford University Press, 1997.

Vertovec, Steven. "Religion and Diaspora." In *Textual, Comparative, Sociological, and Cognitive Approaches,* edited by Peter Antes et al., 275–304. New Approaches to the Study of Religion 2. Berlin: de Gruyter, 2008.

Walker, Alice. *We Are the Ones We Have Been Waiting For: Inner Light in a Time of Darkness.* New York: New Press, 2006.

Washington, Jr., Joseph R. *Black Sects and Cults: The Power Axis in an Ethnic Ethic.* Garden City, NY: Anchor, 1973.

Washington, Sylvia Hood. "'We've Come This Far by Faith': Memories of Race, Religion, and Environmental Disparity." In *Echoes from the Poisoned Well: Global Memories of Environmental Injustice,* edited by Sylvia Hood Washington et al., 195–208. Lanham, MD: Lexington, 2006.

West, Cornel, and Eddie Glaude Jr. *African American Religious Thought: An Anthology.* Louisville: Westminster John Knox, 2003.

Winant, Howard. "Teaching Race and Racism in the Twenty-First Century: Thematic Considerations." In *The New Black Renaissance: The Souls Anthology of Critical African-American Studies,* edited by Manning Marable et al., 14–22. Boulder, CO: Paradigm, 2005.

Yai, Olabiyi B. "African Diasporan Concepts and Practice of the Nation and Their Implications in the Modern World." In *African Roots/American Cultures: Africa in the Creation of the Americas,* edited by Shelia S. Walker, 244–55. Lanham, MD: Rowman & Littlefield, 2001.

9

Saving the World (and the People in It, Too)

Religion in Eco-Justice and Environmental Justice

RICHARD R. BOHANNON II AND KEVIN J. O'BRIEN

Today ecology is in vogue and many people are talking about our endangered planet. I want to urge us to deepen our conversation by linking the earth's crisis with the crisis in the human family. If it is important
to save the habitats of birds and other species, then it is at least equally
important to save black lives in the ghettos and prisons of America.

—James Cone[1]

Environmental devastation stands as a single great crisis of our time,
surpassing and encompassing all others. It is preeminent because
it must be solved now, today, in this generation. Human hatred and
division and strife and poverty must be solved now, too—terrorism is
just one sign of this low-grade fever. But if they are not—and human
beings have been slow to solve them over the centuries—they will be
around for the next generation to solve. . . . the environmental crisis is
not an historic and eternal crisis. It is new, and it is a timed exam—a

1. Cone, "Whose Earth Is It, Anyway?" 32.

hundred years from now, our descendents will not be trying to solve the greenhouse effect. We will solve it, or it will be too late to solve.

—Bill McKibben[2]

The two quotations above share an important moral idea: environmental problems are related to social problems, the needs of human beings and the needs of ecosystems are connected. This is the primary thrust of James Cone's quote, and of the essay from which it is drawn, "Whose Earth Is It, Anyway?" where he urges those who work for racial justice to take environmental issues seriously and those who work for environmental sustainability to take racial issues seriously.[3]

Essayist and environmental leader Bill McKibben also works to relate these two spheres of attention, noting that environmental degradation and human injustices are both urgent crises. However, McKibben suggests that the former crisis encompasses and surpasses the latter, that environmental issues are more immediate and more comprehensive; he introduces the idea that, although these two sets of moral complaints are related, they may also compete for attention. Cone seems to anticipate the possibility of such a competition, as well, arguing that social justice for African Americans is "at least" as important as environmental conservation, leaving open the possibility that he finds social issues to be more urgent and encompassing. These quotes therefore introduce two ideas (1) social justice is relevant and connected to environmental issues, and (2) there is nevertheless a possibility of choices which must be made between them, between the crises in "the ghettos and prisons of America" and climate change.

Neither James Cone nor Bill McKibben writes within the academic field of Religion and Ecology, but both have been influential upon it. More importantly, in these brief quotes they outline a central question that must be asked deliberately, carefully, and repeatedly by scholars of Religion and Ecology: what does our work—explicitly motivated by an environmental impulse— have to do with the work of social justice, of

2. McKibben, *Comforting Whirlwind*, 15.

3. Unfortunately, conversations about race within Religion and Ecology have most often been limited to environmental justice and eco-justice. For a critique of this and a more nuanced discussion on race in Religion and Ecology, see Elonda Clay's chapter in this volume, above.

ensuring equality and flourishing for all human lives? Is it always possible to do scholarship that helps to save the world and the people in it, too, or must we sometimes face conflicts and distinctions between these two goals?

This chapter works to begin a conversation about these questions by arguing that there should be a clear distinction made between "eco-justice"—a popular moral principle based on faith that human and non-human interests can be synthesized—and "environmental justice"—the goal of a movement that has taken shape over the last three decades to defend equity and democracy in the distribution of environmental benefits and burdens among divergent human communities. Assuming that there is and must be a connection between these perspectives, we will nevertheless argue here that it is also vital to carefully attend to the distinctions between them.

Offering a brief history of the terms eco-justice and environmental justice, we will particularly attend to the different roles religion has played in each within the United States, which is a key reason we argue for a distinction between them.[4] The chapter then concludes by offering a methodological argument and raising some questions for the field of Religion and Ecology in light of the differences between eco-justice and environmental justice.

Eco-Justice: An Integrative Norm of Religion and Ecology

Integration has long been a central principle among scholars concerned with environmental issues. The holistic perspectives of ecology and cosmology, the ecumenical desire to rally distinct denominations and faith traditions around environmentalist causes, and the increasing awareness that the long litany of environmental and social ills have common

4. Of course, we can only begin to defend this claim in one chapter, and two limits to the scope of our argument are particularly important to note. First, we consider Religion and Ecology, eco-justice, and the environmental justice movement solely within the context of the United States (simply because that is our own context), and are open to the possibility that our conclusions would change if we changed our focus to other parts of the world. Second, we are focusing our attention on social justice as it refers to issues of class and race, which have been the primary objects of attention in the environmental justice movement. Many other justice issues—gender, sexuality, and disability, to name a few—also deserve consideration; their relationship to the environmental justice movement has and should continue to be studied. However, such work is beyond the scope of this chapter.

roots have led environmentalists to focus on bringing ideas, peoples, and solutions together. Given this emphasis on integration, it comes as no surprise that most writing about issues of social justice in Religion and Ecology has focused on their compatibility and coherence with environmental concerns.

To emphasize this connection between environmental and social issues, the term "eco-justice" emerged in the early 1970s among North American theologians and ethicists, almost all Christian. As Dieter Hessel writes, the term arose to "express a spiritually grounded moral posture of respect and fairness toward all creation, human and nonhuman."[5] Hessel himself played a role in this development, as Director of the Committee on Social Witness Policy for the US Presbyterian Church when it formed an "Eco-Justice Task Force." This group released a resource paper in 1989, *Keeping and Healing the Creation*, urging the church to recognize the "eco-justice crisis—the historic turning point at which the abuse of nature and the injustice to human beings place the future in grave jeopardy, both for natural systems and for human society." In response to this crisis, the paper argues, the church is called to reevaluate its life and mission to "fully incorporate the keeping and healing of the creation—the protection and restoration of the vulnerable and the oppressed, both human and nonhuman."[6] The emphasis in this document is on the synthesis of justice and ecology, a single mission of religious reform responding to both environmental degradation and human oppression.

William Gibson, the principle author of *Keeping and Healing the Creation*, also edited a journal focused on the subject and helped to found the Eco-Justice Project and Network.[7] Gibson's writings on the subject emphasize the holistic interconnections of humanity with the rest of nature, based on a theological belief in the coherence of God's creation. For example: "The love of earth and people is the eco-justice agenda—one agenda, because earth and people are one creation. To call it creation points to the Creator, the author, source, and sustainer of creation, who has a purpose for it, who relates to it lovingly, wills its well-being, and

---

5. Hessel, "Eco-Justice Ethics," lines 14–15.

6. Presbyterian Eco-Justice Task Force, *Keeping and Healing the Creation*, 3 & 60.

7. The journal began publication in 1981 under the title *The Egg: A Journal of Eco-Justice*, and its name was changed to *Eco-Justice Quarterly* in 1993. For Gibson's own history of the organization, the journal, and the core idea behind both, see Gibson, "Introduction to the Journey."

influences and beckons it toward its destiny and fulfillment."[8] Eco-justice is here an explicitly theological, Christian call for faithful striving toward an ideal of social justice that extends to the entirety of creation.[9]

Hessel also emphasizes the Christian theology of holism inherent in eco-justice: "In sharp contrast to modern church and culture, biblical thought poses no either/or choice between caring for people and caring for the earth. Covenant theology emphasizes that the way people treat the land is as important a sign of faithfulness as is the way they treat each other."[10] Justice, in this context, is about common cause, about recognizing the connections between people and the earth as consistent parts of the same system and therefore treating them with the same level of concern.

Hessel and Gibson's work are clear examples of what eco-justice was coined to represent and what it has come to mean in Religion and Ecology: a theological affirmation that social and environmental interests have common cause and can be addressed in united, complementary ways. Another example of this use of eco-justice comes in Roger Gottlieb's recent introductory text on religious environmentalism, *A Greener Faith*. Observing that "If we love redwoods and dolphins because they are kin, that does not mean we should cease to love our human kin as well," Gottlieb argues that Religion and Ecology entails a necessary commitment to eco-justice.[11] Any authentically religious environmentalism, Gottlieb argues, must integrate concern for human beings with concern for the interconnected natural world as a whole.

Gottlieb emphasizes that the interconnected ideal of eco-justice is a response to interconnected forms of oppression, and his primary example is environmental racism, the disproportionate burden that people

---

8. Gibson, "Creation and Liberation as a Continuing Story," 55.

9. Gibson is cautious to note that eco-justice is not "utopian" in a sense that is simplistic or idealistic, but he relates it to the kingdom of God as a model of that to which Christians should strive: "We do not imagine that the journey to eco-justice leads to a utopian future. Neither eco-justice nor the kingdom of God will come to more than partial realization in the historical drama. But we are called to participate in the drama, the continuing story, and to respond to our best discernment of God's project in our time" (Gibson, "Introduction to the Journey," 9)

10. Hessel, "Introduction": Hessel, "Eco-Justice Theology after Nature's Revolt."

11. Gottlieb, *Greener Faith*, 45. Gottlieb's own definition of eco-justice is very similar to Hessel's and Gibson's: on the same page, he defines "ecojustice" as "a prophetic vision of a social order in which both nature and people are treated with respect and care."

of color and the poor bear from the degradation of natural systems. He asserts: "It does not make sense to ask if the widespread siting of toxic incinerators in African American communities is an environmental, a racial, or a class issue. Clearly, it is all three."[12] As evidence for this claim, Gottlieb calls upon the environmental justice movement. Indeed, this movement is marshaled to demonstrate the main point of his book—that such an integrated effort is powerfully motivated by religious impulses. He cites the 17 "Principles of Environmental Justice" approved at the first National People of Color Environmental Leadership Summit in 1991, finding in them an example of the holistic thinking that characterizes religious environmentalism: "the integration of the spiritual and the political, concern for nature and for human beings."[13]

It is not difficult to see where Gottlieb finds such integration. The preamble to the Principles of Environmental Justice insists upon "our spiritual interdependence to the sacredness of our Mother Earth," and the first principle again "affirms the sacredness of Mother Earth." The third principle calls for responsible use of land and resources "in the interest of a sustainable planet for humans and other living things."[14] This is an integrative view, including humans with the natural world and linking social concerns to environmental, and it matches the core claim of eco-justice. Many in the field of Religion and Ecology have made the same connection as Gottlieb, using the environmental justice movement as an example of this perspective. However, before evaluating the accuracy of this connection, it is important to understand the environmental justice movement on its own terms.

Environmental Justice: A History of a Political Movement

As a term, environmental justice has a distinct history from eco-justice.[15] In 1978, polychlorinated biphenyl (PCB)—a recently-banned, highly toxic chemical—was illegally dumped along 240 miles of rural highway

---

12. Ibid., 49.

13. Ibid., 136.

14. First National People of Color Environmental Leadership Summit, "Principles."

15. That is, we are concerned here with the term *environmental justice*, and not with the history of the environmental justice *movement*, which many have successfully argued began well before the word originated in the 1980s. See the first chapter of Cole and Foster, *From the Ground Up*.

in North Carolina. A landfill for the chemicals was designated on former agricultural land in Warren County, North Carolina, a rural and predominantly black part of the state. The local community was outraged and organized a campaign of opposition, largely based in two churches, one Baptist and the other United Church of Christ (UCC). Dollie Burwell, a member of the latter congregation who was also an active member of the Southern Christian Leadership Conference (SCLC), became a leader of the protests.[16] This was not the first time toxic dumping had been protested in the U.S., and obviously not the first time the SCLC had been involved in community organizing, but these events proved to be a catalyst for environmental justice as a national, organized movement.

The UCC became institutionally involved in the struggles of Warren County in 1982, when church leaders began to lead protests, organizing congregations and integrating prayers and religious songs into their activism. In 1986, the denomination's Commission of Racial Justice also became involved, and one of their primary contributions was a national survey of every registered toxic waste facility in the United States placed in geographic correlation to local racial demographics. This survey led to a watershed document, first published in 1987 (updated in 1994 and again in 2007): *Toxic Wastes and Race.*[17] This was the first time a widespread survey dealt with the connections between race and environmental pollution, and the results were disturbing: even when socioeconomic factors are considered, race is the most statistically significant predictor in the siting of hazardous wastes. The 2007 update to this report used a more precise methodology, which solidified the earlier findings; in fact, the new methodology showed that in some instances racial disparities are *higher* than previously estimated.

Benjamin Chavis, executive director of the UCC's Commission in 1987, is credited with coining the term "environmental racism" to describe these findings, and *Toxic Wastes and Race* helped to define a movement dedicated to combating this trend, a movement for environmental justice.

What motivates *Toxic Wastes and Race* more than anything is a drive for data to prove the reality of environmental racism. This is explicit in the preface to the 1987 draft: "We realize that involvement in this type

16. See McGurty, *Transforming Environmentalism.*

17. For the 1994 edition, see Goldman and Fitton, *Toxic Wastes and Race Revisited*; and for the 2007 edition, see Bullard, et al. *Toxic Wastes and Race at Twenty.*

of research is a departure from our traditional protest methodology. However, if we are to advance our struggle in the future, it will depend largely on the availability of timely and reliable information."[18] Charles Lee, who directed the research for that draft, writes that it "marked a clear departure from [the UCC Commission for Racial Justice's] traditional protest and direct action activities."[19] The report's focus on data has been one of its key strengths: whether or not one shares the commitments or faith of the institution that sponsored *Toxic Wastes and Race*, the troubling facts it presents demand a response. This emphasis on data has become a characteristic of the environmental justice movement, the academic literature of which is prominently social scientific, with extensive quantitative analysis and carefully researched case studies on particular instances of environmental racism.[20]

Toxic Waste and Race was focused on data so as to equip grassroots organizations with a solid resource and to influence public policy. Thus, the 1987 draft concludes with four pages of policy and organizational recommendations; the first one, for instance, is for the "President of the United States to issue an executive order mandating federal agencies to consider the impact of current policies and regulations on racial and ethnic communities."[21] This proposal was an impressive success: seven years later, in 1994, President Bill Clinton signed executive order 12898, titled "Federal Actions To Address Environmental Justice in Minority Populations and Low-Income Populations," a landmark piece of government policy addressing environmental racism.[22] Inspired by such success, the environmental justice movement continues to thrive and struggle today to raise awareness about and overcome environmental racism.

One striking aspect of this history is the fact that religious and theological language is not explicit in the foundations and methods of the

18. United Church of Christ, Commission for Racial Justice, *Toxic Wastes and Race*, x.

19. Lee "Beyond Toxic Wastes and Race," 43.

20. See, for instance, Westra and Lawson, *Faces of Environmental Racism*; and Camacho, *Environmental Injustices, Political Struggles*.

21. United Church of Christ, Commission for Racial Justice, *Toxic Wastes and Race*, xv; see also 24.

22. While executive order 12898 is a significant piece of policy for the environmental justice movement, it has unfortunately not been well implemented or funded. There is evidence, for instance, that poor and minority communities have had *less* success in getting sites listed on the EPA's Superfund listing since the order was passed in 1994; see O'Neil, "Superfund."

environmental justice movement. The foundational study of the movement was commissioned by an office —or, in their current terminology, a "ministry"—of the United Church of Christ, and many of the activists involved came from churches; however, the rhetoric of this movement is not prominently Christian or explicitly religious. A close reading of *Toxic Wastes and Race* reveals no discussion of values, no mention of God or faith, and no emphasis on connecting the fight against injustice to the ministry of the church. This is a practical and political document, seeking to support community organizing and change public policy for the sake of social justice. While its authors and many who use it are clearly motivated by faith, only one small section offers suggestions to "churches," and they are lumped together with "community organizations" for a series of recommendations that offer no special attention to religious or environmental themes.[23] Were it not for a brief reference on the title page of the original 1987 document, readers would have little reason to assume that this is a church-sponsored report at all.[24]

Of course, we do not mean to suggest that the environmental justice movement has no religious elements or is not religiously motivated.[25] Just as the civil rights movement of the mid-twentieth century—out of which environmental justice arose[26]—had a strong religious foundation, many of the primary environmental justice actors and organizations are religious. However, this religious influence does not detract from the importance of noticing when the language of faith and theology is largely absent and secondary to other primary justifications. In the public face of environmental justice movement, even as it has been shaped by the work of the United Church of Christ and the black church, religion has not been prominent or explicit.

23. United Church of Christ, Committee for Racial Justce, *Toxic Wastes and Race*, 26–27.

24. The two updates since 1987 (see fn 17, above) likewise hold only minimal references to religious language or institutions.

25. Indeed, as the discussions, above, in chapters 1 and 2 of this volume make clear, definitions of *religion* in religious studies generally, and Religion and Ecology particularly, are far too broad and complicated to think one could easily declare any social or cultural movement free from religious motivation.

26. Bryant and Hockman argue that the environmental justice movement should be primarily understood as a child of the civil rights movement, and specifically cite the Black church as having "played a significant role" in the formation of the civil rights movement and (as its child) the environmental movement. See Bryant and Hockman, "Brief Comparison."

Instead, this movement emphasizes a political appeal to the rights of citizens to be free from the negative impacts of pollution and to have a participatory role in determining their own future and relationships to the nonhuman world. Defining what he calls the "environmental justice paradigm," Robert Melchior Figueroa highlights these two elements, identifying the core of the movement as "the interrelatednesss of distributive justice and political recognition."[27] Environmental justice understood this way emphasizes not the cosmic or theological interrelatedness of all beings, but rather the intersection of two types of social justice.

This philosophical and political characterization of environmental justice is well demonstrated by an analysis of the First National People of Color Environmental Leadership Summit in 1991. Six hundred delegates gathered at this meeting to share information and insight about the disproportionate burden poor and minority peoples feel from environmental degradation and the disproportionate environmental benefits enjoyed by wealthy people of European descent. Together, the delegates developed and affirmed the seventeen "Principles of Environmental Justice," which have been used ever since to summarize the moral impulse behind the movement.

As discussed above, Roger Gottlieb and others see these principles as most fundamentally about a sacred integration. It is possible to read them differently, however. The advocacy on behalf of "Mother Earth" that Gottlieb mentions occurs only at the beginning and end of the principles, and beyond these occurrences it is difficult to demonstrate that concern for nature is easily compatible with concern for human beings. The principles call for a series of rights for citizens, workers, and "all peoples," but they express very little direct concern for "nature," and repeatedly emphasize the rights and needs of human beings rather than "all creatures."

It is true that the final principle ends with a call for individuals to "make the conscious decision to challenge and reprioritize our lifestyles to insure the health of the natural world for present and future generations."[28] This is an important sentiment, and it clearly justifies environmental concern with an appeal to human health and flourishing. At no point, however, does it explicitly advocate on behalf of the nonhuman world for its own sake—the "health" of the nonhuman world is implicitly

27. Figueroa, "Evaluating Environmental Justice Claims," 360. For a different and more extensive discussion of the ways *justice* is and should be defined by the environmental justice movement, see Schlosberg, *Defining Environmental Justice.*

28. First National People of Color Environmental Leadership Summit, "Principles."

for the benefit of "present and future generations" of humans—and so it would not be fully accurate to claim that social ethics and environmental concerns are integrated in the Principles of Environmental Justice. These principles may be framed by a vague language of "sacredness," but they are fundamentally and overwhelmingly political, calling for human rights and human justice.

Distinguishing Environmental Justice and Eco-Justice

Two key distinctions between eco-justice and the environmental justice movement have emerged in looking at how the terms originated: First, the environmental justice movement often does not understand itself primarily and explicitly in religious terms, a fact which clearly distinguishes it from the largely Christian ideal of eco-justice. A second distinction is related: while eco-justice is a ideal of cosmic connection, environmental justice appeals to a more procedural and political set of concrete tasks.[29] Willis Jenkins captures both distinctions when he asserts that these two approaches to environmental issues have different standards of justice: "While the ethics of ecojustice evaluated right relations directly in reference to creation's own dignity, advocates of 'environmental justice' critiqued environmental degradations with respect to human dignity."[30] Eco-justice points toward a world of theological integration and harmony, while environmental justice points toward distributive equity and wider political participation.

Thus, eco-justice and environmental justice are different. The former uses theological claims to argue for a holistic ethic attending to all creation. The latter is academically dedicated to social scientific analysis, not explicitly animated by religious commitments, and driven primarily by a concern that our current practices promote inequity and the exclusion of some human citizens. Eco-justice is about bringing all of creation together as a locus of moral concern; environmental justice is about quantifying injustice against marginalized human communities and establishing a clean environment for human life. These are both admirable and important goals, but they are distinct.

29. The contrast here is reminiscent of arguments surrounding environmental philosophy and pragmatism; see Lucas Johnston and Samuel Snyder's chapter, above, in this volume.

30. Jenkins, *Ecologies of Grace*, 63.

To distinguish these two ideas is not to claim that they are utterly different or incompatible. On the contrary, both eco-justice and environmental justice emphasize that human interests cannot be separated from those of thriving ecosystems, and both seek to fundamentally transform contemporary industrialized societies in order to move toward healthier and more sustainable ways of life. However, as scholars and teachers of religion, we believe it is vital to notice the differences in the ways religion is used to support these ideas.[31] As participants in the field of Religion and Ecology, we believe it is vital to notice the scope and theological undergirding of the popular idea of eco-justice. Finally, as citizens concerned to respect the voices and perspectives of the oppressed and marginalized, we believe it is crucial to let the environmental justice movement define itself.

The distinction between eco-justice and environmental justice can be helpfully related to the distinction many environmental justice advocates have previously made between their movement and environmentalism more broadly. While the "Big 10" environmental organizations have been influenced to take issues of race, class, gender, and other forms of oppression seriously, many in the environmental justice movement and in mainstream environmentalism nevertheless continue to stress that "the two movements should not be merged. As important as finding ways to work together—and indeed imperative to being able to do so—is appreciating that both movements also, at times, have to work apart."[32] To protect "the environment" is not always the same thing as defending social and environmental justice, and the distinction between the two goals and the movements that support them is vitally important.

Sociologist Dorceta Taylor argues that environmentalists and environmental justice activists are divided in part by "different social locations" and therefore "have vastly different environmental experiences." While mainstream environmentalists "Might count lawmakers among their personal, political, or professional networks" and so are predisposed to take legal action, environmental justice activists tend to organize in community settings, and so "are more likely to use direct-action strate-

---

31. For one demonstration of the pedagogical value we see in drawing a strong distinction between eco-justice and environmental justice, see Bohannon and O'Brien "Environmental Justice and Eco-Justice."

32. Sandler and Pezzullo, "Conclusion," 313.

gies such as protests and rallies."[33] Furthermore, while both movements are founded on what Taylor calls "ecocentric" principles, environmental justice uniquely expands from those principles "to link environment and race, class, gender, and social justice concerns in an explicit framework" because the experiences and priorities of these activists push them to take these concerns seriously.[34]

Taylor's discussion of these two movements raises a third distinction to be made between environmental justice and eco-justice: the social location of its advocates. While environmental justice is a movement that emerged in inner cities and poor rural areas, eco-justice was developed by scholars, ministers, and academic theologians on university campuses. This suggests that differences between the two ideas are appropriate and inevitable, and it means that neither will be a complete and accurate ideal for all people for all time.

Recognizing this, Christian ethicist Larry Rasmussen has suggested that an understanding of justice compatible with an "earth ethic" cannot be completely defined by someone who is white and male, like himself, but rather must be learned from the environmental justice movement. A crucial lesson emerging from this movement, Rasmussen argues, is that environmentalists and ethicists who come from dominant and comfortable social status must be deeply cautious about suggesting that all human beings cause environmental degradation and suffer from the problems it creates. Environmental justice activists clearly teach "that not all are being poisoned equally, or even breathing the same air."[35] In light of this lesson, Rasmussen suggests, it is not enough for religious ethics to simply "extend moral community to the full community of life," to teach an ideal of eco-justice that straightforwardly includes human and nonhuman creatures. Ethicists must also attend to the concrete realities of the oppressed human beings who suffer poverty and cruelty.[36] To truly embrace "eco-justice" and seek a holistic and comprehensive view of environmental degradation and social injustice, we must step outside of the sphere of those who advocate eco-justice and also learn from those who seek environmental justice.

---

33. Taylor, "Rise of the Environmental Justice Paradigm," 509-10.

34. Ibid., 541–42.

35. Rasmussen, "Environmental Racism and Environmental Justice," 8.

36. Ibid., 22.

Those of us in Religion and Ecology who do not come from oppressed communities must be cautious about claiming that we can fully understand or summarize the interests and ideas of environmental justice activists, and we must allow these activists to speak for themselves. Those of us who care about the environment and come from privileged social positions and secure economic standing have something to learn about justice from those who have been marginalized and oppressed. Along these lines, as white, heterosexual males who work in the field of Religion and Ecology and do not live in communities under unique environmental threats, the authors of this chapter feel it is important to propose that our field pay rigorous attention to environmental justice on its own terms. Even those of us who advocate eco-justice must acknowledge that there is considerable work left to do to take the struggles of marginalized peoples seriously.

More broadly, when environmental justice advocates stress that their movement is not the same as environmentalism, they offer a lesson to advocates of eco-justice: it is not always pragmatic and may not always be possible to advocate for every worthy cause simultaneously, and the social location of an activist or scholar will influence which concerns are most prominent within a given context. Eco-justice may give those of us who share its theological claims and foundations a hope and a vision of an integrated world in which "creation" is united and whole, but this hope cannot blind us to the difficult and real choices that must be made in our world today. For this reason, it is vital to recognize that eco-justice and environmental justice have different approaches to religion, different goals, and emerge from different social locations.

Religion and Ecology, Eco-Justice, and Environmental Justice: A Methodological Argument

To recognize the distinction between environmental justice and eco-justice is more than just semantic pickiness; it is a call for caution. Advocates of eco-justice should work to understand the environmental justice movement on its own terms, and should not simplistically assume that their work will be compatible with the concerns of those who suffer environmental racism or the marginalized and oppressed more generally. Scholars in Religion and Ecology should make links between human and environmental interests, but should be careful and explicit about whether they approach this linkage through the lens of eco-justice by emphasizing the basic harmony of all creation or environmental justice by seeking social change to empower oppressed peoples.

The quotations that began this chapter emphasize why we feel this distinction is so important. When he notes that saving "black lives in the ghettos and prisons of America" is "at least equally important" as saving "the habitats of birds and other species," James Cone clearly demonstrates an environmental justice perspective, recognizing the fundamental connections between human beings and the natural world but primarily emphasizing the importance of human well-being and the particular needs of oppressed human populations. Cone implies that there may be times when we are forced to choose: will we devote our energies to helping the non-human environment or to ensuring greater justice for racial minorities? The two projects may ultimately be linked, but the limited energy and time of any one person inevitably means that we cannot do it all. As an advocate for environmental justice, Cone has chosen to emphasize the needs and interests of oppressed human beings. Those of us who would make a different choice should be prepared to justify and explain it.

In contrast to Cone, Bill McKibben seems to think from the perspective of eco-justice, affirming the holistic integrity of creation and the common roots of its destruction when he writes that "environmental devastation stands as a single great crisis of our time, surpassing and encompassing all others." From his perspective, the most urgent problem is the most universal and dangerous: the degradation of the global environment upon which all human beings and all other living creatures depend. McKibben shows that it is possible to emphasize a holistic attention to the whole earth, to see social justice as one subsidiary claim within a larger and broader goal. Those of us who disagree with him, and seek to pay more focused and narrow attention to the needs of particular human communities while the global environment is degraded, should be prepared to justify and explain that decision.

It is worth emphasizing once more that this chapter does not advocate a return to the days when social justice and environmental concerns were perceived as unrelated and irrelevant to each other. Both environmental justice and eco-justice represent vital movements demonstrating that human society cannot be separated from its environmental contexts. However, scholarship will be able to move forward more robustly if it distinguishes between the claims of eco-justice ethics and the environmental justice movement, without necessarily forcing an absolute choice between them. Religion and Ecology is a field about integration, and it is important that scholars in this field continue to hope that these interests can be integrated, that we can contribute in some small way toward saving the world and the people in it, too. However, unless we distinguish between the ideals of environmental justice and eco-justice, we will not be able to have an honest conversation about whether that is truly possible or how we should respond in situations where it is not.

Bibliography

Bohannon, Richard, and Kevin J. O'Brien. "Environmental Justice and Eco-Justice." In *Grounding Religion: A Field Guide to Religion and Ecology*, edited by Whitney Bauman et al., 163–80. New York: Routledge, 2010.

Bullard, Robert D. et al. *Toxic Wastes and Race at Twenty: Grassroots Struggles to Dismantle Environmental Racism in the United States*. Cleveland: United Church of Christ Justice and Witness Ministries, 2007.

Bryant, Bunyan, and Elaine Hockman. "A Brief Comparison of the Civil Rights Movement and the Environmental Justice Movement." In *Power, Justice, and the Environment: A Critical Appraisal of the Environmental Justice Movement*, edited by David Naguib Pellow and Robert J. Brulle, 23–36. Urban and Industrial Envrionments. Cambridge: MIT Press, 2005.

Camacho, David E., editor. *Environmental Injustices, Political Struggles: Race, Class, and the Environment*. Durham: Duke University Press, 1998.

Cole, Luke W., and Sheila R. Foster. *From the Ground Up: Environmental Racism and the Rise of the Environmental Justice Movement*. Critical America. New York: New York University Press, 2001.

Cone, James H. "Whose Earth Is It, Anyway?" In *Earth Habitat: Eco-Injustice and the Church's Response*, edited by Dieter T. Hessel and Larry L. Rasmussen, 23–32. Minneapolis: Fortress, 2001.

Figueroa, Robert Melchior. "Evaluating Environmental Justice Claims." In *Forging Environmentalism: Justice, Livelihood, and Contested Environments*, edited by Joanne Bauer, 360–76. Armonk, NY: Sharpe, 2006.

First National People of Color Environmental Leadership Summit. "The Principles of Environmental Justice." Online: http://www.ejnet.org/ej/principles.html/.

Gibson, William E. "Creation and Liberation as a Continuing Story." In *Eco-Justice—The Unfinished Journey*, 53–68. Albany: State University of New York Press, 2004.

———. "Introduction to the Journey." In *Eco-Justice—The Unfinished Journey*, 1–12. Albany: State University of New York Press, 2004.

Goldman, Benjamin A., and Laura J. Fitton. *Toxic Wastes and Race Revisited: An Update on the 1987 Report on the Racial and Socioeconomic Characteristics of Communities with Hazardous Waste Sites*. Washington DC: Center for Policy Alternatives, 1994.

Gottlieb, Roger S. *A Greener Faith: Religious Environmentalism and Our Planet's Future*. Oxford: Oxford University Press, 2006.

Hessel, Dieter T. "Introduction: Eco-Justice Theology after Nature's Revolt." In *After Nature's Revolt: Eco-Justice and Theology*, 1–20. Minneapolis: Fortress, 1992.

———. "Eco-Justice Ethics." *Forum on Religion and Ecology* 2007. Online: http://fore.research.yale.edu/disciplines/ethics/eco-justice.html/.

Jenkins, Willis. *Ecologies of Grace: Environmental Ethics and Christian Theology.* Oxford: Oxford University Press, 2008.

Lee, Charles. "Beyond Toxic Wastes and Race." In *Confronting Environmental Racism: Voices from the Grassroots*, edited by Robert D. Bullard, 41–52. Boston: South End, 1993.

McGurty, Eileen. *Transforming Environmentalism: Warren County, PCBs, and the Origins of Environmental Justice.* New Brunswick, NJ: Rutgers University Press, 2007.

McKibben, Bill. *The Comforting Whirlwind: God, Job, and the Scale of Creation.* Cambridge: Cowley, 2005.

O'Neil, Sandra George. "Superfund: Evaluating the Impact of Executive Order 12898." *Environmental Health Perspectives* 115 (2007) 1087–93.

Presbyterian Eco-Justice Task Force. *Keeping and Healing the Creation: A Resource Paper.* Louisville: Committee on Social Witness Policy of the Presbyterian Church (USA), 1989.

Rasmussen, Larry L. "Environmental Racism and Environmental Justice: Moral Theory in the Making?" *Journal of the Society of Christian Ethics* 24 (2004) 3–28.

Sandler, Ronald, and Phaedra Pezzullo. "Conclusion: Working Together and Working Apart." In *Environmental Justice and Environmentalism: The Social Justice Challenge to the Environmental Movement*, edited by Ronald Sandler and Phaedra Pezzullo, 309–20. Urban and Industrial Environments. Cambridge: MIT Press, 2007.

Schlosberg, David. *Defining Environmental Justice: Theories, Movements, and Nature.* Oxford: Oxford University Press, 2007.

Taylor, Dorceta E. "The Rise of the Environmental Justice Paradigm: Injustice Framing and the Social Construction of Environmental Discourses." *American Behavioral Scientist* 43 (2000) 508–80.

United Church of Christ, Commission for Racial Justice. *Toxic Wastes and Race in the United States: A National Report on the Racial and Socio-Economic Characteristics of Communities with Hazardous Wastes Sites.* New York: Public Data Access, 1987.

Westra, Laura, and Bill E. Lawson. *Faces of Environmental Racism: Confronting Issues of Global Justice.* 2nd ed. Studies in Social, Political, and Legal Philosophy. Lanham, MD: Roman & Littlefield, 2001.

10

Religion and Ecology on the Ground

"Practice" and "Place" as Key Concepts

BRIAN G. CAMPBELL

" Practice" and "place" are two increasingly important concepts in the study of Religion and Ecology. These buzzwords serve as markers for several interlocking trends in the field, including 1) the incorporation of empirical and ethnographic methods; 2) attention to local, particular places, cases and contexts; 3) focus on lived practices; and 4) concern for the practical implications of our scholarship. These are signs of the maturing of the field. As our work grows in its breadth and diversity, we also recognize the need for greater depth and specificity, for attention to particular practices and places.

In this chapter, I examine the turn to practice and place within Religion and Ecology scholarship, and I suggest ways this trend holds promise for how we approach our research and teaching. Because these concepts are used so widely, they can serve as bridges between the multiple disciplines and discourses in the field, a shared vocabulary that invites conversation. These terms can also serve to mask real differences. In this chapter, I survey some of the ways these terms have been used in recent work within Religion and Ecology, then compare these with broader trends in scholarship on practices and place. In this context, I argue for approaches that focus attention firmly on the local and also the global, and approaches that foreground issues of power and difference.

Our attention to particular contexts cannot be a retreat from the broader world. The "everyday life" and "lived experience" we study are always situated within social and material structures that are powerful in part because we view them as distant or take them for granted.

Place and Practice within Religion and Ecology

Three recent monographs exemplify the emerging attention to practice and place within Religion and Ecology: Sarah McFarland Taylor's *Green Sisters: A Spiritual Ecology*, Rebecca Kneale Gould's *At Home in Nature: Modern Homesteading and Spiritual Practice in America*, and Adrian Ivakhiv's *Claiming Sacred Ground: Pilgrims and Politics at Glastonbury and Sedona*.[1] These texts reflect the spread of diverse cultures and practices of Religion and Ecology "on the ground." They also demonstrate a key shift among scholars toward the ethnographic study of particular places and practices, one key direction of expansion of the field beyond the questions of worldview and anthropocentrism raised by Lynn White.[2]

Taylor, Gould and Ivakhiv each reflect at length on the value of ethnographic research and its implications for broader methodological and theoretical issues in the field. These works model ethnography as a partnership with the people and places we study, and recognize that in such work, we are always negotiating differences of power and knowledge. Taylor and Gould situate themselves among the historians of religion in America engaged in the study of "lived religion," examining particular constellations of everyday religious practice. This focus on lived religion reflects a commitment to take seriously communities that have often been ignored by scholars focused on intellectual and institutional history: women, ethnic minorities, children, the working class, and those not affiliated with traditional religious communities.[3] Because of their sustained and sensitive participant-observation, Taylor and Gould are able to describe a complex set of religious and ecological practice. As

1. Among others, Anna Peterson, Bron Taylor, Laurel Kearns, David Haberman and Marthinus Daneel have also done important ethnographic work in Religion and Ecology. See, for example, Peterson, *Seeds of the Kingdom*; Taylor, "Resacralizing Earth"; Kearns and Immergut, "When Nature Is Rats and Roaches"; Haberman, *River of Love*; and Daneel, *African Earthkeepers*.

2. A number of scholars have advocated such a shift toward ethnographic research. See, for example Kearns, "Greening Ethnography"; Jenkins, "After Lynn White."

3. For an overview of this lived religion approach, see Orsi, "Everyday Miracles"; McGuire, *Lived Religion*.

historians, they situate these within prominent American philosophical, theological, ethical, and cultural traditions, and they bring these into conversation with key scholarly debates. These works reveal their deep and lasting relationships with their subjects, whom they recognize as partners in the research.[4]

Ivakhiv's project involves extensive ethnographic research at two sites. He highlights not only the ways that human communities participate, but also the places themselves participate in their interpretation. Places, especially ones like Glastonbury and Sedona with extraordinary or unusual geographic features, have a kind of agency and power in shaping the way groups imagine and make use of them. He advocates a "hermeneutic-phenomenological" approach to ethnography, attentive to cultural practices and discourses that shape the identity of a place, but also to the researcher's "actual embodied experience of encountering the landscape." He describes, for example, Sedona's "rockscapes," noting their "solidity and monumentality" that "seem to *call for* some sort of interpretation."[5]

These scholars' commitment to ethnographic methods reflects not only a different way of gathering data, but also a different way of defining what it is we aim to study. These scholars prioritize practice in defining and describing religion. Taylor argues that a focus on religious practice is part of a "renaturing" of the concept of religion. This approach treats religion as an "organic system . . . embedded in stories, everyday practices, foodways, material culture, common sense, humor, practical ways of life, and so forth."[6] She argues that green sisters are defined by a complex "ecology" of religious practices—how they pray and worship, cook and clean, conserve farmland and heirloom seeds—linking them to a wider web of social and theological movements.

Gould uses a practice-based approach to make the case that homesteading is a vital religious culture, an example of what Robert Wuthnow calls "practice-oriented spirituality."[7] This is not individualistic, nature-

---

4. Sarah McFarland Taylor describes her commitment to "reciprocal ethnography." She invites the green sisters to "talk back" during interviews, shares drafts of her work with them, and includes their responses to her interpretive metaphors. (xix).

5. Ivakhiv, *Claiming Sacred Ground*, 212–13.

6. Taylor, *Green Sisters*, 283

7. Wuthnow, *After Heaven*. For both Wuthnow and Gould, this "practice-oriented" third way represents an alternative to the picture presented in Bellah's *Habits of the Heart*, which, on the one hand, decries the rise of morally impotent "expressive individualism"

oriented spiritual seeking, but a defined set of individual and collective practices, embedded in strong social networks, rooted in a historic tradition, and morally committed to the broader human community and the natural world. Gould draws on Catherine Bell's notion of "ritualization" to highlight the process by which certain activities come to be privileged among homesteaders. These "homemade rituals" become markers for a whole set of collective values - particular disciplines of growing and eating food, home construction techniques, and community sauna gatherings. Rather than debating whether homesteading is in fact religious, or whether nature is sacred for homesteaders, Gould focuses on particular practices and processes of ritualization, allowing her to examine how this particular community works out such categories of meaning.

Adrian Ivakhiv examines what he describes as "spatial practices" or "practices of place" of the New Age pilgrims: hiking, meditation, visualization, chanting, 'chakra activation,' invocation or channeling of guides or spirits, and the arrangement of stone or rocks in medicine wheels and the conducting of ceremonies within them.[8] Organizing his research around particular places, Ivakhiv stresses the multiplicity of competing practices that develop at a given site. He demonstrates that New Agers practices must be interpreted within the context of "interpretive disputes with other groups, and broader sets of socioeconomic relations."[9] At Glastonbury and Sedona, Forest Service bureaucrats, tourism promoters, real estate developers, Native Americans and Evangelical Christians produce their own senses of place, often contesting the practices and politics of one another. Ivakhiv demonstrates how these religious and spatial practices draw on deep cultural traditions as they negotiate these contemporary contexts. His work shows the necessity for analyzing practices in place, with attention to the immediate, local world but also to complex global flows of culture and capital.

Each of these three works uses "place" as a framing concept. Taylor and Gould use the bioregionalism of their subjects to highlight the importance of understanding religious practice within a local context. Taylor describes the ways green sisters "reinhabit" their local ecosystems, through practices like permaculture farming and straw-bale construc-

---

and "lifestyle enclaves" and, on the other hand, laments the decline of "communities of memory," especially religious communities.

8. Ivakhiv, *Claiming Sacred Ground*, 191–92.

9. Ibid., 193.

tion. She also employs this spatial concept metaphorically, describing the sisters' "reinhabitation" of traditions and structures of religious life. They embrace and adapt old ways of life in response to contemporary environmental concerns. Gould compares contemporary homesteaders to Wendell Berry and Gary Snyder, with their agrarian and bioregionalist commitments to cultivating a sense of place. Homesteaders cultivate their environmental and spiritual lives by staying home, caring for land, family and local community. The homesteaders, like the green sisters, cultivate a lasting sense of place, dwelling in their particular context over many years and learning to live in harmony with the natural environment. Ivakhiv pushes for a concept of place as always more than local, advocating what he calls a "nonessentialist bioreigonalism" that aims to ground cultural and economic activity in its immediate environment, while also highlighting "difference and plurality . . . the ambiguity and mutabililty of borders and cross-border movements, territorialities and deterritorializations."[10] The New Age pilgrims he studies are not long term residents with deep roots in Glastonbury and Sedona, and their practices highlight the dynamic global processes that define these places. His ethnography is attentive to the powerful feelings evoked by the direct encounter with a place, but he situates such seemingly local experience within a much broader political, material, and cultural context.

As these three scholars take up dynamics of place, they each attempt to strike a difficult balance, articulating the particular ways "nature" is socially constructed and the ways the particulars of place insist that nature is always more that a construct. Gould recognizes how going "back to nature" is key to homesteaders' cultivation of a more authentic life and a more authentic self. This indeed reflects abstract, romantic ideas of intimacy with nature, yet she also stresses the way activities like chopping wood, harvesting vegetables, collecting water serve as tangible reminders of interdependence with nature. These practices at once reinforce and challenge socially constructed ideas of nature.

Ivakhiv presents a typology of the four main models for how people conceive of nature: as object, as resource, as home, and as spirit. He argues that these metaphors are not wholly socially constructed, and instead advocates a "co-constructive" view, which recognizes the reciprocal relationship between different social groups and the landscape. Places, especially ones like this with extraordinary or unusual geographic features,

10. Ibid., 235.

have a kind of agency and power in shaping the way people imagine and make use of them. Even as he is attentive to global dynamics, Ivakhiv prioritizes the phenomenological encounters with the most immediate physical space.

These three books demonstrate the promising turn within the study of Religion and Ecology to the analysis of particular practices and places. Taylor, Gould, and Ivakhiv examine particularly remarkable examples—profound commitments to sustainable living and dramatic natural landscapes—but these are by no means the only kinds of cases that warrant attention to practice and place. Scholars of Religion and Ecology can employ similar lenses to analyze the way even more mainstream communities configure practice and place, the way they understand what is natural and what is sacred. Place and practice are increasingly common, and often accommodating analytic categories. They open new opportunities for interdisciplinary dialogue, but they also challenge us to critically reflect on the different ways we use these terms.

Expanding the Conversation beyond Religion and Ecology: Place

Within Religion and Ecology, the turn to place has often meant a turn to what is local and immediate. Scholars often invoke the language of bioregionalism and incorporate phenomenological approaches that prioritize attentiveness to nature. This prioritization of the local often reflects and is reflected in the practitioners and communities who are concerned about religion and the natural world. Whether implicitly or explicitly, many assert that a deep, localized sense of place is the firmest foundation for environmental ethics. If we can only learn to know and connect with a place intimately, sustainable choices will follow. Each of the three communities above reflects this sense of the spiritual and moral power of attachment to place.

There are important tensions and limitations to this localized view of place. In this section I will highlight several ways scholars of Religion and Ecology can develop more nuanced notions of place by engaging with spatial thinkers from religious studies, from cultural geography, and from other disciplines in the emerging "environmental humanities." As I discuss these disciplines, I will point to several key themes: the politics of place-making, and especially issues of power and difference;

globalization and the complex layering of spatial scales that constitutes any place; and the social construction of place and nature.

Within religious studies, Mircea Eliade continues to be a pivotal figure in discussions of space and place. Eliade claims the sacred "irrupts" in a particular place, making it the *axis mundi,* the center and origin of the world, the zone of absolute reality, radically set apart from everything profane.[11] Sacred space is substantively distinct from all else. Jonathan Z. Smith has been one of the most forceful critics of Eliade's substantive view of the sacred. He argues that Eliade depoliticizes the sacred, ignoring the process by which the center becomes central and the resulting dynamics of marginalization. For Smith, constructing a place as sacred center simultaneously constructs other places as marginal or profane, and this mapping of the sacred is also a mapping of political power.[12]

David Chidester and Edward Linenthal share this attention to the "politics of sacred space" in their introduction to *American Sacred Space.* They urge a shift from phenomenological to sociological perspectives on the sacred, demanding focus on the "symbolic labor" by which sacred space is constructed—the "choosing, setting aside, consecrating, venerating, protecting, defending and refining" of sacred spaces.[13] Chidester and Linenthal note the ways space is "naturalized" to obscure the politics of this place-making. Focused on the American context, they highlight the romanticization of "nature," which often serves to hide the conquest of people and land. They argue that because sacred space asserts a particular symbolic and social order, it is inherently contested. Sacred spaces mark "hierarchical power relations of domination and subordination, inclusion and exclusion, appropriation and dispossession."[14] Focused on the lived practices that produce an intimate, localized sense

11. See, for example, Eliade, *Myth of the Eternal Return,* 17

12. See Smith, *To Take Place,* 104. Smith proposes two basic structures of spatiality in religions, the "locative" and "utopian." The former is characteristic of closed, static systems that affirm and celebrate the sacred order of the cosmos, often ritually producing correspondingly ordered, bounded physical spaces. Here, the greatest threat to the sacred is vast, open, chaotic space that lies beyond the bounds of the ritually ordered sacred. Smith contrasts this with the utopian vision of space, which sees highly structured space as static and oppressive. Here, the sacred lies beyond the social structure, and individuals strive for freedom by escaping the bounded, ordered social space. See Smith, *Map Is Not Territory,* 129–46.

13. Chidester and Linenthal, "Introduction," 17.

14. Ibid.

of place, scholars of Religion and Ecology are not always attentive to such dynamics of power.

Chidester and Linenthal bring religious scholarship on sacred space into conversation with cultural geographers, particularly those working in Marxist traditions, who examine the power dynamics and economic exchanges that constitute a place. These scholars offer important critiques of local and phenomenological approaches to place, challenging us to attend to both the local and the global. Doreen Massey calls for a "global," and "progressive" sense of place as an alternative to conservative notions of place, ranging from "reactionary nationalisms to competitive localisms, to sanitized, introverted obsessions with 'heritage.'"[15] She critiques dominant notions of place that start with the philosophy of Martin Heidegger, who characterized places as cohering around an essential identity, one constructed from an inward-looking history and the maintenance of boundaries. Using her London neighborhood as an example, Massey writes, "It is (or ought to be) impossible even to begin thinking about Kilburn High Road without bringing into play half the world and a considerable amount of British imperialist history. Imagining it this way provokes in you (or at least in me) a really global sense of place."[16] Places in fact have multiple identities that coexist, often contested. Places have permeable boundaries, with webs of social relations extending across vast expanses of time and space. Places, she argues, are constantly in process, not fixed but ever evolving to deal with new forms of difference.

Massey notes that globalization creates new configurations of time and space, with constantly changing networks and flows, highly mobile information, capital, people, and more. If we only view this at the most global or most local level, however, we often fail to see the ways this process is socially differentiated. Individuals and groups are placed in very different ways relative to these interconnections and exercise very different kinds of power over these movements. Massey insists that in analyzing the dynamics of any place, we must be attentive to this "power-geometry."[17] How do the communities we study fit into these global-local dynamics? How does this compare to other communities? How do we navigate this web of connections as scholars?

15. Massey, "Power-Geometry," 64. See also Massey, "Global Sense of Place."

16. Massey, "Power Geometry," 66.

17. Ibid, 61.

Neil Smith echoes this attention to social differentiation and scale, arguing, that the very notions of "geographical scale is hierarchically produced as part of the social and cultural, economic and political landscapes of contemporary capitalism and patriarchy."[18] He calls for attention to different spatial scales - body, home, community, urban, region, nation, and globe—and to the practices and processes by which the boundaries between these are established and maintained. As scholars of Religion and Ecology, we should be particularly aware of the way environmental discourse negotiates the tension between the ideals of global citizenship and the local "sense of place." Modern environmentalism became a mass movement in the 1970s, often using invoking concern for the "whole earth" and the iconic image of earth from outer space. Geographer Denis Cosgrove stresses the danger of such global visions that pull "diverse life on earth into a vision of unity."[19] He traces visions of the globe through history, arguing that these are not just detached or distant, but implicitly represent the global itself as local, our common home and dwelling place. Cosgrove argues that visions of the global and the local are always dialectically related, and both are shaped by the history of Western imperialism and colonialism.

David Harvey is particularly critical of the way "nature" functions in the discourse of localism, and he warns against making romantic feelings toward nature the basis for environmental politics. Harvey acknowledges the "depth and intensity of feeling" people have in "intimate and immediate relations to nature or to others," yet he argues for critical analysis of the social relations that produce and are produced by particular ideas of nature and community. "There can be no going back, as many ecologists seem to propose, to an *unmediated* relation to nature (or a world built solely on face-to-face relations)."[20] Our phenomenological experience of the immediate feels so "authentic" that it tempts us to ignore the larger material processes and structures.[21] Just as Marx warns against the "fetishism of commodities," Harvey warns against the fetishism of the local, often a fetishism of nature. Instead, he proposes a materialist approach to place, attentive to global fluxes and flows, to dynamics of race and class, and to the social construction of nature.

18. Smith, "Homeless/Global," 101.
19. Cosgrove, *Apollo's Eye*, 16.
20. Harvey, *Justice, Nature*, 198–99.
21. Ibid., 313–14.

Experiential, phenomenological knowing must be held in tension with critical analysis of social and material relations beyond the local.

These cultural geographers are among the many voices within the emerging disciplines of the "environmental humanities" advocating more nuanced approaches to nature as a socially constructed and contested category. The collection called *Uncommon Ground*, edited by William Cronon, exemplifies this multidisciplinary field of inquiry, with essays by historians, philosophers, literary scholars, and others. Cronon's influential opening essay, "The Trouble with Wilderness," notes the ways environmentalism and those who study it have prioritized nature as wilderness, meanwhile ignoring the health of other ecosystems and places, especially urban environments.[22] In recent years, environmental historians have struggled to expand their view to include diverse kinds of places, but also diverse kinds of people, highlighting the contributions of urban reformers, workplace safety and public health advocates, and grassroots activists around the globe.[23] Philosophers and literary eco-critics are engaged in similar debates over the place of wilderness, the framing of the category "nature," and the breadth of environmental politics.[24] As these disciplines are expanding and maturing, they are examining the theoretical assumptions underlying predominant ideas of nature and the limits of both literary and ecological theories.[25] We can learn a great deal by observing the shifting landscapes of these related disciplines. They challenge us to develop more nuanced theories of place and to be attentive not only to wild nature, but also to urban, suburban and built environments as key contexts for the study of Religion and Ecology.

Expanding the Conversation beyond Religion and Ecology: Practice

Alongside this interdisciplinary spatial turn, there has been a broad turn toward "practice" in social theory.[26] Practice theorists like Michel

22. Cronon, "Trouble with Wilderness."

23. See, for example, Gottlieb, *Forcing the Spring*.

24. Among eco-critics, for example, the pluralist move was asserted most distinctly in Adamson, et al., *Environmental Justice Reader*.

25. Among eco-critics, for example, there is now a lively debate about the ways nature is and is not socially constructed, See Morton, *Truth of Ecology*; Phillips, *Truth of Ecology*; Mazel, *American Literary Environmentalism*.

26. See Schatzki et al., *Practice Turn*; Ortner, "Theory in Anthropology."

Foucault, Pierre Bourdieu, and Michel de Certeau examine the interplay between the individual actors and the larger structures that both constitute and constrain particular embodied activities. Power operates not only from the top-down but throughout social and cultural systems, in the routine activities of individuals' lives. However, these activities also represent the possibility for improvisation and innovation, for resistance to the present social order. De Certeau is particularly attentive to everyday practices and their spatial context. His influential essay "Walking in the City" contrasts two views of urban space. He begins looking down at Manhattan from atop the World Trade Center, describing the panoptical, "god-like" view of the city as an orderly, unified, and well-mapped concept that reflects the strategies of powerful institutions. He contrasts this with the view of "ordinary practitioners of the city" who "live down below" and experience the city on foot, improvising new paths and creating new spaces of possibility.[27] These practice theorists have helped usher broad shifts in the humanities and social science focusing attention on the world of everyday activity and the tensions between subjects and systems, creativity and control. Like the cultural geographers noted above, many of these practice theorists draw on Marxist political and intellectual tradition, highlighting class and power dynamics.

The turn to practice in religious and theological studies has likewise been influenced by Marxist theory, especially through Latin American liberation theology, which prioritizes the praxis of liberation from oppression, displacing texts and doctrine as the prime focus of scholars. This has ushered in a wave of contextual theologies (such as black, feminist, womanist, mujerista, and queer theologies) that focus attention on both structures of injustice and the experience of particular marginalized groups. These theologies are "practical" in the sense that they emerge from and respond to day-to-day social, political, and economic realities.

Theologians have also turned to practice as a way to overcome the gap between beliefs and behaviors.[28] Protestant theologians such as Dorothy Bass and Craig Dykstra have also argued that theology is about practices and not just ideas.[29] Drawing on Alasdair MacIntyre's definition

---

27. Certeau, *Practice of Everyday Life.*

28. This gap is an increasingly important concern for environmental ethicists and scholars of Religion and Ecology. See chapter 7, above, by Lucas Johnston and Samuel Snyder.

29. See, for example Volf and Bass, *Practicing Theology* and Dykstra, *Growing in the Life of Faith.*

of practice, they locate theology in the collective practices of religious communities. Individuals are formed in the wisdom and virtues of their religious tradition through its particular practices.[30] As vice-president for religion at the Lilly Endowment, Dykstra has helped support this practical turn in the study of religion and theology. Lilly has helped fund individual and collective research and publishing,[31] conferences and websites,[32] graduate programs,[33] a new journal,[34] and resources aimed at popular audiences and faith communities.[35] While the majority of these initiatives are focused on North American Christian practices, Lilly has also funded comparative projects and research examining historic and contemporary religious practices in various non-Christian traditions, including in the sort of "spiritual, not religious" practices exhibited by Gould's homesteaders.

This turn to practice in critical theory and Christian theology is now visible in several increasingly important approaches within the study of religion: concern for "lived" or "everyday" religion,[36] material culture,[37]

30. MacIntyre's oft-quoted definition reads, "By a practice I am going to mean any coherent and complex form of socially established co-operative human activity through which goods internal to that form of activity are realised in the course of trying to achieve those standards of excellence which are appropriate to, and partially definitive of, that form of activity, with the result that human powers to achieve excellence, and human conceptions of the ends and goods involved, are systematically extended" (MacIntyre, *After Virtue*, 187).

31. See, for example, The History of American Christian Practice Project (http://www.unc.edu/depts/practice/index.html) and Maffly-Kipp, Schmidt, and Valeri, *Practicing Protestants*

32. See, for example, http://www.waytolive.org/.

33. Lilly is currently funding graduate programs at Duke, Emory, Vanderbilt, and Boston University. The primary mission of these grants is to encourage doctoral training in practical theology. Emory structured its initiative more broadly to foster conversation between those who study Christian practical theology and those who study religious practices from diverse traditions and contexts, pioneering an interdisciplinary and comparative approach to practice.

34. See http://www.practicalmattersjournal.org/, another example of Emory's interdisciplinary and comparative approach.

35. See, for example http://www.practicingourfaith.com/.

36. Hall, *Lived Religion in America*; Ammerman, *Everyday Religion*; McGuire, *Lived Religion*.

37. McDannell, *Material Christianity*.

religion in practice,[38] and religious practices.[39] There are important differences in these approaches, not unlike the differences between those who examine place phenomenologically and locally and those who examine place as a global and local, social and political production. Mary McClintock Fulkerson is among those who have critiqued the MacIntyre-influenced approach to theology. She challenges these theologians for uncritically promoting practice as a way to preserve community and tradition, not "recognizing the racialized, gendered, and otherwise power-laden nature of Christian tradition."[40] Fulkerson stresses that all practice is socially located, and argues that scholars must be attentive to the political and global forces that shape religious practice and also the practice of scholarship. Robert Orsi, one of the most influential scholars of lived religion stresses that this approach "emphasizes dissent, subversion, and resistance, rather than harmony, consensus, and social legitimation."[41] Orsi, like Fulkerson, wants to foreground the politics of religious practice. His own research highlights the particular practices of working-class and immigrant American Catholics, making him particularly attuned to the way practices reflect and reinforce social differences and hierarchies.

Theorists of practice, both within and beyond the field of religion, provide useful vocabularies for analyzing the complex religious phenomena produced at the intersection of established traditions and innovative, ecologically-oriented practices. We have much to gain and much to contribute to this growing body of work. Taylor, Gould, and Ivakhiv demonstrate, for example, that ecological systems and environmental challenges are important parts of the structure that both constrains religious practice and generates new eco-religious practices. While we highlight these more-than-human structures, we should not ignore the social dynamics of such practice. This means not only examining the environmental politics asserted by green sisters, homesteaders, new age pilgrims, and other eco-religious communities, but also the way these groups use eco-religious practices to situate themselves within

38. McDannell, *Religions of the United States in Practice*; Lopez, *Religions of China in Practice*; Lopez, *Religions of India in Practice*; Bowen, *Religions in Practice*.

39. Bass and Richter, *Way to Live*; Volf and Bass, *Practicing* Theology; Bass, *Practicing Our Faith*.

40. Fulkerson, "Theology and the Lure of the Practical: An Overview," 300.

41. Orsi, "Everyday Miracles,"15.

hierarchies of social class, race, etc. As scholars, we are often skilled at examining such dynamics when focused on oppressed communities and skilled at avoiding such analysis when dealing with the privileged. These theorists of practice challenge scholars of Religion and Ecology to critically assess issues of power and difference not only in traditional cases of "environmental justice," but also in contexts and communities that are closer to our own social location.

The Practice and Place of Religion and Ecology

Bourdieu stresses that as we focus our attention on complex social worlds "out there," we must also analyze the habits and disciplines of our own scholarly practice, the symbolic and material structures that shapes our subjectivity.[42] *Inherited Land* takes up this very task, assessing the texts and theories, institutions and structures that have shaped the field and shaped us as disciplined professionals. In the final section of this chapter, I want to use the notions of practice and place to reflect on our individual and collective work as scholars of Religion and Ecology. I have suggested a number of ways the turn to practice and place can shape our research, so here I will focus in particular on the practice of teaching.

Teaching in Place

Within the world of environmental education, there is now a well-established tradition of "place-based education," which seeks to help students understand their local ecosystems and to give them experiences of place that foster greater concern for their environment through a combination of environmental science fieldwork and exploration of the history, folk culture, aesthetics, and economics of local communities.[43] Education theorist David Gruenewald has been instrumental in pushing this place-based education movement beyond its rural and environmental roots. He incorporates Marxist-influenced critical pedagogies in the tradition of Paulo Freire that prioritize social justice concerns, and he draws on Marxist-influenced theorists of place, including cultural geographers,

---

42. Bourdieu, *Homo Academicus.*

43. See Woodhouse and Knapp, "Place-Based Curriculum and Instruction"; Orr, *Ecological Literacy*; Sobel, *Place-Based Education*; Christensen and Crimmel, *Teaching about Place.*

who emphasize the social production of space, power and difference, and the dynamics of globalization.[44]

What would it look like for scholars of Religion and Ecology to re-orient our teaching around issues of place, informed by these pedagogical movements? To begin, such a shift would force us to humbly acknowledge that most of us have relatively shallow roots in the bioregions where we now live. We have spent years developing our expertise within particular academic fields, but in the process we have joined the ranks of a mobile, cosmopolitan class lacking in local knowledge.[45] To teach in place, we need to learn about place, and we need to partner with people and organizations that can help our students to engage with local social and ecological issues. Our colleges and universities have all sorts of local experts, some of them faculty, and there are abundant resources beyond the campus as well.

As we engage in teaching beyond the classroom, we must remember that our colleges and universities are themselves very much part of the surrounding communities, often the most important institutions producing particular arrangements of social, economic, political and ecological space. Together with our students, we have the responsibility to critically examine our institutions within their local and global contexts. Understanding our place takes listening to the variety of voices that can help us learn this institutional history.

We must critically examine dynamics of power and difference at this institutional level, but also in our classrooms. The classroom we inhabit together is itself a porous place with its own political geography. As teachers and students we are simultaneously networked with cultures and communities across the globe. We often teach a variety of social classes, nationalities, religious traditions, racial and ethnic groups; addressing these different identities and experiences of place often reveals dynamics at play beyond the classroom. Making space to discuss these differences also helps reveal the ways our experiences of place are always mediated.

---

44. See Gruenewald, "Best of Both Worlds"; Gruenewald, "Foundations of Place"; Gruenewald and Smith, *Place-Based Education*.

45. On the culture of academic rootlessness, see Zencey, "Rootless Professors."

Teaching and Practice

The turn to practices also presents important challenges and opportunities for our teaching. Just as we expand our students' capacities to critically assess key texts and concepts, we have a responsibility to nurture their skill at observing religious and ecological phenomena in lived contexts, including their own everyday lives. We should consider not only what particular practices we want our students to learn about, but also what practices we want them to explore and experience. Depending on our contexts and courses, this could include particular sorts of eco-religious practices (e.g., mindfulness meditation or liturgical leadership), personal sustainability practices (e.g., eating local, seasonal foods), practices of citizenship and political advocacy (e.g. effective letter-writing or public demonstration), or practices of ecological observation (e.g., testing water quality).

Many universities are now pursuing well-publicized campus "greening" initiatives, and these often offer a variety of ways for individual students and classes to engage with sustainability issues in practice.[46] As we support and participate in such initiatives, we should also reflect critically on the ways these practices reflect and reinforce particular structures of social difference and power. Drawing on theorists of practice, we can ask a number of important questions: What constituencies most benefit from campus greening? Who makes the greatest sacrifices? What environmental issues are prioritized? What is not? Who has the power to make decisions regarding campus sustainability? How are particular practices promoted as a way communicate the university's particular status and identity to wider publics (donors, prospective students, etc.)? What practices are not prominently promoted and why?

Theologian John Cobb, who was active in some of the earliest environmental efforts in theological schools, articulates a holistic vision of sustainability touching all aspects of institutional life. In addition to key questions of curriculum and pedagogy, he expresses concern for equity

---

46. The Association for the Advancement of Sustainability in Higher Education (http://www.aashe.org/) is the primary national clearinghouse for information on campus sustainability. Scholars of Religion and Ecology have been involved in these efforts, and have been particularly instrumental in promoting sustainability initiatives at theological institutions. The "Green Seminary Initiative" (http://www.webofcreation.org/GreenSeminary/aboutus.htm/) is the current umbrella for this effort, building on the work of Theological Education to Meet the Environmental Challenge (TEMEC) in the 1990s.

in hiring practices, rank, tenure, salary and institutional governance; for socially responsible investments and funding sources; and for sustainable purchasing practices, buildings, and grounds. He calls for seminaries to become communities that practice simplicity, consuming fewer resources and reducing the financial burden on students.[47] We and our students might investigate how the particular practices prioritized in our contexts reflect particular notions of nature and sustainability, particular structures of power, and particular social and economic concerns.

Practice can serve as valuable bridge concept within the field of Religion and Ecology, framing collaboration between scholars who approach this work in varied ways. The study of practices provides a language to talk about both traditional "world religions" as well as new and emerging "nature religions." Practice can be a bridge between those who study *about* eco-religious practices, those who *teach* them, and those who see themselves as *practitioners*. Scholars of Religion and Ecology have done important work on theological concepts (anthropology, cosmology, etc.) but we can do much better at engaging with those who study and teach practices (for example, the disciplines of practical theology and religious leadership within Christian theological education.)[48]

Practice is one emerging ground on which scholars of Religion and Ecology can explore complex yet generative tensions within the field, particularly between normative and descriptive approaches. In part, this tension reflects longstanding differences between religious studies and theological studies, but these differences are easily exaggerated. In fact, both religious and theological studies depend on careful description, and both are motivated by values and commitments. How should our scholarship reflect our individual and collective ethical commitments? How are environmental concerns similar or different from other kinds of personal and professional commitments? In what ways should we, like Taylor,

47. Cobb, "Some Critical Questions for Evaluating Theological Education in Response to the Environmental Challenge," in Hessel, *Theology for Earth Community*. 232–36.

48. The 2005 conference at Drew University, "Ground for Hope: Faith, Justice, and the Earth," and the subsequent book, *Ecospirit*, is one example of an effort to incorporate these multiple approaches to practice. The text includes essays that are highly philosophical, theological, and theoretical, together with place-based case studies and practical, liturgical resources. Our national and international academic gatherings are vital, but local and regional conferences like this one create unique opportunities to build ongoing partnerships among academic and religious communities, environmental organizations and concerned citizens. See Kearns and Keller, *Ecospirit*.

Gould, and Ivakhiv, weave our first person voice and embodied experience together with the people, places, and practices we study? How do we engage a broader public through our teaching, research and writing? The field will inevitably include a variety of answers to these questions, and we should not shy away from asking one another hard questions about our divergent positions. Rigorous scholarship can take many forms, including many forms of public engagement. We have a responsibility to expose our students to many models of engaged scholarly practice, challenging them to consider these questions and their own emerging identity as concerned, critically reflective citizens and scholars.

In my own course on Religion and Ecology, I have tried to incorporate commitments to place and practice in a number of ways.[49] At the outset, we focus on our immediate "natural" context, doing a walking tour of the urban forest Emory has preserved adjacent to campus. We learn some key ecological features of our bioregion as well as the cultural history of this landscape, and how different waves of local residents have transformed it and adapted to it. In this first week of the course, we practice skills of observation, paying attention to place through our senses. This tour also aims to demonstrate the ways our local natural area is embedded in a larger web of connections—sewer flows and air pollution patterns, plant and animal habitats, and more. Its boundaries are in fact quite permeable - points of connection as much as separation. We then leave the greenspace and split into smaller groups to investigate other ways our lives at Emory are connected beyond our immediate ecosystem. Students learn about where our power is generated, where the campus food comes from, where our trash and recycling go, and more. This exercise demonstrates that it is not only when we are out of the classroom or off campus that we are engaging with the broader world.

In subsequent classes, we travel to other parts of Atlanta to pay attention to the environmental realities in some quite different contexts. Students volunteer and learn with a variety of secular and faith-based organizations that work on environmental justice issues in parts of the city that are primarily poor or African American, in contrast to the largely white, affluent neighborhood surrounding Emory. Through these

---

49. The course is part of the Youth Theological Initiative at Emory's Candler School of Theology, also supported by Lilly. The extended class sessions in this intensive summer program allow for great flexibility, making possible the many fieldtrips described here.

experiences, I demonstrate that paying attention to nature, especially in a diverse urban context, inevitably leads to questions of justice. Why does one place have cleaner water than another? Why are green spaces less accessible to African Americans in Atlanta than whites? Answering these questions requires more than simply paying attention to what is immediately observable. These questions of justice challenge students to learn the history of how the landscape came to be structured in this way, how systems of power operate to distribute environmental burdens and benefits. Working with these organizations, students come to see that this kind of knowledge is located in the local community as much as in any archive or academic text. They see the wide variety of practices through which various groups respond to issues of social and environmental justice: grassroots organizing, legislative advocacy, personal lifestyle choices, public protests, educational programming, etc.

Throughout the remainder of the course, we continue to visit sites throughout the city and we continue to learn more about the history of Atlanta, paying particular attention to the way power and difference map onto geographical space. The city has a long history of racial segregation, and this dynamic is now even more complex as Atlanta has emerged as a global city that is home to growing communities of immigrants and refugees along with highly mobile classes of professional and service workers. The course examines religion and environmental ethics on the ground, in the practices of diverse cultures and religious communities, viewing broader issues through the particular landscape and lens of Atlanta.

The classroom community is itself quite diverse, and I structure discussions and writing assignments to examine the different ways we experience the city's social, religious and environmental dynamics. Individually and together, the class reflects on why particular experiences surprise, inspire, and trouble. Hearing each other describe the city, students begin to understand that we never simply leave the classroom and see the "real world." Places do not have an essence that direct experience reveals. Our knowledge is always situated, shaped by what we bring to our experience.[50] Knowing one's place demands knowing one's self, and we come to know ourselves in and through a diverse community. Critical self-reflection makes students more engaged learners and more effective citizens.

---

50. Haraway, *Simians, Cyborgs and Women*, 187.

I have outlined a number of ways concepts of practice and place can inform the way we teach Religion and Ecology. We could extend this line of thinking to reflect on other aspects of our professional identity—how we participate in colleges and universities, in academic guilds, in religious communities, in environmental organizations, and in local, regional, national and global politics. I have highlighted a number of ways that nuanced notions of place and practice can strengthen our research, our writing, our teaching, and these other fields of practice. Drawing on resources from bioregionalism, phenomenology, and place-based education, we should be attentive to the natural world we encounter in our local contexts, cultivating a rich sense of place.

This alone is not enough, however. Informed by the work of cultural geographers and theorists of practice, we must also be attentive to structures of power and difference, to the complex layering of local and global scales, and to the ways our very notions of what is natural, local, and global are shaped by social processes. Such analysis sharpens our understanding of Religion and Ecology on the ground, and it makes us more aware of the social structures and processes that constitute and constrain our own scholarly practice.

Bibliography

Adamson, Joni et al., editors. *The Environmental Justice Reader: Politics, Poetics, & Pedagogy*. Tucson: University of Arizona Press, 2002.

Ammerman, Nancy Tatom. *Everyday Religion: Observing Modern Religious Lives*. Oxford: Oxford University Press, 2007.

Bass, Dorothy C. *Practicing Our Faith: A Way of Life for a Searching People*. San Francisco: Jossey-Bass, 1997.

Bass, Dorothy C., and Don C. Richter. *Way to Live: Christian Practices for Teens*. Nashville: Upper Room, 2002.

Bellah, Robert N., et al. *Habits of the Heart: Individualism and Commitment in American Life*. Berkeley: University of California Press, 1985.

Bourdieu, Pierre. *Homo Academicus*. Translated by Peter Collier. Stanford: Stanford University Press, 1988.

Bowen, John Richard. *Religions in Practice: An Approach to the Anthropology of Religion*. Boston: Allyn and Bacon, 1998.

Certeau, Michel de. *The Practice of Everyday Life*. Berkeley: University of California Press, 1984.

Chidester, David, and Edward T. Linenthal. "Introduction." In *American Sacred Space*. Religion in North America. Bloomington: Indiana University Press, 1995.

Christensen, Laird, and Hal Crimmel. *Teaching about Place: Learning from the Land*. Reno: University of Nevada Press, 2008.

Cobb, John B., Jr. "Some Critical Questions for Evaluating Theological Education in Response to the Environmental Challenge." In *Theology for Earth Community: A Field Guide*, edited by Dieter T. Hessel, 232–36. Maryknoll, NY: Oribs, 1996.

Cosgrove, Denis E. *Apollo's Eye: A Cartographic Genealogy of the Earth in the Western Imagination*. Baltimore: Johns Hopkins University Press, 2001.

Cronon, William. "The Trouble with Wilderness; or, Getting Back to the Wrong Nature." In *Uncommon Ground: Rethinking the Human Place in Nature*, edited by William Cronon, 69–90. New York: Norton, 1996.

Daneel, M. L. *African Earthkeepers*. 2 vols. African Initiatives in Christian Mission 2–3. Pretoria: UNISA, 1998.

Dykstra, Craig R. *Growing in the Life of Faith: Education and Christian Practices*. 2nd ed. Louisville: Westminster John Knox, 2005.

Eliade, Mircea. *The Myth of the Eternal Return*. Translated by Willard R. Trask. New York: Pantheon, 1954.

Fulkerson, Mary McClintock. "Theology and the Lure of the Practical: An Overview." *Religion Compass* 1 (2007) 294–304.

Gottlieb, Robert S. *Forcing the Spring: The Transformation of the American Environmental Movement*. Rev. and updated ed. Washington DC: Island, 2005.

Gould, Rebecca Kneale. *At Home in Nature: Modern Homesteading and Spiritual Practice in America*. Berkeley: University of California Press, 2005.

Gruenewald, David A. "The Best of Both Worlds: A Critical Pedagogy of Place." *Educational Researcher* 32 (2003) 3–12.

———. "Foundations of Place: A Multidisciplinary Framework for Place-Conscious Education." *American Educational Research Journal* 40 (2003): 619–54.

Gruenewald, David A., and Gregory A. Smith. *Place-Based Education in the Global Age: Local Diversity*. New York: Erlbaum, 2008.

Haberman, David L. *River of Love in an Age of Pollution: The Yamuna River of Northern India*. Berkeley: University of California Press, 2006.

Hall, David D. *Lived Religion in America: Toward a History of Practice*. Princeton: Princeton University Press, 1997.

Haraway, Donna. *Simians, Cyborgs and Women: The Reinvention of Nature*. New York: Routledge, 1991.

Harvey, David. *Justice, Nature, and the Geography of Difference*. Cambridge: Blackwell, 1996.

Hessel, Dieter T., editor. *Theology for Earth Community: A Field Guide*. Ecology and Justice Series. Maryknoll, NY: Orbis, 1996.

Ivakhiv, Adrian J. *Claiming Sacred Ground: Pilgrims and Politics at Glastonbury and Sedona*. Bloomington: Indiana University Press, 2002.

Jenkins, Willis. "After Lynn White: Religious Ethics and Environmental Problems." *Journal of Religious Ethics* 39 (2009) 283–309.

Kearns, Laurel. "Greening Ethnography and the Study of Religion." In *Personal Knowledge and Beyond: Reshaping the Ethnography of Religion*, edited by James V. Spickard et al. New York: New York University Press, 2002.

Kearns, Laurel, and Matthew Immergut. "When Nature Is Rats and Roaches: Religious Eco-Justice in Newark, NJ." In *Lived Religion in an Urban Context: Ethnographic Portraits of Religion in Newark*, edited by Karen McCarthy Brown, n.p. Berkeley: University of California Press, forthcoming.

Kearns, Laurel, and Catherine Keller. *Ecospirit: Religions and Philosophies for the Earth.* Transdisciplinary Theological Colloquia. New York: Fordham University Press, 2007.

Lopez, Donald S., Jr. *Religions of China in Practice.* Princeton Readings in Religions. Princeton: Princeton University Press, 1996.

————. *Religions of India in Practice.* Princeton Readings in Religions. Princeton: Princeton University Press, 1995.

MacIntyre, Alasdair C. *After Virtue: A Study in Moral Theory.* Notre Dame: University of Notre Dame Press, 1981.

Maffly-Kipp, Laurie F. et al., editors. *Practicing Protestants: Histories of Christian Life in America, 1630–1965.* Lived Religions. Baltimore: Johns Hopkins University Press, 2006.

Massey, Doreen. "A Global Sense of Place." *Marxism Today* (1991) 24–29.

————. "Power-Geometry and a Progressive Sense of Place." In *Mapping the Futures: Local Cultures, Global Change,* edited by Barry Curtis et al., 59–69. Futures, New Perspectives for Social Analysis. London: Routledge, 1993.

Mazel, David. *American Literary Environmentalism.* Athens: University of Georgia Press, 2000.

McDannell, Colleen. *Material Christianity: Religion and Popular Culture in America.* New Haven: Yale University Press, 1995.

————. *Religions of the United States in Practice.* 2 vols. Princeton Readings in Religions. Princeton: Princeton University Press, 2001.

McGuire, Meredith B. *Lived Religion: Faith and Practice in Everyday Life.* Oxford: Oxford University Press, 2008.

Morton, Timothy. *Ecology without Nature: Rethinking Environmental Aesthetics.* Cambridge: Harvard University Press, 2007.

Orr, David W. *Ecological Literacy: Education and the Transition to a Postmodern World.* Edited by David Ray Griffin. SUNY Series in Constructive Postmodern Thought. Albany: State University of New York Press, 1992.

Orsi, Robert. "Everyday Miracles: The Study of Lived Religion." In *Lived Religion in America: Toward a History of Practice,* edited by David D. Hall, 3–21. Princeton: Princeton University Press, 1997.

Ortner, Sherry B. "Theory in Anthropology since the Sixties." *Comparative Studies in Society and History* 26 (1984) 126–66.

Peterson, Anna L. *Seeds of the Kingdom: Utopian Communities in the Americas.* Oxford: Oxford University Press, 2005.

Phillips, Dana. *The Truth of Ecology: Nature, Culture, and Literature in America.* Oxford: Oxford University Press, 2003.

Schatzki, Theodore R. et al., editors. *The Practice Turn in Contemporary Theory.* London: Routledge, 2000.

Smith, Jonathan Z. *Map Is Not Territory: Studies in the History of Religions.* Studies in Judaism in Late Antiquity 23. Leiden: Brill, 1978.

————. *To Take Place: Toward Theory in Ritual.* Chicago Studies in the History of Judaism. Chicago: University of Chicago Press, 1987.

Smith, Neil. "Homeless/Global: Scaling Places." In *Mapping the Futures: Local Cultures, Global Change,* edited by Barry Curtis et al., 87–119. Futures, New Perspectives for Social Analysis. London: Routledge, 1993.

Sobel, David. *Place-Based Education: Connecting Classrooms & Communities.* Nature Literacy Series 4. Great Barrington, MA: The Orion Society, 2004.

Taylor, Bron Raymond. "Resacralizing Earth: Pagan Environmentalism and the Restoration of Turtle Island" In *American Sacred Space*, edited by David Chidester and Edward T. Linenthal. Religion in North America. Bloomington: Indiana University Press, 1995.

Taylor, Sarah McFarland. *Green Sisters: A Spiritual Ecology*. Cambridge: Harvard University Press, 2007.

Volf, Miroslav, and Dorothy C. Bass. *Practicing Theology: Beliefs and Practices in Christian Life*. Grand Rapids: Eerdmans, 2002.

Woodhouse, Janice L., and Clifford E. Knapp. "Place-Based Curriculum and Instruction: Outdoor and Environmental Education Approaches." *ERIC Clearinghouse on Rural Education and Small Schools* (2000). Online: http://www.eric.ed.gov:80/PDFS/ED448012.pdf

Wuthnow, Robert. *After Heaven: Spirituality in America since the 1950s*. Berkeley: University of California Press, 1998.

Zencey, Eric. "The Rootless Professors." In *Rooted in the Land: Essays on Community and Place*, edited by William Vitek and Wes Jackson, 15–19. New Haven: Yale University Press, 1996.

11

Religion and the Urban Environment

RICHARD R. BOHANNON II

When we speak of the natural environment—saving the environment, for instance—we can generally assume that we're talking about something away from where we live. Places like the forests, oceans, and the wilderness come to mind. This is not without consequences. William Cronon, for instance, has famously (or infamously) critiqued the environmental movement's concern over saving the wilderness, arguing that concern over the wilderness often accompanies a *lack* of environmental concern over the environments we actually live in[1]—and an increasing majority of people across the globe, and certainly the overwhelming majority of academics, live in or near cities.

Thus for many people, a primary encounter with the non-human world comes from interactions with cities and towns, which encompass our homes, our workplaces, our grocery stores. Cities are material worlds, they are environments, but they are decidedly not natural environments (at least not according to how those words are usually understood). Cities are human artifacts. They are, we tell ourselves, the opposite of natural.

This chapter is about religious perceptions of the "city," in scare quotes, and particularly the contemporary city in the United States.[2] The

---

1. Cronon, "The Trouble with Wilderness."

2. I vary between talking about cities, in the plural, and the "city," in the singular as an idea, because speaking of the "city" is helpful, but also tends to erase difference. Jennifer Robinson has forcefully argued that the focus on "global" cities in urban

211

first half argues for two broad, related conclusions: 1) we need more critical engagement from religious scholars on cities as environmental entities, and 2) understanding the city is of critical concern for those who study Religion and Ecology. This second point—that Religion and Ecology scholars need to take cities seriously—dominates this essay's second half, where several possibilities are outlined for what that might mean.

Religion, Nature, City: Connections

Over the past four decades, a substantial body of literature has surveyed a variety of religious perceptions of "nature" in the United States. Within such scholarship, it has become common to assume that Christianity in particular has heavily influenced the stories we tell about nature, for good or ill—indeed, this volume is based on the fact that this assumption has become commonplace among a critical mass of religion scholars.

As other essays in this volume describe in more detail, Religion and Ecology scholarship is sometimes divided between two exaggerated poles—one that analyzes environmental and religious practices as they are actually "lived," the other which analyzes theological traditions and convictions. This latter approach has certainly been more widespread. Theologians and scholars from a variety of faiths have sifted through their various traditions in search of beliefs and practices that might lead their communities into a more sustainable future; the series published by the Forum on Religion and Ecology[3] is the most prominent and exhaustive example of this work. Taking a different, though not inherently incompatible, approach, a recent edition of *Journal of the American Academy of Religion* argues for the existence of "aquatic nature religion,"

---

studies, for instance (e.g., Sassen, *Global City*), has caused us to ignore the majority of cities that are "ordinary," especially in the global South—that is, cities that are relatively unimportant for the global economy. Furthermore, when scholars have looked at smaller, more ordinary cities, they tend to only look at those characteristics that fit into the global city paradigm—to look at, for instance, how globalization has reshaped the urban landscape—and to ignore all other factors. Much like the term "nature," then, which numerous scholars have critiqued for its normative, exclusionary power (e.g., Latour, *Politics of Nature*), but which nevertheless has an explanatory power, speaking of the "city" can be problematic. In this chapter I thus tend to use the plural, "cities," to refer to actual urban environments or literature about such places (e.g., Chicago or New Orleans), and "city," in the singular, to refer to normative, socially fabricated images of the urban world. See Robinson, "Global and World Cities"; Robinson, *Ordinary Cities*.

3. Mary Evelyn Tucker and John A. Grim's Religions of the World and Ecology series.

tied together not by shared theological convictions but by religious experiences tied with specific ways of physically encountering nature.[4] What concerns me here is not the differences between these two camps, but the fact that among them lies a shared conviction: there is something religious about how many of us in the United States understand and interact with "nature." Equally important, only in rare instances does this scholarship deal substantively with notions of the city, and even then the subject is often pre–twentieth century and/or non-Western cities.[5]

Religion and the City

There is, however, a vibrant body of literature concerned with religion and the city in the U.S. Most of this work has followed the Chicago school of sociology and primarily focused on the distinctive characteristics of religion in an urban context, such as pluralism or immigration.[6] Some of this work, such as Nancy Eiesland's investigation of the affects of suburban growth on religious practice, even encompasses a notion of "urban ecology," a term coined in Chicago by Robert Park in the 1920s.[7] This research, however, uses ecology in a purely analogical sense, and simply means to convey that urban social networks function with a multi-layered complexity akin to that found in more natural ecosystems.

When literature on religion and the city has stepped back to ask how the "city" has been constructed as a symbol or idea, it has largely done so from an historical perceptive. Perhaps most famously, Augustine's *City of God* was written after the destruction of Rome in 410. Early colonists in New England, among others, famously used the "city on a hill" metaphor to describe the new Puritan society they wished to establish, and images of a "new Jerusalem" have appeared throughout Christian history—though these images have most often been used to describe an ideal morality rather than as a prescription for the built environment.

4. E.g., Snyder, "New Streams of Religion."
5. E.g., Fumagalli, *Landscapes of Fear.*
6. E.g., Orsi, *Gods of the City.* This field has begun to recently organize itself more formally. In 2007, for instance, the Religion and Cities Consultation, which began meeting at the American Academy of Religion.
7. Eiesland, *Particular Place*; Park, "Concept of Position in Sociology"; Ganziano, "Ecological Metaphors as Scientific Boundary Work."

Only a small portion of scholarship on such images has dealt with nature, but a number of sources nevertheless exist. The most detailed has perhaps been Vito Fumagalli's work on medieval Europe (which has unfortunately been largely ignored by Religion and Ecology scholars, at least in the United States), which offers a fascinating depiction of how perceptions of the natural world shifted with the advent of urbanization—as cities grew and people gradually lived further apart from the untamed wilderness, the natural world increasingly became something to be feared (and with it, things associated with nature and physicality, such as "pagan" fertility rites or the body).[8]

Other sources are relevant here, of course. Industrial cities in the nineteenth century, especially in Europe, were frequently described as satanic, hellish, evil places, the effect of both concentrated poverty, oppressive working conditions, and extreme environmental pollution.[9] This provided some of the impetus for socialist revolutions—Friedrich Engels wrote compellingly of Manchester's profound pollution and poverty, for instance[10]—but it also formed a backdrop for sanitized, utopic visions of the city. Tristam Hunt has documented such a rise of visions of the city as a "new Jerusalem" emergent in Victorian England, which formed the precursor to the "garden cities" of the late nineteenth century, both in England and the United States, and eventually was a factor leading to the contemporary suburb.[11]

Before moving on, two things might be said about the literature that exists at the moment: only rarely do discussions of how religion and cities have shaped one another rigorously consider environmental issues, and in the few instances where the environment is brought into the conversation, we are left with an account that says very little directly about contemporary cities in the United States.[12]

8. Fumagalli, *Landscapes of Fear*.

9. See Pike, *Metropolis on the Styx*. In the United States, nineteenth-century cities were also depicted as modern-day "Babylons," centers of sin and temptation; e.g., Todd, "New York, the New Babylon?"

10. Engels, "Working-Class Manchester."

11. Hunt, *Building Jerusalem*.

12. Theologians have not been so silent, as will be discussed later, but theirs is a different project—they are calling for renewed theological visions that help shape the future, rather than analytically describing how religious visions have already shaped contemporary cities.

Cities and the Environment

Scholarship outside religious studies has been far more fecund in questioning the city and its relationship (conceptually and ecologically) with the environment.

"Cities," writes Lewis Mumford, "are a product of the earth."[13] Mumford, among the leading urban theorists of the mid-twentieth century, nonetheless spent little time investigating this premise; it was left to others to question specifically how the city interacts with and has been contrasted with nature. In this vein, two of the most influential works have been Raymond William's study of the city and the rural "countryside" in English literature, and Cronon's study of Chicago as the locus of an environmental and agricultural transformation of the Midwest. [14] According to Cronon's work, one can't understand the history of Chicago without understanding the history of deforestation in Wisconsin, for instance—and, by implication, one can't understand Wisconsin's forests and farms today without taking account of Chicago. Several works have followed, such as environmental histories of New York and New Orleans, and further investigations of the city and nature in literature and art, all with the intent of either documenting or arguing against the broader cultural assumption of the urban as the antithesis of the natural.[15]

Other scholars, particularly within cultural geography, follow Donna Haraway and describe the city as a "cyborg,"[16] with hopes of conveying a space that is neither purely human nor natural. Similarly, scholars such as Erik Swyngedouw describe cities as "metabolizations" of nature—the city is the product of human labor, which refashions nature into a commodity (and thus, according to Swyngedouw, allowing it to also describe human power struggles).[17] While there is disagreement among some scholars as to whether the cyborg or the metabolization of nature more accurately describes the city, they both intend to portray the city not as a human construct, but as a thoroughly enmeshed blend of human and non-human/natural activity.

13. Mumford, *Culture of Cities*, 3.

14. Williams, *Country and the City*; Cronon, *Nature's Metropolis*.

15. Gandy, *Concrete and Clay*; Colten, *Unnatural Metropolis*. On the city and nature in literature and art, see Short, *Imagined Country*.

16. Gandy, "Cyborg Urbanization."

17. Swyngedouw, *Social Power and the Urbanization of Water*. See also Heynen, et al., *In the Nature of Cities*.

Perhaps the largest body of scholarship questions the environmental impact and sustainability of cities and urban life more broadly,[18] usually positing certain urban planning strategies (such as walkable communities, mass transit, or urban agriculture) as the path toward a more sustainable future.

Though there are a variety of claims and emphases within this scholarship, they agree on two basic insights, at least in terms of the question at hand for this essay: the city—either in the abstract or in the particular—must be understood as part of the natural environment, and definitions of the "city" as symbolically separated from "nature" tend to work in the favor of certain social groups to the detriment of others. Furthermore, while the sources for this work are quite broad, it has most often been entirely silent regarding religion.

This points to a curious hole in the literature thus far: an entire subdiscipline has emerged to study religion and the environment, another group of scholars have questioned religious perceptions of the city, and a separate school analyzes the environment and the city. To my knowledge, however, little has been written linking the three, especially in terms of the contemporary United States.

To summarize in another way, I would make three broad assertions which themselves are not particularly controversial: 1) the religious sphere is a significant influence on how we understand and interact with nature; 2) the religious sphere is a significant influence on the social fabric of contemporary US cities; and 3) while "nature" and the "city" are most often constructed as opposite from one another, such distinctions are in fact difficult to maintain. I suggest that two conclusions are thus in order.

First, *in order to understand the city from an environmental perspective, we need to understand the influence of religious perspectives.* That is, insofar as Religion and Ecology scholars have been correct in viewing religion as a key variable in our interaction with the environment, it is also a critical point in understanding the city as the antithesis to untamed nature.

Second, *in order to understand religious perceptions of and interactions with nature, we need to understand something about cities.* I am not arguing that all scholars in Religion and Ecology need to become experts in urban theory or urban planning, but rather that the city, both

---

18. Light, "Urban Blind Spot"; Benton-Short and Short, *Cities and Nature*.

as a concept and as a physical entity, must nonetheless be rigorously engaged with by Religion and Ecology scholars as a component of the environments, ecologies and natures that we study. It is to this second point that the remaining half of this essay is devoted.

Religion, Nature, City: Possibilities

My elevator response for this article's thesis would thus be that Religion and Ecology scholars need to take the city seriously. But what would that look like?

No one, straightforward answer to such a question is possible. As a review of papers at any Religion and Ecology/Nature conference would very quickly prove, our research projects are remarkably diverse in both subject and methodology. A constructive Christian theology raises different questions and research problems than an ethnographic study of Buddhism in Southeast Asia. Nonetheless, there are at least three different, complementary possibilities that might cover a wide array (though not the totality) of Religion and Ecology scholarship: cities as an environmental problem, cities as sites for sustainability, and cities as environments.

Cities as an Environmental Problem

Perhaps the least controversial way of understanding cities among environmentalists (scholars and activists alike) is as an environmental problem. The good news is that a great deal of scholarship is already making this assumption; the bad news is that it is rarely explicit or critically analyzed.

Seeing cities as environmental problems takes at least two forms—cities as sources of pollution, and as sites of alienation from nature. While pollution is a problem for both rural and urban communities—coal mining, for instance, typically occurs far away from cities—cities undoubtedly often hold high concentrations of pollutants stemming from industry, household and toxic waste, energy production, diesel emissions from trucks and buses, and poor indoor air quality. While such pollution has undoubtedly become a theme in Religion and Ecology scholarship, stemming at least partially from influence by the environmental justice movement, cities are perhaps more commonly seen as places where people are *alienated* from nature, where the simple fact that wild(er) nature does not exist in obvious forms is a profound loss in its own right.[19]

Two examples from recent academic work demonstrate how this perspective can provide a critical lens. In Rebecca Kneale Gould's work on the modern homesteading movement as a form of "lived religion," readers are presented with practitioners of "back to nature" spiritualities that most often assume a place that has been left—usually the city specifically. It is important to note that the homesteaders that Gould describes are not reactionary against the built environment itself. The three most well known of her subjects—Helen and Scott Nearing and John Burroughs—both spent a substantial amount of energy creating their homesteads (such as Burrough's Slabsides), but everything about these places, from their stone walls to their unfinished wooden desks, emphasized that they were non-urban spaces.[20]

When I first gave a thorough reading of Gould's book, it was with a class of undergraduate environmental studies majors at a rural university surrounded by farmland, where at least half the students grew up in farming communities and one was a farmer. The students' reactions to Gould's subject were interesting: those from farming communities all felt, and some quite vociferously so, that the farmers they knew would have a very different perspective on nature and what it means to farm. Most were third, fourth or fifth generation farmers, and many of their families (at least in my students' perspectives) experienced farming as an obligation and economic necessity, some felt trapped, and held few if any of the spiritual or moral concerns of the homesteaders that Gould lived among.

These students' reactions demonstrate, and Gould herself notes, that the homesteaders' perception of nature is dependent on an exodus from the city. Just as Thoreau left Concord for his experiment in Walden Pond, many homesteaders are ex-urbanites seeking an alternative to the vices (moral, environmental, or both) of the city. John Burroughs, for instance, held the curious position that cities emerged to teach humans how to interact with each other and the environment; after learning their lessons in the city, "God promoted him to life in the country."[21]

---

19. In popular literature, this has been popularized most by the diagnosis of a "nature deficit disorder" affecting today's children. See Louv, *Last Child in the Woods*.

20. Gould, *At Home in Nature*.

21. Quoted in ibid., 135.

In environmental literature more broadly, it is assumed that caring for nature/environment/creation is about something outside the city. This is a central (and helpful) assumption in Kimberly Smith's recent book on African-American environmental thought, for example. Smith takes a standard question of environmental scholarship—how does a certain community understand or relate to "nature"—and applies it to a demographic (African-Americans) that modern popular culture has stereotypically seen as urban and environmentalists have largely ignored.[22]

To do this, Smith spends significant time discussing the lingering effects of an agricultural society (both slave and free) on urbanized African-American culture in the twentieth century, and assumes that there is no meaningful encounter with nature in the city—work, for instance, shifts from agricultural to industrial.[23] This shift forms an interesting problematic, and certainly perceptions of nature shifted as communities moved from an agricultural environment to an urban one. However, emphasis on the shift from agriculture to industry masks the continuities between the urban and natural/agricultural environments. The environmental differences are rather obvious, for instance, between working a small personal garden as a slave in a rural community and working in a factory in New York or Chicago. But they are both *environments*, and in more than simply the broadest meaning of the term. The "nature" encountered is controlled in both instances, though they differ in order of magnitude in the separation from things wild.

That the city is in fact an environment, and more specifically an environmental problem, becomes clear in Smith's own work as she briefly moves into contemporary times and discusses the environmental justice movement, where cities are not only sites of environmental problems, but of racially mis-distributed environmental problems.

Seeing the city as an environmental problem—which necessitates, to a significant degree, seeing the city as part of the environment—has applicability outside of distinctly urban environmental issues, such as encountered in the environmental justice movement.

To use a very different example, in restoration ecology there are vigorous debates on what it means to restore an ecosystem—Is restoration

---

22. Smith. *African American Environmental Thought*.

23. Chad Montrie's recent natural history of work in the US follows a similar logic with a broader number of communities, often asking what happens when agricultural or manual labor becomes industrialized. See Montrie, *Making a Living*.

even possible? Is it desirable? Does it depend on a (largely unscientific) view of ecosystems as stable and pure? These debates often revolve around understandings of an ideal nature and ideal environments. But they also either assume or call for renewed visions of the city. Cities are the problem—directly (when the restoration is in an urban setting) or indirectly (such as pollution from mining, logging, or other forms of environmental destruction most often closely linked to urban growth elsewhere)—but cities are also the solution. Systemic ecological restoration, at least in most places, would call for a total rearrangement of how cities relate to their environments.[24]

Cities as Sites for Sustainability

Such visions lead us to a different conception of cities as places that make sustainable lifestyles possible. Urban environmentalism, as both a subject of academic study and as a form of activism, is growing in a variety of ways.

In one mutation, nature is brought back into the city. There has been a recent growth in popular nonfiction, for instance, that leads readers on "wilderness adventures" in the Meadowlands between New York City and Newark, NJ, takes them on "suburban safaris," or explores the wildlife in Central Park.[25] Such "nature" in the city is nonetheless kept as distinct categories in these formulizations: the spectacle is the intermingling of the wild and the civilized, the temporary breakdown of the borders between nature and city. Nature is seen in the park or the undevelopable wetlands, but not as part of the actual city streets.

A second approach advocates for urban living as a more sustainable lifestyle. This can be subdivided at least one further step still. Scholars such as Steve Kellert want to "green" the city, by changing existing urban structures to make them more environmentally responsive.[26] Others have argued that residents of dense, urban environments have inherently more sustainable lifestyles. Andrew Light, for instance, has argued that environmentalists have an "urban blind spot," having ignored the fact that, on average, urban residents live in smaller spaces, often in apartments that are more energy-efficient than free-standing homes, use less

24. See, for instance, Kellert, *Building for Life*.

25. Sullivan, *Meadowlands*; Holmes, *Suburban Safari*; Winn, *Red-Tails in Love*.

26. Kellert, *Building for Life*.

land, and are able (in some cities, at least) to get around by walking and using public transit.[27] To use energy as one measure, for instance, urban apartment dwellers who receive their heat in winter using oil, gas, or electricity create much less pollution than back-to-earth homesteaders who rely on wood-burning stoves (both because more modern forms are much cleaner, and because apartment dwellers share heat through walls and ceilings).

While this has not caught the attention of a large number of Religion and Ecology scholars, there have been a handful of religious attempts at creating sustainable cities. Perhaps the most intensive has been Paolo Soleri's Arcosanti, a small city he began developing in the Arizona desert in the 1960s. Inspired in part by Teilhard de Chardin's evolutionary cosmology,[28] Soleri and his followers are striving to make Arcosanti a thoroughly sustainable re-visioning of what cities might be; Soleri's design imagines the city as an organic cell, in which the human inhabitants are but one part of something cohesive. Soleri's writing is often spiritual or theological, and his work attracted substantial attention from John Cobb, who sees in Soleri's "arcologies" a new possibility for building the Christian "City of God."[29]

At least two other Christian eco-theologians, both in Europe, have more recently given direct attention to cities. British theologian Tim Gorringe and Finnish theologian Seppo Kjellberg have both taken what they see as the core tenets of eco-theology (and, in Gorringe's case, social justice) to argue for new ways of understanding and building cities today.[30] The issues raised by this theological work have yet to fully infiltrate the larger sphere of Religion and Ecology scholarship, however.

Interestingly, these thinkers' approaches still assume a basic antagonism between cities as we know/perceive them, and a "nature" that is out there and which urban life must either respond to more adequately or be integrated with more fully. The goal, in other words, is to make cities more like nature, with the "natural" held up as the moral/ethical standard. While there are problems with this in some contexts (many victims of natural disasters, for instance, would hesitate to hold up nature

27. Light, "Urban Blind Spot."

28. While Soleri is clearly influenced by Teilhard de Chardin, it should be noted that (unlike Teilhard's) Soleri's framework is not Christian.

29. Cobb, *Christ in a Pluralistic Age.*

30. Gorringe, *A Theology of the Built Environment*; Kjellberg, *Urban Ecotheology.*

as a moral standard), there is often no denying that our cities have been built in ways that are destructive to many of us and will ultimately be unsustainable for everyone.

An alternative approach is possible, however. Counting both non-human spaces (forests, prairies, etc.) and cities (and other parts of the built environment) as parts of *nature*—or, if this language of nature is abandoned, as *environment(s)*—allows for the entrance of more complex analyses that not only makes politics more visible (as Bruno Latour argues)[31] but also makes more sense of how human social systems affect non-human spaces and entities.

For scholarship that views cities as environmental problems or sustainable possibilities to reach its fullest potential, in other words, the separation between "nature" and the "city" has to be erased—the city must be understood as a (dis)functioning part of a much wider environment.

Cities as Environments

By arguing for cities as environments, I mean two things: 1) reintegrating the city (as a concept) into our existing scope of work on nature, and 2) expanding the scope of Religion and Ecology scholarship to include urban projects that understand cities themselves as environments and as (dis)functioning systems.

Conceiving of cities, with their steel, neon and plastic, as belonging to "nature" or the environment (as indeed they do on the molecular level) allows us to look more directly at how cities influence and are influenced by their surrounding environments; it also allows us to look at how the human adaptations of those environments which work to benefit some people and places to the detriment of others. Latour similarly calls for abandoning the language of "nature" (at least for research purposes) and instead speaking of a "collective" of actors.[32] Rather than looking at either human or natural factors to the exclusion of the other (as the social and natural sciences have historically done), the point is not to lump everything into one category, but instead to draw out all the connections that exist in a given situation. For Religion and Ecology scholars, the point is that the city has had enormous influence on both the non-urban environment and religious practices, and understanding

31. Latour, *Politics of Nature*.
32. Ibid.

these three categories (religion, nature, city) as enmeshed would yield new, and potentially crucial, insights.

Such a shift is already occurring outside of religious studies. For instance, in a recent history of New Orleans, Craig Colten describes a history of that city tied to the Mississippi River and surrounding swampland. Both the physical characteristics of the river and the layout of the city have grown and changed in response to one another—whereas the river had always flooded and shifted course (sometimes by hundreds of miles), it now sits confined in a narrow dike-lined channel, and the city itself has grown as the dikes became more sophisticated and the low-lying swampland was drained.[33]

As many have learned in the aftermath of Katrina, this geography of New Orleans has greatly affected the city's future viability, but it has also evolved to its present state along a less than egalitarian path. David Harvey has argued that landscapes tend to reflect the social relations that created them, and this is especially true of New Orleans.[34] The rigid confinement of the river has radically altered the regional landscape: the safety of the city of New Orleans has always been maintained at the cost of the rural countryside, which is alternatively hit with more devastating floods (the water kept out of New Orleans must go somewhere) and is slowly sinking into the Gulf of Mexico because the Mississippi River can no longer deposit sediment in its annual flood. Within the city itself, houses located on the highest elevations (which are at lowest risk of floods) are home to the wealthier and whiter neighborhoods, along with the financial center and the tourist districts—indeed, the radical dike and pump system was created in order to protect these financial

33. Colten, *Unnatural Metropolis*. Colten's work is loosely based on the historical model used by William Cronon in his environmental history of Chicago (see Cronon, *Nature's Metropolis*).

34. See Harvey, *Justice, Nature, and the Geography of Difference*. In more recent work, Harvey has located four broad conditions to explain "uneven geographical development": 1) capitalist forms of accumulation are "materially embedded" both socially and ecologically; 2) accumulation happens through "dispossession," whereby objects (whether a natural object or person's labor) are turned into capital; 3) such accumulation takes on a "law-like character... in space and time"; and 4) social struggles over wealth occur at multiple levels geographically and socially (Harvey, *Spaces of Global Capitalism*, 75ff). For those versed in the history of New Orleans these four conditions are easy to discover in the city's history.

investments—while the neighborhoods of poorer and predominantly African American residents lie in the most flood-prone areas.[35]

To understand New Orleans, then, it is nonsensical at best to separate the natural environment from the built environment. And while New Orleans might seem to be a unique situation—not many cities lie partially beneath sea level, after all—which makes it particularly vulnerable, this city is not unique in its dependence and reliance on its environment. A quick survey of recent literature demonstrates this: in addition to Cronon's pioneering work on Chicago (1991), Matthew Gandy has written an environmental history of New York, Maria Kaika (2005) has compellingly written on the water systems of London and Paris, and Mike Davis has written rather terrifying essays on Los Angeles, among other cities.[36]

Perhaps the most radical redefining of the environment comes from the environmental justice movement, which takes the "environment" to refer quite literally to a person or community's immediate environs. This move is not intrinsically urban—many environmental justice struggles occur in rural areas—but it is nonetheless an explicit move toward the built environment.

The environment here is not a world of forests, oceans, and wilderness, or a nature distinct from humanity, but a place "where we live, where we work, and where we play," a phrase first used by Dana Alston in her address to First National People of Color Environmental Leadership Summit, in 1991, and since frequently repeated. The environment, remarked Alston, "affords us the platform to address the critical issues of our time: questions of militarism and defense policy; religious freedom; cultural survival; energy and sustainable development; the future of our cities; transportation; housing; land and sovereignty rights; self-determination; and employment."[37] For Allston and many other environmental justice practitioners, the environment is thus an all-encompassing and unapologetically human-centered issue.

In other words, as environmental justice came to be seen as a critical issue by different grassroots organizations made up primarily of racial and ethnic minorities, the "nature" of environmentalism was not unquestioningly adopted as a concern. Patrick Novotny points to organi-

35. For a theological exploration of what this might mean, see Anne Daniell's excellent work; e.g., Daniell, "Divining New Orleans."

36. Cronon, *Unnatural Metropolis*; Gandy, *Concrete and Clay*; Kaika, *City of Flows*; Davis, *Ecology of Fear*.

37. United Church of Christ Commission for Racial Justice. *Proceedings*, 103.

zations such as the Gulf Coast Tenants Organization in Louisiana and Mississippi, which "recast their definition of the environment to connect it with housing, municipal services, workplace safety, health care, and property taxes" (Novotny 2000: 73). Activists were not just adding the environment to their list of concerns, but also redefining the environment. Giovanna Di Chiro, in her work with a grassroots EJ organization in Los Angeles, likewise sees activists as conceiving "of 'nature' and 'environment' as those places and sets of relationships that sustain a local community's way of life."[38]

Such a perspective will not be helpful for all of the questions asked by environmental scholars—as Kevin O'Brien and I argue in a separate essay in this volume, environmental justice holds a narrower range of issues that might be useful for some Religion and Ecology scholars, and we should be wary of assuming that all good environmental scholarship could (or should) fit into an environmental justice framework. In a reverse of William Cronon's critique of wilderness, such an ethic alone would have us ignore (or perhaps even intentionally pollute) nature's wilder places. For the sake of this current essay, the lesson of environmental justice is simply that one must incorporate both the natural and the built environments in order to make sense of the issues at hand.

Where, however, might religion fit into this?

At least two examples, one anthropological and the other theological, might point toward an answer to this question. Representative of the former, Karen McCarthy Brown makes a compelling argument that the practice of Haitian Vodou "stretches and strains" significantly among immigrants to New York City. A primary cause of this strain, Brown argues, is the "ecological dissonance" experienced as practitioners move from Haiti to New York. Brown's argument is helpful in part because it takes the city seriously as an environment in the context of religious practices that express a "longing for contact with the earth." Even though Brown treats the city as a thoroughly *un*natural environment, it is nonetheless an environment that reshapes religious practice. A three-day celebration of the yam harvest changes in meaning and significance, for instance, as yams shift from being a local and inexpensive product, often grown by the celebrants (as it is in Haiti), to an expensive and imported food in Brooklyn.[39]

38. Di Chiro, "Nature as Community," 300.
39. Brown, "Staying Grounded in a High-Rise Building."

In her philosophical and theological exploration of apocalyptic thought, Catherine Keller gives another route for incorporating the city into an exploration of ecological theology. In a section dissecting the image of a "New Jerusalem" in the Christian tradition, Keller observes that eschatological and utopic city envisioned as a thoroughly managed, controlled and un-wild nature. It is a "neo-classical park," in which "the point is . . . that nature did *not* do this."[40] Hesitancy, fear and antagonism toward "nature" within the Christian tradition is part of a larger logic that, among other things, pits the city—the symbol of civilization, of fully controlled and commodified nature—against (wild) nature.

These two examples have not found wide audience in Religion and Ecology scholarship—Brown's work has not moved within the parameters of this field, and this particular aspect of Keller's work has not been widely discussed—and indeed they are both extracted from larger arguments. But, to distill their argument to the simplest level, they might teach us two lessons: a practice-based approach to studying Religion and Ecology should move beyond only those religious practices that occur in "nature," and theoretical and theological constructions of "nature" carry with them an implied "city."

Conclusion: Religion and Ecology (and Cities Too?)

Most scholars in Religion and Ecology are motivated by a love of nature, or at least a fear and anxiety about our increasingly damaged planet. If such an assertion is reasonably correct, it might also be the case that many of us have ambivalent, hesitant feelings toward cities, even if that is where we generally meet for conferences. That is, when we think and talk about cities, it tends heavily toward cities as an environmental problem. When the American Academy of Religion's Religion and Ecology group has organized tours of host cities during annual conferences in the past few years, for instance, they have most often been environmental justice tours of polluted areas, not walking tours of healthy neighborhoods (though this changed with the 2010 meeting in Atlanta). While such tours are a positive development, they also seem indicative of a general disposition within our field: cities are sites of pollution, of corporate power, and of extreme poverty (and sometimes extreme wealth). These statements are all true, but cities are also more than this.

40. Keller, *Apocalypse Now and Then*, 140.

My hope is not to make us all into urban studies scholars, but to more fully recognize that our conceptions of nature are intimately linked with those of the city. This matters because, beyond the fact that most of us live in metropolises, when we're considering the environmental implications of various religious traditions or the religious properties of environmental practices, we need to think not just about their understandings of nature, but also of the city; not only their understanding of creation, but of human creativity. Keller's work on the New Jerusalem is provocative, for instance, because it makes a connection between environmental critique and where we actually live (eschatologically, at least).

Thus, when we're doing more "on the ground" research on lived or practiced religions or spiritualities, that which is environmentally significant moves beyond overtly environmentalist practices and eco-theological rituals, and includes (among other things) patterns of urban development and lifestyles. Work on modern homesteading, for instance, might be put into interesting contrast with a thick description of middle-class suburban real estate development. Such work might be most fruitfully accomplished not by becoming real estate experts, but rather by widening our conversations to include scholarship by those specializing in more urban issues.

As Religion and Ecology scholarship continues to develop, and as we debate questions such as whether or not graduate students in our field need coursework in the natural sciences, or how we can or should use words like "ecology" that have very specific meanings among scientists, we might broaden what is means to be a specialist in this interdisciplinary topic. We might, in other words, study religion and the "environment" in the fullest meaning of the word, natural and otherwise.

Bibliography

Benton-Short, Lisa, and John Rennie Short. *Cities and Nature*. Routledge Critical Introductions to Urbanism and the City. New York: Routledge, 2008.

Brown, Karen McCarthy. "Staying Grounded in a High-Rise Building: Ecological Dissonance and Ritual Accommodation in Haitian Vodou." In *Gods of the City: Religion and the American Urban Landscape*, edited by Robert A. Orsi, 79–102. Religion in North America. Bloomington: Indiana University Press, 1999.

Cobb, John B., Jr. *Christ in a Pluralistic Age*. Philadelphia: Westminster, 1975.

Colten, Craig E. *An Unnatural Metropolis: Wresting New Orleans from Nature*. With a new preface. Baton Rouge: Louisiana State University Press, 2005.

Cronon, William. *Nature's Metropolis: Chicago and the Great West.* New York: Norton, 1991.

———. "The Trouble with Wilderness; or, Getting Back to the Wrong Nature." In *Uncommon Ground: Rethinking the Human Place in Nature,* edited by William Cronon, 69–90. New York: Norton, 1996.

Daniell, Anne. "Divining New Orleans: Invoking Wisdom for the Redemption of Place." In *Ecospirit: Religions and Philosophies for the Earth,* edited by Laurel Kearns and Catherine Keller, 454–67. Transdisciplinary Theological Colloquia. New York: Fordham University Press, 2007.

Davis, Mike. *Dead Cities, and Other Tales.* New York: New Press, 2002.

———. *Ecology of Fear: Los Angeles and the Imagination of Disaster.* New York: Vintage, 1998.

Di Chiro, Giovanna. "Nature as Community: The Convergence of Environment and Social Justice." In *Uncommon Ground: Rethinking the Human Place in Nature,* edited by William Cronon, 298–320. New York: Norton, 1995.

Eiesland, Nancy. *A Particular Place: Urban Restructuring and Religious Ecology in a Southern Exurb.* New Brunswick, NJ: Rutgers University Press, 2000.

Engels, Friedrich. "Working-Class Manchester." In *The Marx-Engels Reader,* edited Robert C. Tucker, 579–85. 2nd ed. New York: Norton, 1978.

Fumagalli, Vito. *Landscapes of Fear: Perceptions of Nature and the City in the Middle Ages.* Translated by Shayne Mitchell. Cambridge: Polity, 1994.

Gandy, Matthew. *Concrete and Clay: Reworking Nature in New York City.* Urban and Industrial Environments Cambridge: MIT Press, 2003.

———. "Cyborg Urbanization: Complexity and Monstrosity in the Contemporary City." *International Journal of Urban and Regional Research* 29 (2005) 26–49.

Ganziano, Emanuel. "Ecological Metaphors as Scientific Boundary Work: Innovation and Authority in Interwar Sociology and Biology." *American Journal of Sociology* 101 (1996) 874–907.

Gorringe, Timothy J. *A Theology of the Built Environment: Justice, Empowerment, Redemption.* Cambridge: Cambridge University Press, 2002.

Gould, Rebecca Kneale. *At Home in Nature: Modern Homesteading and Spiritual Practice in America.* Berkeley: University of California Press, 2005.

Harvey, David. *Justice, Nature, and the Geography of Difference.* Malden, MA: Blackwell, 1996.

———. *Spaces of Global Capitalism: Toward a Theory of Uneven Geographic Development.* London: Verso, 2006.

Heynen, Nik et al., editors. *In the Nature of Cities: Urban Political Ecology and the Politics of Urban Metabolism.* Questioning Cities Series. London: Routledge, 2006.

Holmes, Hannah. *Suburban Safari: A Year on the Lawn.* New York: Bloomsbury, 2005.

Hunt, Tristam. *Building Jerusalem: The Rise and Fall of the Victorian City.* New York: Metropolitan, 2005.

Jenkins, Willis, editor. *The Spirit of Sustainability.* Berkshire Encyclopedia of Sustainability, vol. 1. Great Barrington, MA: Berkshire, 2009.

Kaika, Maria. *City of Flows: Modernity, Nature, and the City.* New York: Routledge, 2005.

Keller, Catherine M. *Apocalypse Now and Then: A Feminist Guide to the End of the World.* Boston: Beacon, 1996.

Kellert, Stephen. *Building for Life: Designing and Understanding the Human-Nature Connection.* Washington DC: Island, 2005.

Kjellberg, Seppo. *Urban Ecotheology.* Utrecht: International, 2000.

Latour, Bruno. *The Politics of Nature: How to Bring the Sciences into Democracy.* Translated by Catherine Porter. Cambridge: Harvard University Press, 2004.

Light, Andrew. "The Urban Blind Spot in Environmental Ethics." *Environmental Politics* 10 (2001) 7–35.

Louv, Richard. *Last Child in the Woods: Saving Our Children from Nature-Deficit Disorder.* Updated and expanded edition. Chapel Hill, NC: Algonquin: 2008.

Montrie, Chad. *Making a Living: Work and Environment in the United States.* Chapel Hill: University of North Carolina Press, 2008.

Mumford, Lewis. *The Culture of Cities.* New York: Harcourt, Brace, 1938.

Orsi, Robert A., editor. *Gods of the City: Religion and the American Urban Landscape.* Religion in North America. Bloomington: Indiana University Press, 1999.

Novotny, Patrick. *Where We Live, Work and Play: The Environmental Justice Movement and the Struggle for a New Environmentalism.* Praeger Series in Transformational Poolitics and Political Science. Westport: Praeger, 2000

Park, Robert. "The Concept of Position in Sociology." *Papers and Proceedings of the American Sociological Society* 20 (1926) 1–14.

Pike, David L. *Metropolis on the Styx: The Underworlds of Modern Urban Culture, 1800–2001.* Ithaca: Cornell University Press, 2007.

Robinson, Jennifer. "Global and World Cities: A View from off the Map." *International Journal of Urban and Regional Research* 26 (2002) 531–54.

———. *Ordinary Cities: Between Modernity and Development.* Questioning Cities Series. London: Routledge, 2006.

Sassen, Saskia. *The Global City: New York, London, Tokyo.* 2nd ed. Princeton: Princeton University Press, 2001.

Short, John Rennie. *Imagined Country: Society, Culture and Environment.* London: Routledge, Chapman, and Hall, 1991

Smith, Kimberly. *African American Environmental Thought: Foundations.* American Political Thought. Lawrence: University Press of Kansas, 2007.

Snyder, Samuel. "New Streams of Religion: Fly Fishing as a Lived, Religion of Nature." *Journal of the American Academy of Religion* 75 (2007) 896–922.

Sullivan, Robert. *The Meadowlands: Wilderness Adventures on the Edge of a City.* New York: Anchor, 1998.

Swyngedouw, Erik. *Social Power and the Urbanization of Water: Flows of Power.* Oxford Geographical and Environmental Studies. Oxford: Oxford University Press, 2004.

Taylor, Bron Raymond, editor. *The Encyclopedia of Religion and Nature.* 2 vols. London: Thoemmes Continuum, 2005.

Todd, J. Terry. "New York, the New Babylon? Fundamentalism and the Modern City in Reverend Straton's Jazz Age Crusade." In *Faith in the Market: Religion and the Rise of Urban Commercial Culture,* edited by John M. Giggie and Diane Winston, 74–91. New Brunswick, NJ: Rutgers University Press, 2002.

Tucker, Mary Evelyn, and John A. Grim, eds. *Religions of the World and Ecology.* 10 vols. Cambridge: Harvard University Press, 1997–2004.

United Church of Christ, Commission for Racial Justice. *The First National People of Color Environmental Leadership Summit: The Washington Court on Capitol Hill, Washington, D.C., October 24–27, 1991.* Edited by Charles Lee. New York: UCC CRJ, 1992.

Williams, Raymond. *The Country and the City.* New York: Oxford University Press, 1973.

Winn, Marie. *Red-Tails in Love: A Wildlife Drama in Central Park.* New York: Vintage, 1999.

12

The Buzzing, Breathing, Clicking, Clacking, Biting, Stinging, Chirping, Howling Landscape of Religious Studies[1]

Gavin Van Horn

The institutionalization of the field of Religion and Ecology gained a solid footing when the Religion and Ecology consultation held its first sessions in 1991 at the American Academy of Religion's (AAR) annual meeting.[2] As this group attracted participants and interest from scholars

1. I am grateful to Laura Hobgood-Oster, Paul Waldau, and Marti Kheel, all of whom shared their perspectives with me about the founding and future of the field of Animals and Religion. They have each been pioneers in drawing attention to nonhuman animals as important agents, worthy not merely of "objective" academic consideration but of ethical consideration and care.

2. The three primary categories for AAR program units are, in ascending order of status, consultation, group, and section (there are also "seminars" that are topic-specific but not eligible for renewal). *Consultations* are considered exploratory in character, a way to test the response of scholars at the AAR. After a designated period, typically three years, a consultation may apply for *group* status. If attendance numbers and interest are deemed significant by the AAR program committee, then a consultation may be granted group status, which carries with it the privilege of a greater number of meeting sessions. *Sections* are program units that are well established as important fields within religious studies for research and scholarship; they are allotted three to five sessions for each AAR meeting. All of the program units (consultations, groups, and sections) are evaluated on a periodic basis to determine if they warrant their designation. The Religion and Ecology consultation became the Religion and Ecology group in 1993.

in religious studies and other disciplines, a sister group sprouted wings, taking the form of the Animals and Religion consultation, which began holding its own informal sessions at the AAR annual meeting in 1998 and became an officially recognized consultation in 2003. Scholars with allegiances to both groups often move back and forth, both intellectually and physically, between the formal and informal meetings of these groups. Clearly, there are a great many overlapping concerns for those who might be attracted to such fields. However, the Animals and Religion consultation emerged with a focused set of analytic concerns and has assumed its own identity. In addition to asking why nonhuman animals were largely ignored by scholars of religious studies until the end of the twentieth century, my purpose in this chapter is to highlight the indebtedness of the field of Animals and Religion to the Religion and Ecology foment, while arguing for the distinctive contributions of Animals and Religion to the broader field of religious studies.

Omitting Animals: Animals as Signifiers of "Primitive" Religion

If history is written by the winners, as the saying goes, it is clear that valuable, alternative perspectives are frequently overlooked, or worse, actively suppressed, in the writing of such triumphal narratives. Defining religion, and more specifically what constitutes and merits attention as a subject of religious concern, has similarly been impacted by particular academic and cultural discourses. Until rather recently, nonhuman animals have been regarded as peripheral to understanding religious belief and practice.

The elision of nonhuman animals from serious consideration by scholars of religion is tethered to the historical origins of Western definitions of religion. These definitions were influenced by nineteenth-century Christian idioms of what counted as religion, even when the scholars themselves were not Christian or thought that Christianity was destined to be supplanted by science.[3] While it is unnecessary to

3. James Frazer (1854-1941) was particularly influential in this respect. Employing the categories of "magic," "religion," and "science," Frazer posited an evolutionary advance in human cultures that was reflected in the explanatory power of these systems of thought. According to Frazer, the superiority of religious beliefs—despite magic and religion often being comingled—was found in their ability to account for the whims of the natural world by attributing these phenomena to capricious gods. Science, which

recount in detail the early scholarly debate of what counted as religion and what did not,[4] what is important to note is that, at least for the most prominent streams of scholarly theory from the late nineteenth to the mid-twentieth century, religion was often considered synonymous with an intense *belief* in *non-material or supernatural beings*.[5] Such criteria had political and social implications, at times acting as the standard of authenticity by which to judge how close non-European cultures came to having anything approximating (Christian) religion.[6]

Because nonhuman animals were peripheral to such definitions, they remained, religiously speaking, invisible to those concerned with "advanced" civilizations, in which, to put it crudely, high-minded ideals involved lofty gods not earthy animals. There was, however, one way in which animals figured into the calculus of early academic attempts at definitions of religion. The late nineteenth century was a time when academic categories were further clarified—the scientific study of religion among these—and it was also a period of time when scholars were heavily influenced by the metaphorical parallels between the development of societal complexity and the phylogeny of animal species.

---

did not appeal to the gods for its explanations, was seen by Frazer as a better system of rational thought, superseding its "predecessors." As Frazer asserted, "In the last analysis magic, religion, and science are nothing but theories of thought; and as science has supplanted its predecessors, so it may hereafter be itself superseded by some more perfect hypothesis, perhaps by some totally different way of looking at the phenomena—of registering the shadows on the screen—of which we in this generation can form no idea. The advance of knowledge is an infinite progression towards a goal that for ever recedes" (Frazer, *Golden Bough*, 932 / [online] 624b).

4. For summaries of such debates, see Taylor, "Exploring," 9–15; Tweed, *Crossing and Dwelling*, 33–53; and Smith, "Religion," 269–284.

5. A figurehead in comparative anthropology, Edward B. Tylor (1832–1917), for example, defined *religion* as "belief in spiritual beings" (*Primitive Culture*, 424). Psychologist William James (1842–1910) spoke about "individual men in their solitude . . . as they apprehend themselves to stand in relation to whatever they may consider the divine" (*Varieties*, 31–32). Tylor's definitional legacy continues in intellectualist and cognitively based definitions (those that rely on belief as a central term) among contemporary scholars as well; for example, Scott Atran's (*In Gods We Trust*) definition of religion as composed of "counterintuitive supernatural agents." Mark Taylor places the "interiorization of religion" as having its genesis with "Luther's turn to the individual self" (Taylor, "Introduction," 2), thereby underscoring the influence of Protestantism's subjective commitment to salvation through personal faith in particular, and Western constructions of religion influenced by this conception more generally.

6. See Chidester, *Savage Systems*; and Masuzawa, *Invention*.

In this respect, the impact of Darwin's *The Origin of Species* (1859) upon the labors of nineteenth-century religious historians and comparativists cannot be underestimated. This seminal work provided a scientifically respected framework from which to theorize about the roots of religious experience. The evolutionary differences between animal species (popularly conceived through the metaphor of a ladder) came to be considered analogous to the evolution of religious beliefs from a single, primal religion.[7] As Eric J. Sharpe noted, at this point in history, "The West became obsessively historical, bent on drawing its parallels and painting its morals on the largest of all canvases, that of the evolution of the world, and within the world of mankind [sic]."[8] The "evolution" of religion, ironically, meant that the appreciation of animals as sacred sources of meaning or divinized companions acted as confirmation of "lower" religious development.[9]

This has been a difficult academic legacy to countermand.

However, the increasing globalization of religion has fostered exposure to and contact with peoples of various religious allegiances while raising critiques about overbroad assumptions about divinity, the importance of belief above practice, and the identification of religion with institutions, among other definitional conventions.[10] Scholars of

7. For an excellent overview of the search in comparative religious studies for the origins of religious belief, and the ways in which this was influenced by evolutionary theory, see: Sharpe, *Comparative Religion*. On the ladder metaphor of height (unlike, say, the metaphor of a strawberry plant) as applied to evolutionary theory, and what she convincingly argues are its misappropriations in social Darwinism and sociobiology, see Midgley, *Beast and Man*, 145–64; and Midgley, *Evolution as a Religion*, 33–39.

8. Sharpe, *Comparative Religion*, 25.

9. For Darwin's own account of religion as comparable to the mistaken attribution of life to inanimate objects, which he supported with observations of his dog's behavior, see Darwin, *Descent*, 65–69, esp. 67. On developmentalist models of religious theory, see: Patton, "Caught," 32; on early psychological theory in relation to animals, and the particular influence of Piaget and Freud, see: Melson, *Why the Wild Things Are*; and Midgley, *Animals*, 118–24; on the dismissal of "animism" as a "primal" religious understanding on which more "advanced" religions are purportedly to be built, see Harvey, *Animism*, 3–16; and Chidester, "Animism."

10. Because most scholarly religious education prior to the 1960s tended to be located within divinity schools, Protestant paradigms and frames of comparison dominated the study of "non-Western" religions. Mark Taylor underscores two fateful developments that untethered religious studies from Protestant paradigms: US Supreme Court decisions that allowed teaching *about* religion instead of teaching religion in public schools, and multicultural and countercultural sensibilities that challenged Eurocentrism. Taylor notes, "As attention shifted from a more or less exclusive focus on

religion now typically understand religious definitions to be provisional, culturally constituted, and plural—helpful tools for framing research questions rather than definitive means of exposing the inadequacies of some religions in comparison to others.[11] Religion is also increasingly evaluated by many scholars according to what it *does*, its active role in meaningfully orienting people toward what is regarded as sacred and to one another, rather than by some unchanging standard or "essence."

One aspect of this broader approach to analyzing the power and function of religion was to re-open the door to the inclusion of nonhuman animals, bringing back into focus the importance of how human identity is shaped by interaction with other animals—among all peoples, not just so-called "primitive" societies or Eastern cultures.[12]

Including Animals: Creating an Academic Habitat for Studying Animals and Religion

Beginning in the last decades of the twentieth century, a body of religious studies scholarship began to coalesce around questions regarding nonhuman animals.[13] Paul Waldau, who has contributed to this growing field, called this scholarly attention "the renewal of an ancient inquiry"

Western religion to a broader range of religious beliefs and practices, it quickly became apparent that it was imperative to rethink not only *which* religions were to be investigated but *how* they were to be studied" ("Introduction," 12).

11. For an overview of the ways that such pluralism has impacted religious studies texts, see Russell McCutcheon's ("Words") review on the proliferation of edited volumes dealing with religious terminology.

12. In the early 1990s, a subfield of the social sciences, *animal studies*, began to develop and attempt to move discussion about animals outside the province of anthropologists, who, according to Steve Baker, continued to focus their attention on societies and cultures other than their own (Baker, *Picturing*, xxxii, xxxv, 6–7). In part, this move is consistent with a larger project of cultural examination and reflexivity inspired by poststructuralism and postmodern theory. For a seminal essay on animals as cultural "objects," see: Berger, "Why Look at Animals?" One of the contributions of animal studies, in my view, is that it rejects wholesale distinctions between "us" (our culture) and "them" (other people's cultures) in favor of highlighting the taken-for-granted assumptions that may be operative in many cultures, including those closest to home.

13. See, for example, Birch and Cobb, *Liberation*; Regan, *Case*; McDaniel, *On God and Pelicans*; Chapple, *Nonviolence*; Linzey, *Animal Theology*; Linzey and Yamamoto, *Animals*; Webb, *On God and Dogs*; Waldau, *Specter*; Foltz, *Animals*; Waldau and Patton, *Communion*; Kheel, *Nature Ethics*; Hobgood-Oster, *Holy Dogs*; and Deane-Drummond and Clough, *Creaturely Theology*.

since "nonhuman life-forms have, from ancient times, had a remarkable presence in religious beliefs, practices, images, and ethics . . . [and] have served as fellow travelers, communal society members and workers, and, often, intermediaries between the physical world and the supernatural realm."[14] This is welcome and needed scholarly inquiry, for religion is deeply implicated in how humans interact with the nonhuman, not only with disembodied beings and forces but also with the living organisms that occupy and move through our common geographies.

Still, a reliable academic habitat was lacking for furthering this dialogue. Throughout the 1990s, the Religion and Ecology group offered a forum for scholars who shared similar concerns about how religion was both influenced by and influenced the larger landscape that humans share with other beings. Despite these overlapping interests as well as the hospitality and encouragement of the Religion and Ecology group,[15] however, it was clear that academic attention to nonhuman animals, in part due to practical constraints of space and time, could not be given the necessary attention it deserved within the AAR without additional sessions.

Discussions began in 1997 about whether an animals-focused group should pursue formal status as an AAR program unit, followed by extended correspondence among a handful of concerned scholars.[16] However, the first petition for formal recognition of an "Animals and Religion" consultation was rejected by the AAR program committee in 2001. Tellingly, the program committee was unconvinced that an "animals" meeting could not be well sheltered by the Religion and Ecology group and believed that the Religion and Women section adequately covered concerns about issues of marginalization. While nonhuman animals and women have both suffered as "silenced subjects," as feminist and ecofeminist scholars have noted, and a good deal of scholarly work has highlighted the "twin oppressions" of women/nature and women/

14. Waldau, "Animals," 356.

15. This support included, for example, a May 1999 conference on Animals and Religion that was sponsored by the Forum on Religion and Ecology (FORE).

16. The information in this paragraph is drawn primarily from an interview by the author with Laura Hobgood-Oster (15 December 2008). I am grateful as well for the perspective of Forrest Clingerman (personal communication, 28 February 2009), who was one of the earliest participants in the discussions about the formation of an Animals and Religion group at the AAR.

animals,[17] the common denominator for resistance to a new AAR grouping may have been due to a more perennial academic reluctance on the topic: Do nonhuman animals *really* merit attention from scholars of religion? Isn't religion about humans and their (human) communities?

As with any field of scholarly inquiry, one need not have a group to justify the worth of the subject. Such recognition does, however, provide a reliable niche for those seeking formal recognition of their interests. The scholars interested in forming an Animals and Religion consultation pressed on and, in the following year, were able to make a more convincing case that the consultation offered a conceptually distinct subject area. Part of this clarification process involved sufficiently distinguishing between the Religion and Ecology group and a separate field devoted to the study of Animals and Religion.

I spoke with three scholars who have been long-time supporters of the Animals and Religion consultation in order to gain a better sense of what sets this group apart from the Religion and Ecology group. These scholars were animal law expert Paul Waldau and ecofeminist historian Laura Hobgood-Oster, both of whom were co-chairs of the Animals and Religion consultation during its first six years; and ecofeminist ethicist Marti Kheel, who, along with Anwar Ghazzala, first proposed the idea for an Animals and Religion group at the AAR.[18] Each of these scholars underscored that the two fields (Religion and Ecology, and Animals and Religion) are not mutually exclusive and clearly complement one another in their subject matter. Waldau explained to me that though he considered many scholars in the Religion and Ecology group to be "true visionaries and elders" and the Animals and Religion consultation "definitely [exists] in their wake," studying animals and religion offers "different kinds of music" when it comes to addressing environmental concerns.

If indeed the Animals and Religion consultation offers a complementary harmony to the Religion and Ecology group, it nonetheless has a focused set of analytic emphases that distinguish it. The most prominent distinctions mentioned by the scholars with whom I spoke included

17. See, for example: Ruether, *New Woman*; Merchant, *Death*; Warren, "Power"; and Adams and Donovan, *Animals and Women*.

18. Unless otherwise noted, quotations from Hobgood-Oster, Waldau, and Kheel are taken from responses to a series of questions I asked each of them on 15 December 2008, 18 December 2008, and 7 January 2009 respectively.

1) "fundamental" ethical and religious questions about person-hood; that is, scholarly inquiries about which nonhumans are valued as "persons" by religious communities and individuals, who is determined to be an "other," and what the consequences of such ideas of personhood are;

2) a focus on *individual* animals and personal relationships that intersects with issues regarding animal welfare and rights, vegetarianism, and animal advocacy, and which places the weight of concern on specific and particular animals rather than "aggregate" or "meta-environmental" concerns for bio-diversity, species populations, or ecosystem functionality;[19]

3) a challenge to and disclosure of religious and cultural ideolo-gies (including anthropo- and andro-centrism) that encourage human exceptionalism or "speciesism" based on taken-for-granted assumptions about what divides humans from other animal species.

Beyond how one might distinguish Religion and Ecology from Animals and Religion as separate fields with different foci, Waldau, Hobgood-Oster, and Kheel felt that research about animals had much to contribute to the study of religion and the humanities as a whole. Focusing on nonhuman animals necessarily leads one into the particu-larities and intimacies of how individual humans and cultures relate to "otherkind." Such research is consistent with recent trends in religious scholarship that have explored mundane or everyday gestures and rituals as critical sites of religious expression and devotion. As Waldau put it, "Religion is not about big metaphysical issues; it's about the next step you take out the door. Religion resides in ordinary, daily acts . . . [and] you cannot possible understand humanity without understanding other living beings."

Moreover, Hobgood-Oster asserted that studying animals in reli-gious traditions served as a corrective that "completes incomplete his-tories." Her own work has highlighted the prevalence of animal subjects in religious art and narrative, particularly in the Middle Ages, which may not have been previously noticed simply because the presence of some animals is so taken for granted.[20] Understanding and making the presence of animals visible, in Hobgood-Oster's view, may serve

19. Kheel was particularly appreciative of this distinction, though Hobgood-Oster and Waldau also noted its importance.

20. See Hobgood-Oster, *Holy Dogs*.

as a counterweight to exclusively text-based studies of religion and a lingering Protestant bias for the Word as an immutable and enduring religious anchor.

In sum, the field of Animals and Religion contributes a distinctive voice to how religion is implicated in what human ecologist Paul Shepard called the "middle ground"—the everyday, earthy material interactions that we share with other organisms, as opposed to "omniscient saviors, transcendent heavens, and . . . metaphysics too grand for trees [and] crested flycatchers."[21] It also seems a way to move the conversation further in the direction of what people are actually doing on this "middle ground"—that is, the ways in which human behavior and identity, including notions of "animality," are constituted and informed by daily relationships with other animals. Such a focus may serve to move questions about environmental behaviors beyond assumptions about the most eco-friendly parts or potential of religious traditions into a deeper consideration of the underlying ideologies that inform widespread cultural views of "nature" and the "animal."

Animal Disruptions

Animal "blessings" are increasing in Christian churches, particularly in the United States. Such ritual blessings are typically held according to the church calendar, on or close to the feast day of St. Francis of Assisi, to honor his deep appreciation for other animals as dependent creatures of God. One of the first and certainly one of the largest animal blessings takes place at the Cathedral of St. John the Divine, an Episcopal church in New York City, where the numbers of nonhumans far outnumbers humans on the day of blessing.[22] In past services, in addition to the usual abundance of dogs and cats, many other animals with which most people less frequently come into contact were present for the celebration— ants, bees, llamas, elephants, and even cyanobacteria (blue-green algae). Hobgood-Oster commented that at one service she attended, the dogs were okay with it, the cats were somewhat bemused, but one particular camel simply, in her words, "did not want to be there."

21. Shepard, *Others*, 8.

22. For more information on the Cathedral of St. John the Divine's creaturely rituals, see McFarland Taylor, "Gaian Mass"; and on the ritual of animal blessings more generally, as well as their moral ambiguities, see Hobgood-Oster, *Holy Dogs*, 107–28.

This camel's discomfort begs a broader question for those who study animals as agents of religious significance: What kinds of "blessings" would a particular animal *want* to receive from humans? In other words, while explicit acknowledgment of the relationships that people share with other animals may be fostered by bringing them into a place of worship, even if only for one Sunday of the year, what might it mean to recognize the lived realities of those animals who would rather *not* be subject to our well-meaning ministrations? Does a "blessing" really disrupt more deeply held cultural assumptions about human dominance over other species? I would like to suggest that the camel's discomfort—not to mention the many animals who necessarily must be absent from such services because they are not domesticated or socialized to humans—speaks to a shortcoming that transcends a single church service. There is perhaps a larger parable here for others, scholars included: We tend to approach other animals, if at all, on our terms.

Despite the gains made in various fields regarding the importance of animals, Waldau wryly noted that humans "are just one species among millions of others, and yet we get 99%—or more—of all the attention at AAR and elsewhere." The very term under which the field of religious studies is housed, *human*ities, indicates the polestar around which most scholarly investigation revolves. What would happen if scholars seriously considered the lived realities of nonhuman beings as worthy of attention?

Attending to Animals

"The world, we are told, was made especially for man—a presumption not supported by all the facts."[23] So said John Muir, the famed late nineteenth and early twentieth century environmental preservationist, a statement inspired by his own near-death experience from malaria.[24]

23. Muir, "Cedar Keys," 825.

24. Muir contracted his ailment on the coast of western Florida. After losing consciousness as a result of his fever, and stumbling toward a boarding house in the throes of delirium, Muir was kindly nursed back to health by the owners of a local sawmill. His sickness lasted three months and no doubt gave him time and reason to reflect on the tenuousness of human existence in the face of "plagues of cholera and yellow fever that come and go suddenly like storms, prostrating the population and cutting gaps in it like hurricanes in woods" as well as yucca plants that were like "vegetable cats" that would surprise an unfortunate traveler and "rob him of his clothes and claw his flesh, while dwarf palmettos will saw his bones, and the bayonets will glide to his joints and marrow without the smallest consideration for Lord Man" (Muir, "Cedar Keys," 822).

Muir went on to suggest that humans, especially the religiously minded of his time, had adopted the role of theological contortionists in order to explain every animal as part of God's plan *for humans*. Thus, whales were merely large gifts of lamp oil, sheep were predestined grass-to-wool convertors, and so on. Nonhuman animals, in other words, were valuable for their God-ordained utility; they were on earth to serve human ends alone. By a similar benighted theological anthropocentrism, those animals that did not easily fit into such useful categories were dismissed as evil—fit to be avoided at best, eliminated without compunction if the circumstances warranted.

This essay highlighted Muir's disdain for a certain species of "just-so" theology,[25] which explained natural phenomena by shaping the evidence to meet an assumption: that humans are the end to which the rest of the natural world must conform. Muir, an unrepentant lover of all things wild, of course saw the evidence differently. For him, the thorns and poisons, claws and fangs, even the power of water to drown, supported a view that human beings were *not* the centerpiece of creation. All creatures had interests of their own, which "might possibly be first of all the happiness of each one of them, not the creation of all for the happiness of one."[26] In other words, Muir's contact with the complexity and diversity of organisms that "smack their lips over raw man" or "destroy labor and drink his blood" led him to scoff at the "presumption" of human exceptionalism. The world was certainly not made for humans alone, and though he granted that "The universe would be incomplete without [hu]man[s]," his spirited holism and understanding of evolution led him to believe that the world "would also be incomplete without the smallest transmicroscopic creature that dwells beyond our conceitful eyes and knowledge . . . [since] they are earth-born companions and our fellow mortals."[27]

Muir was making a point that is well worth dwelling upon—for scholars as much as anyone else. What does it mean to be persons-in-

---

25. I borrow the term "just-so" from Rudyard Kipling's infamous just-so stories. Kipling created a number of memorable fables that took for their starting point the physical feature of an animal and then explained the feature through wonderfully imaginative tales; for example, "The Elephant's Child" tells the story of how the elephant got its lengthy trunk due to its insatiable desire to find out what a crocodile eats for dinner.

26. Muir, "Cedar Keys," 826.

27. Ibid.

relation to other persons, human *and* nonhuman, in a way that carefully considers their own interests?

I would like to suggest that there are two ways in which restoring animals to religious studies scholarship can be critical, provoking a change not only in *what* scholars look for when studying religion (the content of their research) but also opening up different possibilities for *how* scholars go about doing their work (the methods that they use).

Let us start with the *what*. First, attending to animals—as critical to religious and cultural understandings of humanness and community— can decenter scholarly inquiry about religion in productive ways, bringing into sharper focus the manner in which various religious groups order the world with reference to nonhuman animals. In other words, attending to animals changes what one looks for—the *subject* matters— when considering religious practice and ideology.

When people practice religion, they negotiate what it means to be human in a more-than-human world.[28] As I argued previously, due to "classic" Western definitions of religion, divine beings or the "supernatural" have received inordinate emphasis to the exclusion of those beings and/or forces that are construed as human, suprahuman, or subhuman. Nonhuman animals, depending on the cultural tradition and its particular religious expressions, may be placed in one or all of these categories.[29] Attending to the ways in which people actively locate themselves and negotiate with reference to these categories of being (human, suprahu-

---

28. The term "more-than-human world," was coined by David Abram as a way of designating the lateral, intersubjective relationships that humans share with other earthen beings and forces. Employing a phenomenological approach (and a sometimes very personal narrative) to the study of religion, Abram argued that humans are "tuned for relationship" by the body's senses, and that we are dependent on the more-than-human world for our sense of identity: "The simple premise of this book is that we are human only in contact, and conviviality, with what is not human" (Abram, *Spell*, ix). Abram has had an influence on what Graham Harvey refers to as the "new animism," which is premised on recognizing personhood and developing relationships with non-human "persons." In addition to Harvey, who more often relies on Irving Hallowell's description of "other-than-human persons," ethologist Marc Bekoff, ethicist William Lynn, and religionists John Grim and Mary Evelyn Tucker are among those who have used "more-than-human" to underscore notions of interdependence and multiple intelligences among animals. For my purposes here, I mean only to highlight that religion involves much more than human activities and ideas, and need not exclusively involve relationships with beings that are believed to transcend the earth.

29. For important treatments of this topic, see Harvey, *Animism*; Bird-David, "'Animism' Revisited"; and Descola and Pálsson, *Nature and Society*.

man and subhuman) can serve to broaden scholarly understandings of how religion functions.

Notably, defining what is human through religious practices does not merely involve *affirming* what is *included* within a community. The other side of the coin of inclusion is the exclusion (sometimes through dehumanization) of others. In other words, a religious community defines itself by whom it claims is important *and* by whom it claims is not important; by whom it acknowledges as participants worthy of religious attention and by whom it claims as unworthy of religious attention.

Thus, religious practice functions as a way of marking and reinforcing boundaries—ideological, ontological, and geographical—providing them with ultimate meaning and emotional resonance. Religions "label, prescribe, and cultivate some emotions and obscure, condemn, and redirect others," religion theorist Thomas Tweed notes.[30] Religion thus provides ways to direct and channel affective intensities that endow the ways people mark, claim, and map their worlds with ultimate significance. This is not typically a private matter. In other words, religious boundaries (who counts as "in", and who remains "out") are enacted, performed, and concretized through physical and external demonstrations that impact the larger landscape. Such acts identify and reinforce *what is human, what is not, what types of beings appear to cross these boundaries,* and *why it matters*. In human relationships with nonhuman animals, religious practice may serve to reinforce kinship relations and concomitant ethical obligations with specific species or individual animals. Religious practices may also, inasmuch as they indicate what is outside the realm of sacred consideration, reinforce the unworthiness or the "object" status of certain or all animals.

For example, the reintroduction of endangered species, such as wolves, can be regarded as a set of tangible efforts to inscribe conflicting values on the American landscape—a way of ordering the land to reflect variant visions of human relationships to the natural world. In the United States, the presence of animals dangerous to humans and their livestock often delineated between the "civilized" (i.e., domesticated animals and settled lands) and the "wild" (i.e., nondomesticated animals and relatively uninhabited lands), and fewer animal threats were taken as a sign of economic and spiritual progress. Now, it is increasingly the case that more large predators (not fewer) are believed to signify moral progress,

30. Tweed, *Crossing and Dwelling*, 70.

a sign of humans coming to terms with animals in a non-dominionistic manner, and even a recognition of the intrinsic worth of animals that were once despised as useless or evil.

In North America, excluding wolves from proximity to human communities by killing them, while deeply influenced by socioeconomic factors, also is reflective of a vision of humanity (or divinely favored groups of humans) as entitled to the land's (God-given) "resources." Where such views have been prominent, destroying wolves has been variously framed as a mandate, a right, or a responsibility that liberates the land and its commodities for those ordained—or bold, bright, or powerful enough—to make proper use of these raw provisions. In contrast, celebrating wolves as valued members of human and biotic communities tends to rely on a cosmological vision of organic interconnectivity and typically emphasizes human dependence on the natural world. To restore wolves to landscapes they once inhabited, in this context, has been frequently understood as an affirmation of respect for nonhuman animals and sometimes conceived as a sacred healing of ecologically wounded lands.

Take for example these very different viewpoints about the reintroduction of wolves:

> We believe [that wolves] are a ploy or a tool to limit our access to public lands. . . . Wolf lovers worship the created, not the Creator. We believe the wolf was created by God and wasn't intended to be set aside and worshiped in a pagan manner. They [supporters of wolf reintroduction] hold wolves in higher esteem than their fellow man.[31]

> This is the renaissance of the land. The wolf sings it into being. The wolf is all the connections of the land, and that includes our connection, too. As we make room for the wolf we take another step toward embracing the complexity of the world—the glorious, magical complexity that is the expression of God in all things—and we begin to stitch ourselves into the fabric of place.[32]

To look closely at how these conflicting views are enacted is to delve into the tangled webs of narrative, myth, and landscape. Doing so highlights that religion is not limited to human ideas about and traffic with gods, spirits, divine beings, or invisible forces, even if that is what many people find to be one of its most remarkable or distinguishing

31. Miniclier, "Arizonans," B-02.
32. Clifford, "Saved," 194.

features. Religion, as a relational process that orients people in social space, also significantly informs how and why various groups of people interact with nonhuman animals, offering models and narratives of inclusion and exclusion that are oftentimes given coherence in a broader cosmological framework.

So, the content of religious studies, *what* we study, stands to be deeply broadened by attending to nonhuman animals. On the one hand, this wider range of exploration disrupts the exclusively humanistic focus of religious studies and Western scholarship generally. On the other hand, it opens up provocative questions about how various cultures (including those of which we are a part) define and interact with nonhuman beings.

But the field of Animals and Religion may also contribute its own distinctive momentum to a methodological shift that has been underway in religious studies since the 1970s. I am thinking here of historian of religion Robert Orsi and others who have placed a premium on the study of *lived religion*. "Religion," according to Orsi, "is always religion-in-action, religion-in-relationships between people, between the way the world is and the way people imagine or want it to be."[33] In some ways a reaction to theological studies that focused on texts and intellectual traditions, scholarly explorations of lived religion pioneered work that analyzed the meanings people create through their everyday gestures, conversation, ritual participation, and household organization. These studies sought not to abandon texts but to show how they were intertwined with other religious imaginings and practices.

Animals certainly hiss and growl through contexts that are commonly regarded as "religious" spaces—prehistoric cave paintings, petroglyphs, medieval bestiaries, stained glass windows, church or catacomb frescoes, marginal illustrations in sacred texts, hand-carved talismans, and so on—and these symbolic depictions are worthy of study. However, in my view, one of the most exciting possibilities offered by a field like Animals and Religion is that it emphasizes the living agency of other animals as worthy of careful attention. According to Waldau, this brings a scholar into "local worlds." In other words, specific studies of human-animal relationships can illuminate religion as a lived reality that is entangled with the wellbeing of other beings, from the ritualization of a meal (food being the most common point of contact in modern society

33. Orsi, *Madonna*, xx.

with other animals), to canine companionship, to abuses of animals in sport, to the ethics of polar bear migration in a warming world.

It is perhaps apparent that people are not, or at least should not be, passive "objects" for study.[34] It is perhaps less evident, for those of us who are inheritors of dominant Western cultural presuppositions regarding deep ontological fissures between humans and nonhumans, that nonhuman animals are also not passive objects of study. Despite the academic penchant for doing most of our work in the various cubicles of the library, archive, and office, we should not simply *bring animals into* our worlds of writing, symbolic reflection, and well-crafted ethical arguments; for a more robust understanding and appreciation of animal agency, we must go and meet them in their worlds. So, whereas Orsi might take to the streets of the Bronx to analyze the formative power of religious festivals, other religionists might delve into different habitats, from the Amazonian rainforest to city greenbelts.

Donna Haraway—biologist, cultural critic, and a person clearly changed by her relationships with companion species—writes that there is a "kind of doubleness" in how nonhuman animals are present to us: they are "at the same time creatures of imagined possibility and creatures of fierce and ordinary reality."[35] I would like to conclude by focusing on the importance of the latter portion of this animal "doubleness" to scholarly work: the "fierce and ordinary reality" of other living agents.

We need religionists who are willing to become amateur ethologists —in short, those who take the "ontological risk," as Haraway calls it, of being engaged with animals as living, interactive subjects, not merely symbolic curios or artifacts. Elsewhere, this has been referred to as the study of "real animals."[36] What might be gained from this? Haraway suggests one possibility: "all the actors become who they are *in the dance*

---

34. Among others, Merchant and Plumwood have argued this point forcefully, particularly highlighting the influence of Enlightenment science on subject/object, nature/culture, women/men, and emotional/rational dualities.

35. Haraway, *When Species Meet*, 4.

36. This emphasis on "real animals" is beginning to receive greater scholarly attention. In addition to the introductory chapter and afterword in Aftandilian, *What Are the Animals to Us?*, see Hobgood-Oster, *Holy Dogs*. From the perspective of an ethologist, Marc Bekoff has been a consistent advocate for studying the subjectivities and moral behavior of nonhuman animals. He has also been a conversation partner with scholars interested in Animals and Religion. See, for example, Bekoff, *Minding Animals*; and Bekoff, "Wild Justice."

of relating, not from scratch, not *ex nihilo*, but full of the patterns of their sometimes-joined, sometimes-separate heritages both before and lateral to *this* encounter. All the dancers are redone through the patterns they enact."[37] Risky business indeed. And, so too, our scholarship may be redone in this dance, disrupted and reconstituted by attending to the nonhuman presences that surround us and move within us—the buzzing, breathing, clicking, clacking, biting, stinging, chirping, howling landscape of religious studies.

The field of Animals and Religion should be commended for furthering scholarly attention to "ordinary" sites of religious experience and agency, sites where careful engagement with nonhuman animals may deepen understandings of the representational significance of nonhuman animals to religious groups as well as their importance as living subjects in the lives of us all. If open to these possibilities, we can be lured into a world abuzz with creatures who shape the way we think of humanness.[38] Drawn further into these explorations, we may discover a greater appreciation for the genetic kinship we share with nonhuman species, deepen our emotional connections to imperiled creatures, or be astounded at the remarkable and complex behaviors of individual animals; we may also unwittingly be offered lessons in humility from critters who do not always, or ever, share our immediate interests. We may also unwittingly be offered lessons in humility from critters who do not always, or ever, share our immediate interests, perhaps confirming John Muir's ruminations: "The world, we are told, was made especially for man—a presumption not supported by all the facts."[39]

---

37. Harway, *When Species Meet*, 25.

38. Depending on what organisms we are researching, we might find that we are already in the midst of them— indeed, our existence is uniquely reliant upon them, for as Haraway notes, "human genomes can be found in only about 10 percent of all the cells that occupy the mundane space I call my body; the other 90 percent of the cells are filled with the genomes of bacteria, fungi, protists, and such, some of which play in a symphony necessary to my being alive at all, and some of which are hitching a ride and doing the rest of me, of us, no harm. I am vastly outnumbered by my tiny companions; better put, I become an adult human being in company with these tiny messmates" (*When Species Meet*, 4).

39. Muir, "Cedar Keys," 825.

If it is accurate that "religion has often been the primary source for answers to questions such as, 'Which living beings really should matter to me and my community?'",[40] then there is much to gain from paying close attention to human-animal relationships. Studying religion elucidates the ways that different groups of humans understand community and negotiate the boundaries of those communities. Studying nonhuman animals in this context illustrates the way various people understand humanness. Studying the two together opens up broad areas of terrain for addressing issues related to how the landscape is shaped—for better or worse—by the human imagination.

The field of Religion and Ecology has offered a forum for much needed scholarly analysis—an "inherited land"—that the field of Animals and Religion is broadening and deepening still further. In the meantime, nonhuman animals will continue to move across the physical borders of human-created geographies as well as the less apparent but perhaps more potent imaginative borders created by the human mind. Scholars who wish to understand how religion influences environmental concerns and the concrete impacts of human exclusivity would do well to attend to both sets of borders.

Bibliography

Abram, David. *The Spell of the Sensuous: Perception and Language in a More-Than-Human World*. New York: Pantheon, 1996.

Adams, Carol, and Josephine Donovan. *Animals & Women: Feminist Theoretical Explorations*. Durham: Duke University Press, 1995.

Aftandilian, Dave, editor. *What Are the Animals to Us? Approaches from Science, Religion, Folklore, Literature, and Art*. Knoxville: University of Tennessee Press, 2006.

Atran, Scott. *In Gods We Trust: The Evolutionary Landscape of Religion*. Evolution and Cognition. Oxford: Oxford University Press, 2002.

Baker, Steve. *Picturing the Beast: Animals, Identity, and Representation*. Urbana: University of Illinois Press, 2001.

Bekoff, Marc. *Minding Animals: Awareness, Emotions, and Heart*. Oxford: Oxford University Press, 2002.

———. "Wild Justice, Social Cognition, Fairness, and Morality: A Deep Appreciation for the Subjective Lives of Animals." In *A Communion of Subjects: Animals in Religion, Science, and Ethics*, edited by Paul Waldau and Kimberley Patton, 461–80. New York: Columbia University Press, 2006.

40. Waldau and Patton, "Introduction," 14.

Berger, John. "Why Look at Animals?" In *About Looking*, 1–26. New York: Pantheon, 1980.

Birch, Charles and John B. Cobb Jr. *The Liberation of Life: From the Cell to the Community.* Cambridge: Cambridge University Press, 1981.

Bird-David, Nurit. "'Animism' Revisited: Personhood, Environment, and Relational Epistemology." *Current Anthropology* 40 (1999) 67–91.

Chapple, Christopher Key. *Nonviolence to Animals, Earth, and Self in Asian Traditions.* SUNY Series in Religious Studies. Albany: State University of New York Press, 1993.

Chidester, David. "Animism." In *Encyclopedia of Religion and Nature*, edited by Bron Raymond Taylor et al., 1:78–81. 2 vols. London: Thoemmes Continuum, 2005.

———. *Savage Systems: Colonialism and Comparative Religion in Southern Africa.* Studies in Religion and Culture. Charlottesville: University Press of Virginia, 1996.

Clifford, Hal. "Saved by Wolves." In *Comeback Wolves: Western Writers Welcome the Wolf Home*, edited by Gary Wockner et al., 90–194. Boulder: Johnson, 2005.

Darwin, Charles. *The Descent of Man, and Selection in Relation to Sex.* Princeton: Princeton University Press, 1981.

Deane-Drummond, Celia, and David Clough, editors. *Creaturely Theology: On God, Humans and Other Animals.* London: SCM, 2009.

Descola, Philippe, and Gísli Pálsson, editors. *Nature and Society: Anthropological Perspectives.* European Association of Social Anthropologists. London: Routledge, 1996.

Foltz, Richard C. *Animals in Islamic Tradition and Muslim Cultures.* Oxford: Oneworld, 2006.

Frazer, Sir James George. 1922. *The Golden Bough: A Study of Magic and Religion*, vol. 2. Abridged ed., London: Macmillan, 1957. Temple of Earth Publishing 1998–2000. Online: http://www.templeofearth.com/books/goldenbough.pdf/.

Freud, Sigmund. *Totem and Taboo: Some Points of Agreement between the Mental Lives of Savages and Neurotics.* Translated by James Strachey. New York: Norton, 1950.

Grim, John. "Knowing and Being Known by Animals: Indigenous Perspectives on Personhood." In *A Communion of Subjects: Animals in Religion, Science, and Ethics*, edited by Paul Waldau and Kimberley Patton, 373–90. New York: Columbia University Press, 2006.

Haraway, Donna J. *When Species Meet.* Minneapolis: University of Minnesota Press, 2008.

Harvey, Graham. *Animism: Respecting the Living World.* New York: Columbia University Press, 2006.

Hobgood-Oster, Laura. *Holy Dogs and Asses: Animals in the Christian Tradition.* Urbana: University of Illinois Press, 2008.

James, William. *The Varieties of Religious Experience: A Study in Human Nature.* Gifford Lectures. New York: Random House, 1902.

Kheel, Marti. *Nature Ethics: An Ecofeminist Perspective.* Studies in Social, Political, and Legal Philosophy. Lanham, MD: Rowman & Littlefield, 2008.

Linzey, Andrew. *Animal Theology.* Urbana: University of Illinois Press, 1995.

Linzey, Andrew, and Dorothy Yamamoto, editors. *Animals on the Agenda: Questions about Animals for Theology and Ethics.* Urbana: University of Illinois Press, 1998.

Lynn, William S. "Animals: A More-Than-Human World." In *Patterned Ground: Entanglements of Nature and Culture*, edited by Stephan Harrison et al., 258–60. London: Reaktion, 2004.

Masuzawa, Tomoko. *The Invention of World Religions, Or, How European Universalism Was Preserved in the Language of Pluralism*. Chicago: University of Chicago Press, 2005.

McCutcheon, Russell T. "Words, Words, Words." *Journal of the American Academy of Religion* 75 (2005) 952–87.

McDaniel, Jay. *Of God and Pelicans: A Theology of Reverence for Life*. Louisville: Westminster John Knox, 1989.

McFarland Taylor, Sarah. "Gaian Mass." In *Encyclopedia of Religion and Nature*, edited by Bron Raymond Taylor et al., 1:682–83. London: Thoemmes Continuum, 2005.

Melson, Gail F. *Why the Wild Things Are: Animals in the Lives of Children*. Cambridge: Harvard University Press, 2001.

Merchant, Carolyn. *The Death of Nature: Women, Ecology and the Scientific Revolution*. San Francisco: Harper & Row, 1980.

Midgley, Mary. *Animals and Why They Matter*. Athens: University of Georgia Press, 1983.

———. *Beast and Man: The Roots of Human Nature*. Rev. ed. New York: Routledge, 1995.

———. *Evolution as a Religion: Strange Hopes and Stranger Fears*. Rev. ed. Routledge Classics. London: Routledge, 2002.

Miniclier, Kit. "Arizonans Feel Threatened by Wolf Release; Ranchers Say They're Endangered Species." *Denver* Post, B-02, February 1, 1998.

Muir, John. "Cedar Keys." In *Nature Writings*, selected by William Cronon, 818–27. Library of America 92. New York: The Library of America, 1997.

Orsi, Robert A. *The Madonna of 115th Street: Faith and Community in Italian Harlem, 1880–1950*. 2nd ed. New Haven: Yale University Press, 2002.

Patton, Kimberley. "'Caught with Ourselves in the Net of Life and Time': Traditional Views of Animals in Religion." In *A Communion of Subjects: Animals in Religion, Science, and Ethics*, edited by Paul Waldau and Kimberley Patton, 27–39. New York: Columbia University Press, 2006.

Piaget, Jean. *The Language and Thought of the Child*. Routledge Classics. New York: Routledge, 2002.

Plumwood, Val. *Feminism and the Mastery of Nature*. Opening Out. London: Routledge, 1993.

Regan, Tom. *The Case for Animal Rights*. Berkeley: University of California Press, 1983.

Ruether, Rosemary Radford. *New Woman, New Earth: Sexist Ideologies and Human Liberation*. New York: Seabury, 1975.

Sharpe, Eric J. *Comparative Religion: A History*. 2nd ed. LaSalle, IL: Open Court, 1986.

Shepard, Paul. *The Others: How Animals Made Us Human*. Washington DC: Island, 1996.

Smith, Jonathan Z. "Religion, Religions, Religious." In *Critical Terms for Religious Studies*, edited by Mark C. Taylor, 269–84. Chicago: University of Chicago Press, 1998.

Taylor, Bron Raymond. "Exploring Religion, Nature and Culture: Introducing the *Journal for the Study of Religion, Nature and Culture*." *Journal for the Study of Religion, Nature and Culture* 1 (2007) 5–24.

Taylor, Mark C. "Introduction." In *Critical Terms for Religious Studies*, edited by Mark C. Taylor, 1–19. Chicago: University of Chicago Press, 1998.

Tucker, Mary Evelyn. "A Communion of Subjects and a Multiplicity of Intelligences." In *A Communion of Subjects: Animals in Religion, Science, and Ethics*, edited by Paul Waldau and Kimberley Patton, 645–47. New York: Columbia University Press, 2006.

Tylor, Edward B. *Primitive Culture*. Vol. 1. London: Murray, 1920.

Tweed, Thomas A. *Crossing and Dwelling: A Theory of Religion*. Cambridge: Harvard University Press, 2006.

Waldau, Paul. "Animals." In *Encyclopedia of Religion*, edited by Lindsay Jones et al., 1:355–62. 15 vols. 2nd ed. Farmington Hills, MI: Thomson Gale, 2005.

———. *The Specter of Speciesism: Buddhist and Christian Views of Animals*. New York: Oxford University Press, 2002.

Waldau, Paul, and Kimberley Patton. "Introduction." In *A Communion of Subjects: Animals in Religion, Science, and Ethics*, edited by Paul Waldau and Kimberley Patton, 11–23. New York: Columbia University Press, 2006.

———, editors. *A Communion of Subjects: Animals in Religion, Science, and Ethics*. New York: Columbia University Press, 2006.

Warren, Karen. "The Power and Promise of Ecological Feminism." *Environmental Ethics* 12 (1990) 125–46.

Webb, Stephen H. *On God and Dogs: A Christian Theology of Compassion for Animals*. New York: Oxford University Press, 1998.

Conclusion

The Territory Ahead

Whitney A. Bauman, Richard R. Bohannon II and Kevin J. O'Brien

This book is a response to over forty years of scholarship and activism that have helped to establish widespread acceptance among religious people that the environment matters and a widespread realization among environmentalists that religion matters. This work has established a landscape for the study Religion and Ecology, a field which will inevitably continue to evolve in response to numerous factors —new insights in environmental science, social theory, and other academic disciplines; global and local political shifts; technological developments in the ways information and scholarship can be processed and exchanged; recognition of the ways in which humans are shaped and defined by other animals and the rest of the natural world; and changing patterns of environmental degradation. The grounds and contexts of Religion and Ecology are constantly changing, and the field must respond.

In the essays above, authors have named many such changes and suggested many responses. While it would not be possible or prudent to summarize all of those ideas, we do want to draw out two themes— the interplay between how we think about the world and how we act, and the vital challenges of interdisciplinary and intercultural conversations—and raise some of the most important lingering questions that we see emerging from the essays of this book.

This conclusion attempts in broad strokes to gather and analyze the most central and common ideas and emphases of the preceding chapters, and to attend thoughtfully to the texts, traditions, and practices that have shaped these pages. We hope, therefore, to draw from them a sense of how the field of Religion and Ecology is changing and might continue to change.

The Subjects of Religion and Ecology:
Worldviews and Practices

One of the most common suggestions made in these essays is that the field of Religion and Ecology should pay careful attention to the lived experience and practical behaviors of religious people and avoid any implication that worldviews and beliefs alone make up a religion or a religious life. Many essays have made reference to Lynn White's famous argument that environmental degradation is ultimately rooted in the *ideas* of Christianity. While most (if not all) of the scholars who work in Religion and Ecology are ultimately concerned about the ways people *act* toward each other and the non-human world, a great deal of our academic work has striven to investigate and change the ways people *think* about the world and the relationship of human beings to it. Seeking various correctives to this trend, essays in this book have frequently cited critical analyses that call for new approaches to the study of religion (such as the work of Tomoko Masuzawa and Talal Asad) and recent ethnographic approaches to studying the intersection of Religion and Ecology (such as the work of Sarah McFarland Taylor and Rebecca Kneale Gould).

This argument is ongoing in Religion and Ecology, and most essays in this volume have emphasized the importance of studying practices and experiences over ideas and beliefs. In part, this emerges from a claim about the nature of religion. For example, Sam Snyder and Lucas Johnston argue in chapter 7 that it is a misunderstanding of religious life and religious people to think that beliefs and ideas themselves make up a religion. They argue that a more nuanced view—which will also be more fruitful in discussions with pragmatist philosophers—must therefore pay careful attention to the practices and experience of religious people and communities as well as their values. This is not only a corrective to pragmatists who have ignored or stereotyped religion, but also a call for scholars in our field to emphasize and study religious practices.

The focus on religious practice is also informed by the activist bent of Religion and Ecology, and many authors emphasize that if we want to make a difference in a world of environmental degradation, scholars of religion should focus on practical, material action rather than abstract ideas. Along these lines, Brian Campbell argues in chapter 10 that the turn in our field toward practices and place is informed by a hope that theology and the study of religion can more directly understand and shape human behavior as it exists "on the ground." Tracing the importance of particularized actions and locales in recent literature in and outside the field, Campbell demonstrates that many scholars who want to change the world are choosing to start by investigating its particularities.

A third reason to emphasize the importance of action and experience is a caution about too-quickly or casually universalizing religion or religions. Along these lines, Tovis Page argues in chapter 6 that ethnographic and historical attention to the details of religious life is a vital way in which Religion and Ecology scholars can wrestle with the complexities and diversities of human religiosity. When studying gender and sexuality, Page argues, it is particularly important not to make simplistic and generalized universal claims. Such claims will always and necessarily be complicated by attention to the actualities of religious communities and individuals.

Interestingly, and importantly, none of these authors suggests *abandoning* attention to worldviews, ideas, and general trends. Page argues that critical engagement with broad theory about gender and sexuality will be vital for the future of the field, Campbell explicitly states that attention to particularities should not blind us to global networks of power, and Johnston and Snyder leave room for attention to the ways religious ideas can have a real and pragmatic impact on the world. Values may not straightforwardly lead to action, abstract ideas may not be more important than practical behaviors, and broad claims about religion may need to be tempered by particular cases; but values, ideas, and broad claims nevertheless remain important and relevant to the study of Religion and Ecology.

While Lynn White and some who followed him may have overemphasized the importance of thought, none of the essays in this book suggest that thinking does not matter, or that we should not attend to the ways religious beliefs, worldviews and attitudes have shaped and can shape how people interact with their worlds. Whitney Bauman emphasizes this point in chapter 5, noting that the ideas in religious traditions are a kind of technology, a technology that can have profound impacts on the world around us. As a corrective against misuse of such technology, Bauman urges scholars and those we influence to use ideas as scalpels rather than machetes, to avoid broad universals and simplistic approaches that cause harm, but instead to carefully investigate and apply the nuances of religious thought.

Along similar lines, Evan Berry, in arguing for a multi-layered, genealogical definition of "nature religion" in chapter 2, reminds us that one's definition of "religion" carries great consequences. Within current academic discourse, some use the work of scholars such as David Chidester to argue for broad definitions of religion that can encompass practices like fly-fishing or gardening, while other remain tied to more established religious traditions (such as Christianity). Berry's genealogical approach to religion moves beyond this dichotomy and encourages scholars to provide a "thick" description of what we study, to think deeply about the ways traditions and practices have been shaped by the ideas and experiences from which they emerge.

The most straightforward way to sum up the common thread on worldviews and religious practices in this book is to note that studying either one requires some attention to both. While the emphasis of many essays here is on the importance of practices, this is a corrective to a perceived overemphasis rather than a blanket dismissal of worldviews. Perhaps a point of clear agreement in the field of Religion and Ecology going forward might be that scholars who make claims about worldviews and ideas need to more fully acknowledge the importance of lived religions and practices, and scholars who move into careful study of lived religion and practices need to remain aware of the importance of worldviews and ideas. We may never strike a precise and perfect balance, and such balance would likely change among different research projects. Nevertheless, as long as we remain aware of the tension between these two goals, our scholarship will continue to be a productive and self-corrective analysis of religious behaviors and beliefs.

The Conversation Partners of Religion and Ecology: Interdisciplinarity and Interculturality

Religion and Ecology has always been an interdisciplinary and intercultural field. From its foundations, this academic pursuit brought theologians, ethicists, historians, sociologists, and textual scholars in religious studies into conversations that further drew upon the work of many additional scholarly fields, including the natural sciences. Centered on environmental problems that encompass the entire planet, attending to the major "world religions," and increasingly making room for minority religious voices within and outside those traditions, these conversations have always been global. While western Christians may have been most prominent, they have consistently paid attention to other cultures and other conceptual approaches. The chapters in this volume have continued this trend, engaging "religion" as a diverse and global category and drawing examples from many traditional and new expressions of religion with analytical tools from varied fields including philosophy, cultural studies, ecology, anthropology, sociology, history, and all types of religious studies and theology.

Explicitly building on the interdisciplinarity of the field, Fredericks and O'Brien argue in chapter 3 that the field of Religion and Ecology should pay special attention to the natural sciences, both as an acknowledgement of and a check on the power scientists tend to exercise in environmental conversations. They emphasize that conversations with science must not be a simple exchange of answers, but rather an exploration of complexities, uncertainties, and changing ideas. Richard Bohannon makes a similar kind of argument about alternative conversation partners in chapter 11, arguing that Religion and Ecology should not only study the "environment" in dialogue with natural scientists, but also the urban environment as studied by anthropologists who research religion in the city and geographers and historians who research the ways wild, rural, and urban environments interact and influence one another. While the conversation partners differ, both of these chapters advocate more deliberate and detailed interdisciplinary work in Religion and Ecology.

In chapter 4, Eleanor Finnegan calls for a more intercultural conversation that moves beyond the norms of Christian scholarship and normalized Western ideas about religion and scholarship. She points out that although there is much written on Islam and Ecology, most scholarship is focused on the Islamic mainstream as it is expressed in religious texts. With the example of three Sufi farming communities in the United States, she argues that many emerging and historical examples of ecological religious principles, practices, and beliefs can be found on the margins of cultures and outside of what is considered mainstream tradition. It is thus not only important for Religion and Ecology to more fully encompass traditions and practices outside of the major "world religions," but also to recognize minority streams *within* major religions.

Clearly, a theme throughout this book is the need to continue expanding the field's interdisciplinary and intercultural attention in Religion and Ecology, to work hard to include still more ways of knowing and bring more voices to the table. Another example comes in chapter 8, wherein Elonda Clay makes a strong case that limited attention has been paid to African Americans in Religion and Ecology; far more nuance and work will be required to grasp the richness of diasporic experience and all it can teach us about the ways human culture influences and is influenced by the natural world. Clay calls for a vastly expanded interdisciplinary conversation with ethnographic and cultural studies of the African Diaspora, critical race theory, and scholars of globalization. In addition, she also calls on scholars of Religion and Ecology to pay attention to cultural and multicultural expressions that have been ignored in the past: the varied religious expressions of African and African Diasporic communities beyond Protestant Christianity as well as the spiritual practices and material culture of these communities. Such attention to the practices and "transcultural ecological knowledges" of African diasporic communities will expand the academic and cultural attention of the field in helpful and healthy ways.

In chapter 12, Gavin Van Horn develops an argument that Religion and Ecology—and indeed all of religious studies—must expand its interdisciplinary and intercultural work with attention to interspecies relationships. The study of religion and animals is a reminder that humans are animals, which exist within a larger earth community full of other animals. Ignoring this fact has caused scholars to miss both the interconnectedness of life and important insights about how religion functions to shape the ways human relate to and think about other creatures. Religion and Ecology must therefore engage in dialogues with scholars of animals and religion, with ecofeminists, with ethologists, and with thinkers from other cultures who take animals seriously.

A different attention to intercultural and interdisciplinary work is demonstrated by Richard Bohannon and Kevin O'Brien in chapter 9, which is less about expanding conversations than it is about distinguishing them. By clarifying a distinction between the ideals of eco-justice and the movement for environmental justice, they seek to demonstrate differences between discourses, acknowledging that scholars of Religion and Ecology will have different goals and different approaches to our work depending on who our primary conversation partners might be. This is not an argument against working across academic and cultural boundaries, but rather a caution that such work requires clarity, deliberate attention to differences, and a careful acknowledgement of what scope of attention and priorities inform our work.

As Religion and Ecology continues to engage in conversations with diverse cultures and diverse fields of study, it should understand cultural and academic production as ongoing projects: the behaviors and ideas of those we study and those with whom we work will change over time, and so our attention to them must be persistent, careful, and flexible. Furthermore, as we steadily increase our range of conversation partners, we must be honest about how broad our attention can be if we want to have thorough and meaningful conversations across cultural and disciplinary boundaries.

Persistent Questions

In drawing out these concluding themes about the developments we hope for in the field of Religion and Ecology, we are reminded of the most prominent caution we heard from mentors and reviewers about this book. Some experienced colleagues pointed out as kindly as they could that it might seem foolish and arrogant for a group of emerging scholars to write essays about the future of an existing and thriving field of study. Our goal, however, has not been to prognosticate the future of Religion and Ecology. Rather, we have sought to make some suggestions about the directions the field might take based on our understanding of current realities.

The perspective of the authors in this book is unique only because of our timing: we are the first generation of Religion and Ecology scholars to emerge and begin our work within an *established* field. This perspective allows us space to actively reflect on how Religion and Ecology has been shaped and where there might be room for new and productive questions. This book has offered some observations and arguments from that space, which we share with and hope to discuss with the more experienced colleagues who did the work of establishing the field in which we are working. To encourage such discussion, and to mitigate the danger of being overly presumptuous, we will conclude with a discussion of the questions we know we have not answered, some directly inherited from our teachers in Religion and Ecology and others new or different enough that we may only be just beginning to learn how to ask them.

One perennial question in our field concerns the balance between scholarship and activism. We argued in the introduction that Religion and Ecology is characterized by a commitment to both, but noted that there is a productive tension between them. Such tension has been evident at many points in this book, but nowhere did any author claim to have resolved or overcome it. We continue to struggle with such long-standing concerns such as: Are there important topics in the field of Religion and Ecology that do not relate in any direct way to contemporary environmental crises? Are there environmental crises so clear and urgent that political action and activism are more important and urgent responses than scholarship? When scholarship does have something legitimate to contribute to an environmentalist and/or social cause, how can we reliably communicate our findings to activists outside the academy?

Another, related set of questions concerns the balance between universality and particularity, between the tendency to address global environmental issues and religious trends on the one hand and the desire to dig in to local concerns and traditions on the other. In a world of dramatic global climate change, it is hard to ignore the importance of a global perspective, but responsible scholarship of religion and spiritual practices also call us to focus on particularities and unique local characteristics. Furthermore, as discussions of place in Campbell's chapter note, it is impossible to ignore the ways in which every "place" on the globe always already affects and is affected by global connections. While most scholars of Religion and Ecology could likely agree that we should not choose between the local and global, the immediate and the long-term, rapid over slow changes, it remains important to discuss a number of issues: How should we balance and prioritize these perspectives? Are there levels of attention that can be dismissed as less important to or beyond the scope Religion and Ecology as a field? With what tools can we synthesize the findings and ideas of scholarship working at different scales of attention?

Yet another set of questions emerges when we note, as a few of the essays in this book have, that most scholars of Religion and Ecology are also teachers of Religion and Ecology, and must struggle with how to introduce these ideas to students at various levels of education, preparation, and ability. To what extent should we teach our students to be urgently concerned with environmental degradation, and how will this balance with the work of training diverse students to use scholarly methodologies? How much should we introduce the internal debates within the field and how much should we focus on the points of agreement? What do students need to know about religion and environmental issues before we can introduce them to our field, and what do they truly need to know from our field in order to be good citizens, professionals, and thinkers after they graduate?

A final set of questions concerns the changes wrought by technology upon Religion and Ecology. Many of the essays above cite the work of Donna Haraway to emphasize that technology is not cleanly separable from the natural world and so must be seriously engaged by our field. This is vitally important. Perhaps equally important is the self-critical move Donna Haraway further exemplifies, which is an attention to how technology shapes our scholarship and our scholarly selves. How will we make use of the vast swaths of textual, visual, and cultural resources increasingly available and accessible through the digitization of current and past scholarship? Will the increasingly varied forms of communication available to scholars change what counts as scholarship in our field? What will it do to our interactions with one another if we embrace the speed of instant communication and de-emphasize gathering in physical meetings? In what way does it change our interaction with these technologies to be rigorously aware of their environmental costs?

We will inevitably continue to engage these questions, seeking answers where possible and remaining open to the new and old questions we have not paid enough attention to. This book is about the changing grounds of the field of Religion and Ecology, and we do not expect those grounds to ever stop changing.

If the authors in this book are very fortunate, we will keep thinking and working on these issues for many years to come, we will share that work with many mentors and colleagues, and we will hand on our partial answers and questions to the scholars who emerge after us. The goal we had in bringing the authors of this text together was to allow for a kind of academic cross-pollination to occur as we raised a proliferation of questions, critiques and ideas about the current state of Religion and Ecology. It is our hope that these fertile grounds will sprout even more questions, critiques, and ideas.

Index